Deep Impact

Deep Impact

1999 Keswick Ministry

Edited by Hilary Price

OM
publishing

Copyright © The Keswick Convention Council 1999

First published in 1999 by OM Publishing

05 04 03 02 01 00 99   7 6 5 4 3 2 1

OM Publishing is an imprint of Paternoster Publishing,
P.O. Box 300, Carlisle, Cumbria, CA3 0QS, UK
Website: http://www.paternoster-publishing.com

British Library Cataloguing in Publication Data
A catalogue record for this book is available from the British Library

ISBN 1-85078-347-0

Unless otherwise stated, Scripture quotations are taken from the
HOLY BIBLE, NEW INTERNATIONAL VERSION
Copyright © 1973, 1978, 1984 by the International Bible Society.
Used by permission of Hodder and Stoughton Limited.
All rights reserved.
'NIV' is a registered trademark of the International Bible Society
UK trademark number 1448790

Cover Design by Mainstream, Lancaster
Typeset by David Porter Text & Editorial, Greatham, Hampshire
Printed in Great Britain by
Caledonian International Book Manufacturing Ltd, Glasgow

Contents

The Addresses

The Keswick Lecture

Introduction by the Chairman
of the 1999 Convention

There is an important creative tension at the heart of all
Christian service. Growing churches experience it and mission agencies face its demands all the time. It is the tension
expressed in the two words: deep and wide. Paul was a great
missionary pioneer, longing to see the gospel advance to new
territories, bringing the good news to new audiences, but
always concerned that his work had depth. He struggled
energetically to bring people to maturity, rooted and built up
in Christ and strengthened in the faith (Col.1:28,29, 2:6,7).
That is the challenge for the Keswick Convention too. In an
age when it is easy to succumb to the superficial, we want the
Convention to stand for depth – depth in our knowledge of
God, depth in our spiritual life, depth in our understanding
of God's Word, and depth in our fellowship. The 1999
Convention highlighted that theme, hoping that the teaching
of God's Word and the experience of God's presence at
Keswick would have a deep impact in our lives, our church-
es and our world.

Just as Paul had his eyes on new horizons, looking for new
opportunities and open doors, so by God's grace we want to
extend the ministry of the Convention. We won't sacrifice

depth, but we do want to see new audiences captured and captivated by the power of God's Word and Spirit, responding to the Lord with a commitment to renewed service and radical discipleship. So we were thankful to God for many more attending Keswick from the rising generation, for new audiences amongst those with learning difficulties, for hundreds of young people benefiting from specialised tracks, and for missionaries and church leaders from around the world finding refreshment and renewal. The morning Bible Readings were also broadcast live to a wider audience by Premier Radio and appeared on their website. Many people took advantage of the audio and video recordings (details at the back of the book).

The following chapters are a taster of the Bible teaching from the 1999 event, and our special thanks go to Hilary Price for her careful editorial work. We hope that this volume will further contribute to the impact – deep and wide – of God's living Word around the world.

Jonathan Lamb, Chairman, Keswick Convention

Editor's Introduction

What a privilege it has been to listen to hours of Keswick ministry, and what a challenge it has been to edit the transcripts for the first time. David and Tricia Porter have worked on this project as a husband and wife team for many years and they have still had a huge part to play in the book you have in your hand; Tricia has transcribed the tapes at amazing speed and David has typeset the edited material, constantly giving advice and encouragement throughout the editorial process.

It is of course impossible to include every word spoken. My goal has been to retain each speaker's distinctive style, voice and in some cases accent! If you were actually at the Convention, hopefully as you read you will be transported back into the tent, hearing Derick Bingham's passionate preaching, Don Carson's clipped Canadian or Ron Dunn's soft, drawling American. If you were not – let your imagination run as you sit with an open Bible and allow God to teach through His very different channels; what a feast enriched by each speaker's personal cultural background and heritage.

Sadly, I have had to leave out some of the jokes, illustrations and little asides, but if you want to hear it all, and even see it all, you can get hold of tapes and videos (details at the back of the book).

All Bible references that were included in the talks are included in the text and the New International Version has been used throughout. When speakers paraphrase, the reference is preceded by 'cf', so you can compare their version with the original! Capitalisation is used for the persons of the Trinity unless within a direct quotation from the NIV.

I have included these technical details, not to confuse, but to clarify your understanding and to enable the rich teaching to have the deepest impact possible in your lives.

Hilary Price, Keswick Volume Editor

The Bible Readings

Studies in 1 Peter

by Don Carson

1. Heading Toward Heaven
1 Peter 1:1-12

Introduction: What is hope?

Consider Ian's mother. Ian and I were both ten and in the same class at school. We were friends possibly because we were both eggheads. Ian fell ill with cancer. Eventually he dropped out of school. I used to visit him at his home and saw his body shrivel up and then distend from the mysterious combination of disease and drugs.

Ian's mother was a fine, religious woman. She used to sing on a local radio station that produced an inter-faith religious service. When Ian was deathly ill she sang on the radio a song about hope:

> Soft as the voice of an angel,
> Breathing a message unheard,
> Hope with its gentle persuasion,
> Whispers its comforting word.
> Wait till the darkness is over,
> Wait till the tempest is done,
> Look for the sunrise tomorrow,
> After the showers have gone.
> Whispering hope, Oh how gentle thy voice,
> Making my heart in its sorrow rejoice.

A courageous woman this, clinging to hope. But Ian died.

Consider the brutalising conditions of the worst concentration camps, the worst gulags, the most inhumane maximum security prisons. One of the worst cruelties they can impose is the destruction of hope. If you know you are never going to get out, precisely where does your hope reside, or is it destroyed? Those who retain some sort of hope in such brutal conditions often manage to retain some sort of dignity. Perhaps it's hope of an early release after all: hope of a pardon. Maybe it's religious: hope of eternal life. But the loss of all hope often means degeneration into brutality or suicide.

Victor Frankl, the Austrian psychiatrist who was himself incarcerated for a large part of World War Two in one of the Nazi camps, wrote afterwards:

> The prisoner who had lost faith in the future, his future, was doomed. With his loss of belief in the future he also lost his spiritual hold, he let himself decline and became subject to mental and physical decay. Usually this happened quite suddenly in the form of a crisis, the symptoms of which were familiar to the experienced camp inmate. It began with a prisoner refusing one morning to get dressed and work, or to go out onto the parade grounds. No entreaties, no blows, no threats had any effect, he just lay there hardly moving. If this crisis was brought about by an illness he refused to be taken to the sickbay or to do anything to help himself. He simply gave up. There he remained, lying in his own excreta and nothing bothered him anymore.

Consider the role of hope in a broad sweep of human experience. The small child starting play school, looking forward to seeing his special friend; a teenager hoping for acceptance in a circle of friends; hope of achieving certain grades; hope that your complexion will clear up. Eventually, hope that you will be married and that your first child will be more or less normal, considering who the parents are. Hope that you will be promoted at work, hope that your income will cover the mortgage. Hope that your children won't do all the stupid things that you did at their age. Hope for the well-being of your first grandchild. Hope, hope, hope.

For human beings, hope is necessary for well-being. What happens when hopes die? Well for most of us, when specific hopes die other hopes eventually replace them. But suppose there is no hope? When someone really is giving up we say they have lost all hope, and they roll over and die.

Hope looks into the future. It gives a reason for living, it makes actions and choices significant, it adds zest and focus, it provides a moral compass. This is true even when the hope is not realised. For as long as this forward-looking anticipation exists, there seems to be a reason for living, even when that reason does not finally prove to be well-founded. Hell is where there is no more hope, and Dante's picture is exactly right – 'Abandon hope all you who enter here.'

But the New Testament habitually speaks of hope in a slightly different sense. I've just described how we use hope. Biblical hope also includes the element of forward-looking anticipation. As Paul puts it, 'We do not hope for what is already arrived,' for in that case we have already received it. We hope for that which has not yet come to pass (cf Rom. 8:24-5). But when we speak of hope we automatically include the possibility of frustration. 'I hope to leave at five o'clock this afternoon.' In contemporary English you mean that you may not make it. It may take you a little longer to pack your bags, your car may not start, the taxi may be late, or the plane delayed, or who knows what. But hope in the Bible embraces this forward-looking anticipation intrinsic to all hope, without any implied suspicions that the whole thing might come crashing down and that I might be frustrated.

There are two important implications of this: first, the Bible can speak of 'our certain hope'. In modern English, where hope is not certain, that is almost a contradiction in terms. But in the Bible hope is forward-looking and whether it is certain or not depends on the promise on which it is founded, and if it's God's promise, it's certain. So the New Testament writers can speak of a 'certain hope'. We sing:

We have a hope that is steadfast and certain,
Gone through the curtain and touching the throne.

(Wendy Churchill, 'Jesus is King')

Second, in this framework Christian hope then becomes the great virtue, indeed one of the three cardinal Christian virtues: faith, hope and love.

1 Peter says a great deal about Christian hope. But before going any further we must ask ourselves, to whom does Peter address his exposition of hope and what were the first readers of this first letter like?

Peter addresses them in the name of the Father, the Son and the Holy Spirit (verse 1). Now no doubt the full-orbed doctrine of the Trinity was not entirely formulated, but these Trinitarian styles of referring to Father, Son and Spirit are not uncommon in the New Testament. These are those who (verse 18) formerly followed an 'empty way of life handed down to you from your forefathers,' that is, they were pagans. But now, we are told, they have been 'chosen according to the foreknowledge of God the Father'. Peter applies to them an election category from the Old Testament. This Peter who was once shocked to be told three times by God in a vision that he should be, not only permitted, but mandated to eat non-kosher food:

'Rise, Peter, kill and eat.'

'Oh not me God, no unclean food has ever touched my lips' (cf Acts 11:7-8). And now he understands that the locus of God's redeemed community is anchored in God's fore-knowing election in eternity past, as surely as were His own ancient people, the Jews. These Gentile Christians are not second-class citizens of the kingdom, they were known by God from the beginning. This expression, 'who had been chosen according to the foreknowledge of God the Father', does not mean He chose them according to what He foreknew that they would do. He foreknew them, to use Paul's language, that is, He fore-loved them, and He chose them as surely as He had chosen ancient Israel.

Then in verse 2 again he mentions the Holy Spirit. These 'have been chosen according to the foreknowledge of God the Father, through the sanctifying work of the Spirit'. This sanctifying work, in this context, does not have to do with God making them progressively more holy; rather, they have been made holy by the Spirit's work in making them God's. They belong to God, and thus they are set aside for God's use, they are holy in principle, sanctified already by the work of the Spirit. And this 'for obedience to Jesus Christ and sprinkling by his blood'. This is the initial obedience bound up with our initial repentance, our initial submission to Jesus Christ as Lord, as in verse 22 – 'Now that you have purified yourselves by obeying the truth so that you have sincere love for your brothers'. That is obeying the truth of the gospel, you have come to terms with the gospel.

Now, these people have been sanctified by the Spirit in the sense that they have been set aside for God, for obedience to Jesus Christ and sprinkling by His blood. The sprinkling symbolism is almost certainly drawn from Exodus 24. The mountain shook, the people were assembled to enter into a covenant with God, an altar with twelve pillars representing the twelve tribes, the wholeness of the covenant community was constructed and sacrifice was offered. Half of the blood was sprinkled on the altar, Moses read the words of God's covenant, the people pledged obedience and then Moses sprinkled the rest of the blood on them saying, 'This is the blood of the covenant that the LORD has made with you in accordance with all these words' (Ex. 24:8).

Now Peter speaks of these Gentiles becoming obedient to Christ through the new covenant in Christ's blood. We are sprinkled too, not with an ox's blood, but with the blood of Jesus Christ, cleansed by a sacrifice far superior to any sacrifice offered up of sheep or goat or bull.

So Peter addresses them first of all in the name of the Father, the Son and the Holy Spirit, and then as Christians who still live in the world. And that world can be a hard place. He writes, 'To God's elect, strangers in the world,' aliens if you like, 'scattered throughout Pontus, Galatia, Cappadocia, Asia and Bithynia,' regions of modern-day Turkey. The word rendered 'scattered' is the word that is often mentioned in other literature as the Diaspora – the scattering of the Jews from the time of the exile on. First under the Assyrians, the leaders and many of the middle-class in the northern tribes were taken away, with the final tribes being removed by the Babylonians in 587 BC. These scattered Jews were referred to as the Diaspora. In some ways they saw this as a mark of shame and longed for the time when the Messiah would bring them back together again. Now Peter is saying that the real Diaspora, finally, are Messiah's people, and this is not so much a badge of shame as almost a badge of honour. For they are a Diaspora in a world that does not know God. There is a kind of confrontation, they are aliens.

I married an English woman and when she moved back to Canada with me she became a landed immigrant. It sounds a bit like a beached whale! When we moved down to the United States, we both became resident aliens and still are. This is a polite American way of saying you don't quite belong, you're not citizens. That's what Peter says with respect to these Christians. They are strangers in the world, they are the true Diaspora, in this case scattered in what we call Turkey.

And of course that fits into a broad stream of what the Bible says. Jesus warns in John 14 that Christians will dis-cover this world is not their home, they're 'just a-passing through' as the ancient Negro spiritual puts it. Hebrews says that with respect to Jesus, while the high priest carries the blood of animals into the most holy place as a sin offering, so also Jesus suffered outside the city gate, to make the people holy through His own blood. Let us then go to Him outside the camp, bearing the disgrace He bore, for here we do not have an enduring city, but we are looking for the city that is to come. There is a sense in which Christians remain in a perennial tension – we may be citizens of Great Britain, but it is not our ultimate citizenship. In some ways we just don't fit. Thus Peter addresses them as Christians who still live in this world, but that world can be a hard place.

He then goes on with a traditional Christian blessing – 'Grace and peace be yours in abundance.' Grace, someone has said, is God's love in action in Jesus Christ on behalf of sinners. His peace is His shalom, His well-being. As human beings are reconciled to Him with all that means, both for this world and for the world to come, 'Let this be yours in abundance,' he says.

Then Peter, addressing these believers as a Christian apostle, enmeshed in the life of the church – a church that understands its alien status in the world – develops this theme of being an alien, 'She who is in Babylon, chosen together with you,' – that is almost certainly Peter's way of referring to the church in Rome. The church – she, who is in Babylon – a coded New Testament way of referring to ancient Rome. At this point the historical Babylon was a nonentity, a scrappy little village without political significance. In the Old Testament, Babylon with all its neo-pagan love of self had become such a symbol for all that stood against God, that it becomes almost a stereotype of a world that does not know God. That recurs in other New Testament books, not least the Book of Revelation, where Babylon regularly stands for Rome. And over against Babylon, this vile city, is the New Jerusalem. This ancient Babylon now reincarnate in Rome is like a prostitute, whereas the New Jerusalem, the people of God, is like a bride prepared for her groom. And as a result some have suggested that you could re-title the Book of Revelation, 'A Tale of Two Cities', with a subtitle, 'The Harlot and the Bride'.

Now that's the kind of framework out of which Peter is speaking here. 'She who is in Babylon,' the church who is right at the centre of the empire, and the centre of a great deal of idolatry and paganism, 'chosen together with you, sends you her greetings, and so does my son Mark,' that's John Mark. Peter almost certainly stands behind Mark as apostolic witness to the events of Jesus' life. 'Greet one another with a kiss of love,' a holy kiss. 'Peace to all of you who are in Christ.'

Of course this kiss of love is part of Christian fellowship. How that is exemplified in different cultures will vary. I was brought up in French Canada. I'm reasonably used to kissing on both cheeks, but I know many corners of the world where there are certain cheeks you don't do that to. And I quite sympathise with J.B. Phillips' rendering of the famous Pauline passage, 'Give a hearty handshake all round.' It's distinctly more British, you have to admit! This is simply Christian fellowship that is warm-hearted and without reserve.

Here then is the context in which Peter develops the theme of hope in four different dimensions.

1) Hope God establishes (verse 3)

The form of 'Praise be to God' is common in ancient Jewish liturgy. For example, in one of the famous eighteen benedictions, which may well stretch back to Peter's day, there are some lines of preparation for the blessing and then the blessing itself. 'Speedily cause the offspring of David thy servant to flourish, and let his horn,' horn in this sort of symbolism means kingship or kingdominion or kingly rule, 'be exalted by thy salvation, because we wait for thy salvation all the day.' And then the blessing – 'Blessed art thou oh Lord, who causes the horn of salvation to flourish.' It's the same form as here. 'Blessed be the God and Father of our Lord Jesus Christ.' But do you hear the poignant longing in this ancient Jewish blessing? Very different in tone from the Christian one. This ancient liturgy is still looking forward to the coming of the Messiah.

The Christian liturgy and this Christian blessing insists the Messiah has come. Here indeed, in His great mercy, God has given new birth into a living hope, through the resurrection of Jesus the Messiah, from the dead. This hope is surely based on the sheer facticity of Jesus' resurrection. It is not something we hope for in the modern sense, something that might not come off. It is an anticipation that looks forward to something, still to be unpacked a little more, grounded in Jesus' resurrection.

Of course even at the existential level of Peter's own experience, this hope proved life-transforming didn't it? When Jesus died on the cross, where was Peter existentially, emotionally? From Caesarea Philippi on, Jesus had spoken of His death and resurrection. But Peter, like the others, did not have a category for a crucified Messiah. Messiahs don't die, they win and are triumphant. So when Jesus spoke of His impending death, Peter rebuked him, wanting to be courageous – 'Though all forsake you yet not I' (cf Mt.16:22). Yet later there he is denying he knows Jesus, disowning Him. Where is Peter now? Then come the first reports from the women, Jesus is alive! There's a race to the tomb (John 20) and then according to Paul in Acts 15, a private revelation of the resurrected Jesus to Peter before Jesus met with the eleven. Hope sparked into life, followed by a restoration to service, 'Peter do you love me? Do you love me more than these?' (cf Jn. 21:15).

Yet there were more massive dimensions to this hope. By this point Peter has understood the implications. He knows that with the death and resurrection of Jesus there is God's final provision for the forgiveness of sins. The promised Messianic kingdom was dawning. Eternal life could be experienced now, even if not consummated till the end. And with Jesus' resurrection there was every hope of one day gaining resurrection bodies like Jesus' resurrection body. In fact in due course Jesus' return came to be referred to as the 'blessed hope of the church.' We participate in all of this now in some measure, by means of the new birth. 'Praise be to the God and Father of our Lord Jesus Christ. In his great mercy he has given us new birth into a living hope through the resurrection of Jesus Christ from the dead ...' This is the hope that God establishes.

2) Hope God sustains (verses 4-5)

Notice the parallel in verse 3 and verses 4 and 5 between new birth into a living hope and new birth into an inheritance that can never perish. What does the apostle mean by this? Doubtless Peter recalled Jesus teaching about treasure in the Sermon on the Mount – 'Do not lay up treasures on earth... but lay up treasures for yourself in heaven' (cf Mt. 6).

Yet here the focus is not quite on treasure so much as on inheritance. Peter and his readers have an Old Testament background quite clearly in mind, picturing the Israelites' inheritance first and foremost to be the land – given not only to the Israelites as a whole, but parcelled out to each clan, each extended family, with lasting rights of ownership, at least on paper. The Old Testament people of God were aliens and pilgrims until they entered the promised land and received their inheritance. Abraham was just a stranger. The people were slaves in Egypt, they were pilgrims in the wilderness for years and years – waiting to get their inheritance of the promised land.

This does not mean of course that they were utterly destitute, for there was a sense in which, although they were not in the land the promise had given them, the land was in principle theirs. It was therefore the promised land, they looked forward to it with hope. In due course God brought about the accomplishment of that hope and they entered into their inheritance.

Now all of Peter's description of our inheritance emerges from this God-ordained Old Testament model. We too are aliens and pilgrims. This does not mean that we are paupers waiting for an inheritance that is in no sense ours. We are enriched by the certainty of the promise, and Peter insists that some part of it has already come to us. We have a clear title to the inheritance that God has reserved for us, and also a down payment.

Moreover, our inheritance too can never perish, spoil or fade. These words are used in various Old Testament descriptions in Greek, concerning things that happened to land at one point or the other. The land itself doesn't perish after all. Sometimes the people run out of it or marauding troops come in. Sometimes the people are punished, but the land is still there, it doesn't perish. And for us, finally the whole universe, according to 2 Peter, burns up with a fierce heat such that even the elements are devoured, but our inheritance doesn't burn up, it's reserved in heaven for us. We look for a new heaven and a new earth, the home of righteousness. It doesn't spoil, it's not defiled. In ancient Israel's concept of things the land could be polluted by the sins of the people, but the new heaven and the new earth has no sin in it, it is never defiled. In these Petrine epistles we read of the new heaven and the new earth, the home of righteousness. Isn't that a lovely phrase? There will be no shred of bitterness, no hate, no arrogance, no greed, no lust, no envy, no jealousy, no murder, there will be no harsh tongues, there will be no nasty resentments – nothing to spoil or corrode our inheritance.

The fruitfulness of ancient land could fade as in the days of the drought imposed by God Himself under the ministry of Elijah. But our inheritance is salvation consummated in the new heaven and the new earth where there will never ever be any sort of drought again.

Moreover, this inheritance is kept in heaven for us and we are kept for it. Do you hear the language? In his great mercy God has given us new birth into an inheritance that can never perish, spoil or fade, kept in heaven for you. God keeps your inheritance for *you*. And at the same time, He keeps *you* for the inheritance, shielded by God's power. Otherwise the inheritance can be nicely parked up there while we wander off in rebellion and are damned. But no, God keeps His own people by His power, preserving us as He preserves the inheritance for us; as we hope for it and we eagerly anticipate our inheritance, we are shielded by God's power, through faith. This is God's means of keeping us (verse 5), as it is God's means of saving us. This faith and this hope are both grounded in God. Hence we read (verse 21), 'Through him you believe in God, who raised him from the dead and glorified him, and so your faith and hope are in God.' Here then is hope that God sustains.

3) Hope God introduces (verses 6-9)

We might like to imagine that the hopeful person is the optimist, who lives above the hassles of the world in the perennial pleasure of watching things get better and therefore living in hope. But in these verses Peter places hope in the context of suffering. He says we have only been introduced to that hope; we are now receiving the goal of our faith, the salvation of our souls, yet we have not seen Jesus Christ. We love Him, but we still live with trials, sorrows and opposition. Indeed, in these verses Peter provides several reasons why Christians actually rejoice in this hope while they may have to suffer.

The first reason is intrinsic. The suffering is temporary, it is transient, 'though for a little while you may have had to

suffer grief in all kinds of trials,' over against the fruitfulness
and inheritance of an eternity with God. Small wonder then,
in 2 Corinthians 4, after many brutal experiences both
imposed by the world and by churches that had gone a little
astray, Paul can speak of his light and momentary afflictions,
which cannot be compared with the eternal weight of glory.

That's not how I am inclined to see things when I'm going
through it. My entire horizons can be consumed by some
small aggravation. And anyone who has been in the ministry
for any period of time knows full well that sooner or later you
get kicked in the teeth and then it is difficult to imagine any
reward compensating for it. But that's not the way Peter saw
it. No, these 'light and momentary afflictions' Paul writes of,
'this little while' Peter writes of, cannot be compared with the
eternal weight of glory.

The second reason for rejoicing in trials is that the tension
between present pressures and the ultimate glory to come is
precisely what strengthens our faith. If you had really had a
rough time before you became a Christian, but then everything was just smooth sailing, how would that increase your
faith in this broken self-centred world? Peter knows that the
tension between the glory to come and the present pressures
produces endurance. It demonstrates that our faith is genuine
and it deepens that faith (verse 7).

That's a fairly common theme in a lot of New Testament
writings. For example, 'Consider it joy, my brothers,whenev-
er you face trials of many kinds' (Jas.1:2). Did you hear that?
It doesn't mean that we are masochists, 'Oh boy this is a good
one Lord, hit me again.' It tells us rather we should rejoice
'because you know that the testing of your faith develops perseverance. Perseverance must finish its work so that you may
be mature and complete, not lacking anything.' With God in
charge, what this is really designed to do is to make us
become enduring. Just as the endurance that an athlete pushes himself toward produces endurance characteristic of his
very being, so also with trials on the Christian way. And
Christians prize that as an athlete prizes his endurance.

But it's not just strengthening in maturity and endurance
in this life. There's something more: 'Blessed is the man who

perseveres under trial, *because* when he has stood the test, he will receive the crown of life that God has promised to those who love him' (Jas 1:12). In other words, Christians do not have the same sort of values as the secular world that knows nothing of the rewards of heaven. We can look at trials in a different way precisely because we have this Christian hope. If we do not maintain that hope before our eyes it will be very difficult indeed to manage the trials that most of us will face, some in great severity.

There is a third reason for rejoicing, the rewards are spectacular and actually begin now. According to verse 7 our faith is proved genuine under trial and results in praise, glory and honour when Jesus Christ is revealed.

Now we have to ask, is this praise, glory and honour for us or for God? Commentators divide over it. You can make sense of the text either way. On the one hand you want to say that Peter in his writings constantly says that the ultimate praise goes to God or to Jesus. For example in chapter 4:11 he writes, 'If anyone speaks, he should do it as one speaking the very words of God. If anyone serves, he should do it with the strength God provides, so that in all things God may be praised through Jesus Christ. To him be the glory and the power for ever and ever.' Or again in chapter 2 verse 9, 'You are a chosen people, a royal priesthood, a holy nation, a people belonging to God, that you may declare the praises of him who called you out of darkness into his wonderful light.'

Yet on the other hand we receive a crown of glory at the end, according to chapter 5 verse 4. Grace is given us when Jesus Christ is revealed, in chapter 1 verse 13. Now the two of course are bound together. Any glory we ultimately receive is still a sharing of Christ's glory. Thus the thought of all praise being directed to God at the end is essential to this passage. And we Christians already delight, therefore, to see whatever praise and honour and glory come to God through Jesus Christ, now, even in our sufferings. Hasn't that been the experience of many Christians?

More importantly, all this takes place at the end of verse 7, when Jesus Christ is revealed, that is at His Second Coming. Yet we Christians are related to Him already, hence verses 8 and 9. Peter had seen Jesus from the beginning of Jesus' ministry. He had been called by him personally, he had spent two and a half years literally following Jesus around the countryside, he had seen Jesus perform astonishing miracles, he had been one of His inner three, he had seen Jesus transfigured on the mountain. He had been through the emotional depths as he saw Jesus hang on the cross. He had been exalted heavenward as he had seen Jesus resurrected. Oh, he had seen Jesus.

But he writes to people like you and me who have never seen Jesus, we do not see Jesus, but we will see Jesus. And by faith, Peter says, you love Him as much as I do. We are in a relationship with Him, we have so been saved by Him, the new birth has been given to us, the Holy Spirit has come upon us because of all of God's design work in sending Jesus to sprinkle His blood upon us and clean us up. But already we love Him. We do not see Him now, but we believe in Him and we are filled with an inexpressible and glorious joy. Why? For we are receiving the goal of our faith, the salvation of our souls. This then is the nature of the hope that God introduces to us now as we walk by faith, waiting for the final revelation of Jesus Christ. Do you hear the intertwining of Christian faith and hope in these verses?

> Lord Jesus You're still hidden,
> We cannot see Your face,
> Yet still by faith we love You,
> For we have known Your grace.
> Our faith awaits hope's promise,
> Still inaccessible,
> Our joy is full and glorious
> And inexpressible.

4) Hope God designs (verses 10-12)

Peter does not want us to think that this wonderful salvation was some last-minute quick fix. It was not only in the mind of God, but in its broad outline it had been predicted by God through the Old Testament prophets. They themselves did not always grasp very clearly the facts or the time of the remarkable sequence. First the sufferings of the Messiah, followed by the glories that would follow. Look at verses 10 and 11. They searched intently trying to sort out the facts and the timing to which the Spirit of Christ, already antecedent with them, was pointing, 'when he predicted the sufferings of Christ and the glories that would follow'.

Now of course from our perspective as Christians, we can see something of that pattern, but it is not entirely clear how many first-century followers of Jesus before the cross and resurrection, caught it – Peter and the disciples didn't – 'Get behind me Satan, you do not understand the things of God,' Jesus rebukes him (cf Mt.16:23). Today we look at a passage like Isaiah 53, certain that the ultimate reference there is to Jesus Christ Himself – wounded for our transgressions, bruised for our iniquities, the chastisement of our peace was upon Him and with His stripes we are healed. We look to that sacrificial system in which morning and evening a peace offering is made in the tabernacle, then in the temple. We look at Yom Kippur, the Day of Atonement, when the blood of a goat and the blood of a bull were taken into the most holy place and offered up before God, both for the sins of the priest and for the sins of the people.

But how many of the Old Testament writers understood that God would visit us in this spectacular way in which there would first be suffering, shame, pain, the cross; followed by vindication, glory, triumph, life? They could see some elements but they didn't all have it together. They wanted to, they searched intently and with the greatest care, we are told. And what are the implications? The Christians see these things, because we live this side of their fulfilment, in One who is simultaneously God and man, in One who is simultaneously suffering servant and triumphant king, who was simultaneously the sacrificial lamb and the triumphant promised Messiah.

The entailment of course is that if we go through sufferings on the way to glory. It is the way the Master went and why should we think that we would be exempt? So our suffering is not a sign that Christ is not ruling, or that He has goofed, or that perhaps we have been abandoned – rather it is a sign of our allegiance to Jesus, of our alignment with

Jesus, of our fellowship with Jesus – a sign of the glory to follow. This is the way God has designed our hope.

How privileged then we are, for there has arisen a redeemer
for fallen human beings and not for fallen angels (verse 12),
'Even angels long to look into these things.' Don't lessen so
audacious and gracious a plan of redemption for rebels as this
that God has thought up in eternity past and then executed
for us by sending His Son to redeem us.

Here it is then, hope that God establishes, hope that God
sustains, hope that God introduces, hope that God designs.
Brothers and sisters, walk by faith, live in hope – hope not for
an easy set of outcomes in this life, but hope for eternity,
hope anchored in Jesus Christ, whom we have not seen and
yet love. And even though we do not see Him now we believe
in Him and are filled with an inexpressible and glorious joy,
for we are receiving the goal of our faith, the salvation of our
souls.

2. Holiness Without Stuffiness
1 Peter 1:13-2:3

According to 1 Peter 1:16, God Himself says, 'Be holy, because I am holy.' The theologians call holiness a communicable attribute of God, that is, one He can share with us and demands of us. There is no text that says, 'Be omnipotent because I am omnipotent, be omnipresent because I am omnipresent.' Omnipotence and omnipresence are incommunicable attributes of God, they are attributes of God that cannot be shared with us and cannot be demanded of us. But God does say, 'Be holy, because I am holy.'

Introduction: What does it mean to be holy?
The word 'holy' and its cognate noun 'holiness' have a wide range of meanings. Let us begin with those two remarkable passages that use 'holy' three times. In his vision in Isaiah 6 the prophet hears the seraphim crying, 'Holy, holy, holy is the LORD Almighty; the whole earth is full of his glory.'

The same words are then picked up in the magnificent vision of the throne room of God in Revelation 4. What does this mean? Some think that the word means 'separate'. But are the angels around the throne saying no more than 'separate, separate, separate is the Lord God Almighty'? It leaves something to be desired, doesn't it? Others think it means 'moral'. But are the angels around the throne saying no more than, 'Moral, moral, moral is the Lord God Almighty'? You quickly see that there is more at stake than separateness or morality.

In the wide range of meanings associated with this word, at its heart 'holy' is almost an adjective for God. It has to do first and foremost with the sheer godness of God. In this ultimate sense only God is holy. But what God is, is holy – that is, He is God. And because there is but one God, He is necessarily separate, different from all other beings. His very holiness is what separates Him and in that sense there is an element of separateness bound up with holiness. But God, because it is His universe, establishes also what is right and wrong. At base sin is nothing other than doing what God forbids and failing to do what God commands. God in all His being, God as He is, God in His resplendent holiness, establishes the lines. Outside of those lines is everything that is wrong. Thus holiness is bound up with what we call 'morality'.

And then in the Bible the term 'holy' can extend a little further to that which is associated with God, whether the thing is moral or not – provided it is associated with God, it might be considered holy. For example, the shovel used to take out the ash from the altar, because it not used for anything else, was considered holy. It wasn't moral, just a shovel. But it was restricted for divine use and thus it was holy, it was separate unto God.

And then the word can extend further to refer to those who have been set aside for a time: they have been consecrated, sanctified, made holy for a particular function. It can even refer to pagan priests who a few times in the Old Testament are referred to as holy, because they deal in the domain of the sacred.

So you see the word can stretch out, but at its heart it has to do with what God is. Now clearly when He says, 'Be holy for I am holy,' He is not telling us to be God. He is telling us to be so much bound up with God, so much reserved for Him, so much connected with all that brings honour and praise to Him, so much in line with all that He is in His character and being, that we are rightly said to be holy.

This passage not only commands that we be holy like God Himself, but unpacks some of the dimensions of holiness.

1) Hope and holiness (1:13-16)

In verse 13 the 'therefore' connects the preceding verses with this paragraph, that is, the description of the glorious salvation God has provided, with the exhortations to live in the light of that salvation – it connects the indicative with the imperative. In particular, as the gospel has provided a rich and certain hope, so now Christians are told, 'Set your hope fully on the grace to be given you when Jesus Christ is revealed.' This certain hope is there, as secure as the facticity of the resurrection of Jesus Christ, chapter 1 verse 3 – as sure as God's sovereign promise. Therefore, set your hope, that is your own eager anticipation, fully on this hope that will finally be clear to us when Jesus Himself returns, when Jesus is revealed.

In other words – you who are Christians have already received forgiveness of sin, the gift of the Spirit, the communion with believers, and the promises of God as to what will come in the new heaven and the new earth by grace. And now that same grace will also give us many more things, this verse says, when Jesus Christ is revealed. By grace we will receive our resurrection bodies, we will be ushered into a new heaven and a new earth, the home of righteousness, we will be utterly transformed into the likeness of Jesus Himself, by grace.

So the text says, as we have received, '… prepare your minds for action; be self-controlled; set your hope fully on the grace to be given you when Jesus Christ is revealed.' Clearly that's a mental commitment. He's not saying go and pick up a brick or dig a trench. It is something that we have to do with our minds, with our hearts, it's a volitional stance. How exactly does a person set his or her hope on something? Perhaps that's why Peter begins verse 13 as he does. The NIV's 'prepare your minds for action' is a kind of paraphrase of an expression that is almost meaningless to us today – 'gird up the loins of your mind.' In the ancient world many peo-

ple had long robes and if they were going to engage in stren-
uous action they buckled up their robes and tucked them
under their belt, they were girding their loins for action. Now
this is extended to the mind – gird up the loins of your mind.

The point is, get ready to think hard, be self-controlled.
And then he says, 'set your hope fully on the grace to be given
you when Jesus Christ is revealed.' Now it's vitally important
to understand how this *is* and is *not* done. This cannot be
done by self-consciously improving our ability to hope, as if
it were an independent function, I will hope harder, I will
hope harder, I will hope harder. And then after we've hoped
hard enough, directing our hoping function to what we want
to hope for and thus choosing God and His salvation. It's
completely the opposite of how it works. Christian hope
flows in the other direction.

Christian hope is improved by fastening attention on the
object, by thinking about the object of our hope – this is how
we strengthen our eager anticipation and our subjective hope,
by thinking through again and again what it is we hunger for.
Like the kid who starts thinking about the birthday party –
ooh, all those presents and friends and pizza – and he thinks
about it and thinks about it. He doesn't say, 'I will hope for
my party, I eagerly anticipate my party, I *will* resolve to anticipate my party.' Instead he just fastens attention on the party
and thinks about it, maybe even becoming obsessive about it,
and meanwhile he has in fact greatly increased his eager anticipation for the party. He now hopes, in the biblical sense, in
the party.

Thus, strictly speaking, to set our hope fully on the grace
to be revealed is little different from thoroughly and grow-
ingly believing the gospel, the good news in all of its dimensions – not least its dimensions in the life to come. This
requires, Peter insists, diligence and self-control.

But the chief point in this section as a whole, in verses 13
to 16, connects this hope with holiness. 'Set your hope fully
on the grace to be given you when Jesus Christ is revealed. As
obedient children, do not conform to the evil desires you had
when you lived in ignorance. But just as he who called you is
holy, so be holy In all you do; for it is written: "Be holy,

because I am holy.'" Set your hope then on the grace to be revealed. This brings with it, according to Peter, the kind of obedient resolution that pursues practical holiness. The verse quoted here, 'Be holy, because I am holy', comes from Leviticus 19 and it is worth pausing for a moment to recognise what holiness at the street level looked like in the terms of the old covenant to which Peter has referred.

Almost every dimension of life was constrained – what you wore, what you ate, almost all of the public functions. If you have a baby, then there are certain sacrifices to be offered. There are certain clothes you must not wear, there are certain foods you must not eat and if you do become dirty, then there are certain procedures to go through in order to become clean. All of life was defined by the old covenant in terms of getting dirty or getting clean; becoming polluted or becoming pure. If you found a mould spot in your house, you had to go to the priest who examined it and maybe the house was destroyed; if it was not destroyed certain steps could be taken, more sacrifices offered – an entire system that constrained every aspect of life. You could not go through a day, if you were a devout Jew, without thinking about whether what you were doing was part of what the Lord forbade, then what you needed to do to get clean again – you were getting dirty or you were getting clean! There was an astonishing system – socially all-embracing. It wasn't a bit of religion tacked on the Lord's day.

This was part of the symbol-laden way of teaching the covenant community. First, that God has the sole right to make the distinctions. Second, that God expects His people to be holy, reserved for Him, clean. And third, that God establishes the sole means by which people may become clean. The fact that God has the sole right to make the distinctions ultimately has a great bearing on how we think of sin. Consider David for instance. Though he was a great leader, he sinned horribly when he seduced Bathsheba and had her husband Uriah killed when it turned out that she was pregnant. The narrator sums up the account by saying, 'but the thing displeased the Lord' (cf 2 Sam.11:27).

Eventually he was confronted by the prophet Nathan and,

as far as we can see, it is after David's repentance that he pens Psalm 51 saying to God, 'Against you, you only, have I sinned and done this evil in your sight.' Of course at one level that wasn't true. He had not only sinned against God, he had sinned against Bathsheba, Uriah and the baby in Bathsheba's womb; he had sinned against the nation and the covenant. It was hard to imagine anybody connected with the whole thing that he hadn't sinned against! And yet in a profound sense this was exactly the case. What made this sin, what gave this action its depth of odium, was not simply the social dimension of betrayal and trust, as gross as that was, but that it was defiance of God – that is what makes sin, sin. It is precisely because David understands that, that he says, 'Against you only, have I sinned.'

God expects His people to be holy, reserved for Him, clean. God establishes the sole means by which people may become clean. In the fullness of time many of the specific rules were withdrawn, changed, abrogated, modified, above all fulfilled. Thus Jesus says and does some things, according to Matthew 15, which make all foods clean, and if the apostles didn't get it then Peter had to go through a visionary experience in Acts 10 and 11 three times in order to get it. Yet the three purposes of these Old Testament passages continue. God has the sole right to make the distinctions. To this day He is the one who establishes by His very being, by His words, what sin is. He expects His people to be holy, and He alone establishes the means, the sole means, by which people may become clean.

So, be holy as God is holy. That is the context in which this exhortation from Leviticus is embedded. If then we set our hope on the grace to be revealed, we become obedient to the gospel: 'As obedient children, do not conform to the evil desires you had when you lived in ignorance.' In fact the original expression is stronger again: as children of obedience, abandon these evil desires that you had when you lived in ignorance. Just as He who called you is holy, so be holy in all you do.

Do you hear the connections then? We have received this grace, therefore set your hope on the grace that is coming, the grace of perfection in the new heaven and the new earth. And therefore be holy as you press for that fulfilment. Christians are moving toward the holiness that will be ours in the new heaven and the new earth. To claim that we have had our sins forgiven and that we are pressing on toward this climactic hope when Jesus is revealed, and yet deep down to cherish sin, is so massively inconsistent, so grotesque, that it puts a question mark over all our pretensions.

Hope – what we eagerly anticipate – and behaviour are connected. If what you hope for is a really big house in the Cotswolds and that is what dominates your thinking and your priorities, then other things will be trimmed off so that you can press in that direction. If you tell everybody that that's what you really want, but meanwhile you spend every free moment and every free pound trying to buy a little fishing smack somewhere off the coast of Scotland, people are going to say, 'How can you say this over here when you do this over there? It doesn't make sense.'

That's the connection between hope, then, and holiness. We are called to be holy, objectively we are moving toward climactic holiness in the new heaven and the new earth, so align your conduct then with this ultimate Christian hope and set your hope on the grace to be revealed when Jesus comes.

2) The Father and holiness (1:17)

'Since you call on a Father who judges each man's work impartially, live your lives as strangers here in reverent fear.' It is hard for most of us to hear the power of this verse, because in our culture, three main forces mitigate against it.

First, the democratisation of all opinion. That is, each opinion is as intrinsically worthy as all other opinions are. We don't think that father knows best.

Second, the elevation of youth. This is reflected in many symbols in the culture that use youth in advertising.

Third, the trivialisation of the father in our culture. The father is distant and remote, and might be even a laughing-stock. The father is not wise in the family, he is absent, he's divorced, the father's a joke. But in the ancient Jewish world, there was more respect for the opinion of the elderly and the informed than of the young. There was no democratisation of opinion. Youth were to be disciplined and taught, not lionised, and ideally the father was a figure to be reverenced for he was not only the family's authority, but also the family's arbiter and judge. Yet because he was the father he was compassionate.

You hear these things coming together in a well-known verse like, 'As the father pities his children so the Lord pities those who fear him'(Ps.103:13). We wouldn't speak like that, would we? The father wants to be feared, and within that framework, also exercise compassion. The father's role was to command and instruct, to hold all to account. Now I am not denying for a moment that sin could distort this particular cultural structure. Of course such fathers could be abusive and perverse. I am saying that our culture can be abusive and perverse in somewhat different ways. And meanwhile, if we are to understand the kind of cultural connections that are bound up with the figure of God as Father, we need to understand that they emerge from the first century and earlier, not from the twentieth.

They were bound up in part with the fact that most sons ended up doing what their fathers did. In an agrarian or pre-industrial society, if your father was a baker you were likely to become a baker. But not so in a post-industrial and industrial society, where children go off and do what they want to do. In those days the children did what their fathers did. Thus the fathers were not only the figures who passed on certain family traditions, they were the ones who took the kids out in the fields, personally in a hands-on way instructing the new generation. They disciplined, they instructed, they held to account. They were compassionate, but they were to be reverenced and even feared. And we simply do not think of fathers in that sort of set of categories today.

So now listen again to the text. 'Since you call on a Father who judges each man's work impartially, live your lives as strangers here in reverent fear.' In other words, our family connection means that we belong elsewhere – we don't quite belong here. We have seen this notion of being aliens and strangers from the earlier verses of the chapter. We belong to this family, we belong to this father and in this family this Father judges impartially – He has no favourites. In this sense we are extra-terrestrials, or as Clowney says, neo-terrestrials – waiting for the new heaven and the new earth – we belong to another family, we have a slightly different citizenship, our home is elsewhere. Therefore, because He judges each one's work in this family impartially – He is our Father, a Father on whom we call (verse 17). Yet He is also the Father whom we are to treat with reverent fear.

What does this mean, to treat the Father with reverent fear? One of my friends asked his daughter, 'Are you afraid of me?' 'Oh come on Dad, for goodness sake,' she replied. 'No. Is there any sense in which you are afraid of me?' 'Well yes, sometimes.' 'Is that a good thing?' he asked. She grinned and said, 'Yeah, probably.' And he said, 'Then go and reflect on the fear of God.'

No doubt perfect love casts out fear. But in this sinful order, when we are never all that far away from shoving our fists in God's face and singing with Frank Sinatra, 'I did it my way,' it's a good thing to have a bit of fear. In fact the word 'reverent' here is a bit of an addition – the text just says 'fear'. That's not cringing fear, it's not that we are crouching down like a beaten puppy, crying and waiting for the next blow to fall. No, this is a compassionate Father on whom we call, (verse 17). But we do fear Him and it's a good thing.

So what draws us towards holiness? Well, hope for the future, the direction in which we are moving (verse 13), but now also the commanding, demanding judgement of the Father, which completely fills, us in a certain sense, with anticipation, and in another sense with fear. God holds us to account, yet provides us with a name that we can call upon, our Father. Fear and reverence. This Father does not drive us from Him, but toward Him in obedience to Him for this Father really does know best.

3) Jesus Christ and holiness (1:18-21)

In these verses a further great incentive to holiness is plain enough. Not to pursue holiness is to despise and insult the inestimable value of Christ's sacrifice on our behalf. Peter says we were redeemed by Christ's death, by Christ's blood. The notion of redemption is largely alien to our culture, but not to the first century. The redemption of slaves in the Hellenistic world could take place fairly easily: someone could pay money to the owner, perhaps through a temple treasury, and redeem the slave, and thus free the slave from slavery.

Old Testament law likewise provided for the redemption of slaves, sometimes through a *Goel*, that is to say a near relative, a kinsman-redeemer who could buy back, whether a family member had been sold into slavery, or some family possession. The Old Testament law also provided for redemption money so that a person's life would not be forfeit after this crime or that crime. In the case of murder no redemption money was permitted, that's why capital punishment was insisted upon under the Old Testament law, because no redemption money was considered adequate.

Then again every first-born Israelite boy had to be redeemed, that is, paid for with a ransom, Numbers 18, Exodus 30. This was a sign that all Israel was guilty and spared only by the grace of God who allowed the payment and accepted it.

Now all of this meant that the notion of redemption was not alien to Peter or his first-century readers. Again and again in Isaiah, God discloses Himself as the kinsman-redeemer of His people. He is their creator, He is tied to them in a covenant. But He exercises His right as kinsman and redeemer to buy them from their guilt, to buy them from the slavery, to buy them from the punishment that they are about to undergo.

That is the sort of connection that Peter picks up here. We are redeemed, Peter says. What we are redeemed from (verse18) is the meaninglessness of a pagan life, the sheer slavery of it. We are redeemed from the empty way of life handed down to us from our forefathers. The idea is not that we are redeemed from the odd little sin that we may have accidentally committed, but that our whole outlook, the whole heritage, the whole anti-God stance that the first-century pagans inherited from their tradition, was a form of bondage from which they had to be set free. And increasingly in the West that is the way things are. We live in an age when large swathes of our culture now descend from a tradition without reference to the God who made us, and we have to be set free, redeemed, purchased out of this slavery.

What then does *not* redeem us (verse18)? Well, it's not money, it's not like the redemption money used in freeing a slave. You know that it was not with perishable things such as silver and gold that we were redeemed. What did redeem us (and it was inestimably costly) is the precious blood of Christ, a lamb without blemish or defect. Like the prescribed sacrificial lambs in the Old Testament system by which people were made holy.

We were redeemed by His blood. In the New Testament blood regularly refers not simply to the literal fluid in Christ's veins, but to a violent and sacrificial death on behalf of another. So the very texts that speak of being redeemed by the blood of Christ can speak elsewhere of being redeemed by the death of Christ, or by the sacrifice of Christ. And this cost is beyond calculation. The value of this ransom is clarified by reflecting on who Jesus is (verse 20). 'He was chosen before the creation of the world ...' That is why the book of Revelation can speak of Jesus as the Lamb slain before the foundation of the world – presupposed is His pre-existence. He did not just begin His existence in the womb of Mary, but before the foundation of the world He already was and He entered this world in the plan of God and gave up His life, the just for the unjust, to bring us to God.

The theme keeps recurring in this book. Thus in 2:24, 'He himself bore our sins in his body on the tree, so that we might die to sins and live for righteousness; by his wounds you have been healed.'

Through Him then we have come to believe in God (verse 21), and have hope in God. Merely human traditions, the traditions of a fallen race, are wretched illusions. Our faith is in God. Our hope is in God. This is the framework then in which God speaks to us and says, 'Be holy, for I am holy.'

I know that there are many different views on the significance of Holy Communion. But there are certain elements regarding it with which we all agree, and one of those most central elements is in fact made explicit by the command of Christ. 'Do this,' Jesus says, 'in remembrance of me.' So we take the elements and we remember Christ's broken body and His shed blood. Now supposing we were to take those elements and say by our participation, 'I remember, I remember Christ's death on my behalf, I remember,' and then go out and curse somebody on the street, swear at the kids, gossip about the minister, nurture a little bitterness, cheat on one's income tax. The very act of publicly remembering would not only be a contradiction in terms, it would be like spitting on Christ all over again. 'I remember Christ died for me to pay for my sin. Ha ha ha, what a joke.' That's the effect of it, it's grotesque.

Thus one of the functions of the Lord's Supper is precisely to serve as a public renewal of the covenant by which we remember that by which we are redeemed, Christ's death, and thus pursue holiness. I remember, I remember, I remember. As we grow in grace and in our estimation of the worth of Christ, we are increasingly broken by the horror of our sin, by the shame of it and ugliness of it. That only Christ's death was sufficient to pay for it, the focusing on the death of Christ becomes in itself a God-given means to pursue holiness.

4) The Word of God and holiness (1:22-2:3)

In these verses it is important to follow the flow of the thought. Verse 22, 'Now that you have purified yourselves by obeying the truth so that you have sincere love for your brothers, love one another deeply, from the heart.'

The obedience envisaged here is the initial obedience that is bound up with becoming a Christian, with being submissive to Christ, with repentance, with bowing to the gospel. So that now you have purified yourselves by obeying the truth, now that you have become a Christian, now that you have submitted to the Lordship of Christ, now that you have embraced the gospel – therefore now love one another deeply.

In other words, holiness devoted to God has manifested

itself in love for fellow believers. So we have faith and hope and we have love. Does that remind you of anything? Faith, hope and love are often called the Pauline Triad, but in fact it's not simply Pauline, it's basic New Testament theology; here it's bound up with Peter as well. You can't have one without the other either in biblical theology, they intertwine in a variety of ways. And here, setting our hope on the grace that is to come, and trusting and obeying this Word of truth inevitably manifests itself also in love for fellow believers. Now therefore, Peter says, press on with love, love one another deeply from the heart.

It is as if Peter recognises that Christians cannot truly be holy before God without loving the brothers and sisters. The two are not identical, they are not equivalent. They are always distinguishable, but they are always inseparable, you cannot have one without the other. You cannot genuinely pursue holiness and not love brothers and sisters in Christ. And you cannot grow in love of brothers and sisters in Christ without also pursuing holiness before God.

Love one another deeply from the heart. How shall we do this? Shall we simply command people to love and it will be done? Go ahead, love each other more, go on, do it! Turn it on. No. Such love comes from the heart. It's even bound up in the form of a commandment, 'Love one another deeply, from the heart.' The heart in fact that has been regenerated (verse 23). Christian love can be demonstrated in lots of ways, but it cannot simply be taught.

You can demonstrate love by digging up an elderly person's garden for them, by giving money to the poor, by a thousand things. That doesn't mean that those ways are simply transmissible, because the way that Christian love is generated is from within the heart, and this is bound up by the Gospel, that is the living and enduring Word of God. That's how it starts within us – '… you have been born again, not of perishable seed, but of imperishable, through the living and enduring word of God.' In other words, this life-giving Word of God is likened to human procreation – it is the seed of life, it is sown in us to generate love through the eternal, enduring power of the Word of God, unlike human generation –

we generate people and we all die. Human seed is not enduring (verse 24), we are characterised by change and decay but
God's word abides. Therefore, since this word is enduring,
changeless, powerful, effective, likened to seed that generates
and regenerates and transforms from within, 'Therefore, rid
yourselves of all malice and all deceit, hypocrisy, envy, and
slander of every kind. Like newborn babies, crave pure spiritual milk, so that by it you may grow up in your salvation…'

With Paul and in Hebrews you sometimes get a comparison between milk and meat. Milk is for the immature
Christian and by the time you ought to be eating *filet
mignon*, you are still drinking milk. There is a contrast made
therefore between this person's immaturity and that person's
spiritual maturity. That's not the point here. There's no question of maturity along such lines, a move from milk to meat.
The idea here is that for the baby, milk is not an optional
extra, it's that which keeps the baby alive, it's that which
nourishes the baby. And that's the way we Christians are to
see the word of God in our lives. It is not an optional extra,
it is what keeps us alive, it is what feeds us, it is what makes
us grow: '… crave spiritual milk, so that by it you may grow
up in your salvation …'

One of the motives that will help us in this regard is that
we discover it tastes good. For when you start pursuing
Scripture, in due course the delight is not in the rhetoric, we
begin to taste the Lord Himself. The Lord manifests Himself
through the Word. Now that we have become Christians we
have tasted and seen (verse 3) that the Lord is good. Well
then, let's have more goodness, let's enjoy Him all the more,
the text is saying – crave this spiritual food.

Then how shall we pursue holiness? Shall we pursue holiness by a single revival meeting? Oh the Lord may, in His
great mercy, come down upon us in great strength and suddenly disclose Himself to us, but the ordained means of grace
here is the Word of God, that's the truth.

Do you want to be holy? Do you remember what Jesus
prays on the night that He is betrayed, only hours before the
cross? 'Sanctify them through your truth.' That is, 'sanctify
them, make them holy through your truth, your Word is

truth' (cf Jn.17:17).

How does the book of Psalms begin? 'Blessed is the man who does not walk in the counsel of the wicked or stand in the way of sinners or sit in the seat of mockers.' Here the righteous person is described negatively, what he is *not* like. Blessed is the man who does not do any of these things.

In good poetical style we might have expected verse 2 then to describe righteous persons positively – blessed rather is the man who walks in the counsel of the Godly, who stands in the way of the just, who sits in the seat of the praising. But that's not what the text says. Verse 2, describing a just person, simply, positively says, 'But his delight is in the law of the LORD, and on his law he meditates day and night.'

What is Joshua told when he takes over as head of the nation? This Book of the Law shall not depart from your mouth, you shall meditate on it day and night. Then you shall make your way prosperous and then you shall have good success (cf Josh.1:8).

Conclusion

Here then is a vision of holiness that transcends mere conformity to rules that say do this, don't do that. We watch our young people asking, 'Are Christians allowed to ... ?' and then you fill in the blank. And the question seems to be, 'How far can I shove without being absolutely apostate?' We know that the whole culture has drifted toward the abyss in certain respects, and most of us are a little bit leery about the rule-based forms of evangelicalism that were characteristic twenty-five years ago, but on the other hand we just can't stand this antinomian drift, so what do we do? We are not going to establish holiness in the church by merely imposing rules. What that will do is stifle grace.

On the other hand, if you don't pursue holiness in the church, sooner or later you don't have a church. No. We must set our hope on eternal things, we must enter into this relationship with the Father that calls on him as a child calls, and treats Him with reverent fear. We must reverence the sacrifice of Christ above all, we must hide God's Word in our heart that we may learn not to sin against Him.

Let us be frank. In many of our churches there's all kinds of what Peter describes in verse 2 – malice, deceit, hypocrisy, envy and slander of every kind, nurtured bitterness, one-upmanship, arrogance, all kinds of it. Carelessness, resentments, roast preachers, abused parishioners – all kinds of it.

> I am ashamed. Oh Lord forgive.
> I used to nurture bitterness
> To count up every slight.
> The world's a moral wilderness
> And I have felt its blight...
> Oh God I want so much to trust,
> To follow Jesus on the cross,
> To love and love again.

What does it mean to be holy but to love God with heart and soul and mind and strength and our neighbour as our self? 'Be holy, for I am holy.'

3. A Rock and a People
1 Peter 2:4-12

Introduction: What is a temple?

Have you ever played that game where someone says a word
and everyone owns up to the first thing they think of? For
example, 'car'. Some might say 'A new Jaguar' or 'An Aston
Martin' or 'A yellow Mini,' it's amusing to watch what comes
to mind. If I were to say the following word to you, what
would come to your mind? 'Temple.' A large Baptist church
somewhere perhaps, a magnificent oriental structure, a
mosque, a cathedral, Solomon's temple.

Now the passage before us speaks of Christians collective-
ly as a temple. I doubt if many of us, when we heard the word
'temple', thought immediately, 'church, and I am part of this
temple.' But here that is how Peter wants us to think. If we
are to understand what Peter is getting at there are two things
that we must grasp, things that both he and his readers took
for granted. First is the pattern of the temple on which he
bases his exposition, that is the Old Testament tabernacle and
temple from the time of Solomon on. Some of the things
associated with this temple are of paramount importance if
we are to understand this passage.

The temple, and the tabernacle before it, was God's institution. Repeatedly we find in the book of Exodus that Moses
was to build the tabernacle exactly according to the pattern

he saw on the Mount. The writer to the Hebrews says, the reason is because the exact pattern was symbol-laden, and it pointed in various ways to the ultimate sacrifice offered by the ultimate priest before the ultimate holy of holies to deal finally with our sin. So God wanted the pattern to be exact. It was God's institution, not only because of where it was leading in the sweep of redemptive history, but also to define the people of God. This was for the covenant community; it was for the Israelites and to it they were to gather on their high days. It was moreover the centre of God's self-disclosure, the centre from which the word of the Lord was to spring, the centre where God manifested Himself in glory, especially on the high day of Yom Kippur when the priest would enter into the most holy place just once a year, with the blood of a bull and the blood of a goat, to atone for his sins and the sins of the people, and God would manifest Himself in glory before the priest, who served as a kind of mediating officer, as God displayed Himself between the wings of the carved cherubim over the ark of the covenant.

Moreover, it was the centre of the entire sacrificial system which dealt with sin. It was the centre of corporate praise, and from the time of David with the tabernacle and then Solomon with the temple, there was sophisticated music and choir systems – it was the centre of priestly activity. All of these things both Peter and his readers would presuppose and bear in mind when Peter starts talking about the church as the temple of God.

Second, we must also understand the substance and context of the Old Testament passages that Peter quotes in these verses. First-century Bible readers often understood the Old Testament context and would bring it to bear when a text was cited. If I suddenly said to you, 'There is therefore now no condemnation to those who are in Christ Jesus,' many of you would say, 'Romans chapter 8.' You know the context of Paul's thought there and you would bring it with you if I referred to the verse.

So also when these verses are quoted here about the stone, the stone the builders rejected, the stone that is chosen and precious, the most informed readers and certainly Peter's mind as well, would immediately reflect back on the context of these passages – we must bear them in mind if we are to catch the flow of Peter's thought aright.

1) The construction of the temple (2:4-5)

'As you come to him,' that is Jesus, 'the living Stone – rejected by men but chosen by God and precious to him – you also, like living stones, are being built into a spiritual house to be a holy priesthood, offering spiritual sacrifices acceptable to God through Jesus Christ.'

At one level these two verses are clear enough. Peter is thinking of a spiritual temple, not a granite or marble edifice. In this spiritual temple, we are told, Jesus is the massive cornerstone. Now in the construction of the day this cornerstone would not only be the first stone put in place, but it would constrain the rest of the building. It would have to be firmly based, absolutely level, and exactly positioned so as to determine the angle of the walls – it was a defining stone. This massive stone would have to be straight and true. Yet Peter does not want to think of Jesus as an inert hunk of marble, no matter how magnificent, so he calls Him 'a living stone', which not only means that He is a person, but that He is risen from the dead and alive and shapes this temple by exactly who He is; He constrains the entire construction. And we Christians, Peter goes on to say in verse 5, are also living stones, and so the whole temple is built up into what Peter calls a spiritual house.

But Peter is prepared to mix his metaphors in order to draw into the picture some things associated with the temple. We are not only here the living stones of the temple, but we are the temple's priesthood. We offer spiritual sacrifices acceptable to God through Jesus Christ, which is not what the stones did – that's what the priests did.

More importantly the cornerstone itself, Jesus, Peter tells us, was rejected by the builders. But somehow this rejected stone became the cornerstone anyway, because this stone was, 'chosen by God and precious to Him' – that is, God simply overruled the builders.

So this lays out the shape of the extended metaphor, the

construction of the temple. But what authorises this extended metaphor in Peter's mind? Why should we Christians
think of ourselves in these terms? This brings us to the second major point.

2) The foundation of this temple (2:6-8)

Here we have three Old Testament quotations which we must
examine in turn.

The first is Isaiah 28:16, quoted in 1 Peter 2:6. 'For', here's
the grounding in Peter's mind, 'For in Scripture it says: "See,
I lay a stone in Zion, a chosen and precious cornerstone, and
the one who trusts in him will never be put to shame."' Now
in the context of Isaiah 28, the Old Testament prophet speaks
against the princes and leaders of Jerusalem who thought that
their city could never be overthrown. The northern tribes
could go off into captivity, that's conceivable, and no doubt
God could come upon us in temporal judgements, but to
imagine that Jerusalem could be overthrown, with the temple, that's outside the realm of plausibility. For this is the
place where God has chosen to disclose Himself, this is Zion,
God's holy hill, this is the place of the temple, this is where
God manifests Himself in His glory – to think that this city
could be overthrown is simply unbelievable from their perspective. They think they are secure. And so in due course,
they reject the preaching of Jeremiah who warned that the
city would be destroyed if they continued to rebel against
God; and likewise the exiles can't really believe Ezekiel's message that the city would be overthrown – they just don't have
categories for it because they think they are secure in the
shadow of the temple.

So Isaiah, a century and a half earlier than the destruction
of the temple, begins to mock the kind of overweening confidence of the leaders Isaiah 28:14 – 'Therefore hear the word
of the LORD, you scoffers who rule this people in Jerusalem.
You boast, "We have entered into a covenant with death, with
the grave we have made an agreement. When an overwhelming scourge sweeps by, it cannot touch us, for we have made
a lie our refuge and falsehood our hiding-place."' What they
mean by this first part is what's critical here – 'We have

entered into a covenant with death.' It is as if they are so sure that they are safe, that they have entered into a contract with death and hell, so that even when scourges sweep through the entire region they will be safe.

'So this is what the Sovereign Lord says: "See, I lay a stone in Zion, a tested stone, a precious cornerstone for a sure foundation; the one who trusts will never be dismayed. I will make justice the measuring line and righteousness the plumb-line; hail will sweep away your refuge, the lie, and water will overflow your hiding-place. Your covenant with death will be annulled;"' in other words, your so-called deal will be wiped out – 'your agreement with the grave will not stand. When the overwhelming scourge sweeps by, you will be beaten down by it.'

So you see in God's answer, what He's really saying is, your presumed security isn't secure – I am the one who lays in Zion the secure cornerstone, and only those who are solidly grounded on this cornerstone are secure.

As far as I can see that is part of the background to Jesus' words in Matthew 16: 'I will build my church and the gates of hell will not overcome it.' That is to say, this is the secure cornerstone, that is the people that will not be overthrown. Moreover, already in Jesus' day in the first century, there were some Jews who understood this cornerstone in Isaiah 28:16 to refer to the coming Messiah. Peter is in no doubt at all: Jesus Christ, he insists, is this cornerstone and He is built right into this temple which is here, the church.

But that means that the kind of temple that withstands the torrents of death and hell is not the kind that was built in his day on Mount Zion – more the stone Isaiah says, and Peter quotes the words, is 'chosen and precious'. The word rendered 'precious' in English is used sometimes in the ancient world for what we would call precious gems. But it was also used for building stones of great value, such as a first-class giant cornerstone. We might render 'chosen of God and of enormous value'.

At the level of the metaphor the picture is clear enough – Jesus is this massive constraining cornerstone and the whole church is being built up. A flood of truths and passages come

to mind that echo the notion that Jesus is the chosen and val-
ued one. Even at Jesus' baptism a voice from heaven says,
'You are my Son whom I love, with you I am well pleased' (cf
Mt. 3:17). In Isaiah 42 God says, 'Here is my servant whom
I uphold, my chosen one in whom I delight; I will put my
Spirit on him...' Twice in John's gospel we are told, the
Father loves the Son. We find God is totally satisfied with this
servant, with His Son, and vindicates Him in the resurrection
and ascension.

To some then Christ is indeed precious, to those who
believe (verse 7), and we are built up as living stones.

But this does not mean that everyone thinks so highly of
Him and so we are introduced to the second quotation, this
time from Psalm 118:22, cited in verse 7, 'Now to you who
believe, this stone is precious. But to those who do not
believe, "The stone the builders rejected has become the capstone."' Jesus Himself quotes this verse. Undoubtedly Peter
heard Him do it. On this point Peter learned his hermeneu-
tics, his way of interpreting the Old Testament, from Jesus.
The clearest account is in Matthew 21 verses 33 to 42, the
parable of the wicked tenants, where the master sent his various messengers to collect some of the produce and the prof-
it from the field and they were simply beaten up. Eventually
the master sends his own son saying, 'They will reverence my
son.' But they killed him. Jesus thus speaks of the leaders of
Israel killing the Son of God sent to them to receive what is
but His due. And then He quotes this passage, 'The stone the
builders rejected has become the capstone.'

Then Jesus adds, in Matthew 21, 'Therefore I tell you that
the kingdom of God will be taken away from you and given
to a people who will produce its fruit.' But as for the builders
who rejected God's cornerstone, Jesus goes on so far as to say,
21:44, 'He who falls on this stone will be broken to pieces,
but he on whom it falls will be crushed.' Do you hear the
note of exclusiveness in this? Jesus insists unambiguously that
men and women are redeemed by Him. He is the one who
constrains and defines what the locus of the people of God
really is. He does not see Himself as one optional leader in an
entire history, He sees Himself as the fulfilment of the Old

Testament expectations, the one on whom all of these predictions are now focused. And apart from Him there is no salvation. To defy Him, or to confront Him, to disown Him, to dismiss Him, is in fact to be crushed by Him.

Peter understood that message well too, so that in his sermon in Acts chapter 4 he says to leaders in his own day, 'Salvation is found in no one else for there is no other name under heaven given to men by which we must be saved.'

Do not be confused by the word 'capstone' here. When we think of 'capstone' we might think of a stone at the cap of a peak, and then we start wondering if we've got two stones, a cornerstone down here and then a capstone at the top. It simply means the principal stone, it's still referring to the cornerstone – the stone the builders rejected has become the principal stone, the cornerstone.

The whole point then is further elucidated in Isaiah chapter 8 verse 14. It is important to note something of the context, beginning in Isaiah 8 verse 11. Here the nation is threatened once again, with a preliminary judgement – the people are fearful: 'The LORD' then, according to Isaiah, 'spoke to me with his strong hand upon me, warning me not to follow the way of this people' – the current faddish opinions as to what the solutions should be. This is what God said,

> Do not call conspiracy everything that these people call conspiracy; do not fear what they fear, and do not dread it. The LORD Almighty is the one you are to regard as holy, he is the one you are to fear, he is the one you are to dread, and he will be a sanctuary; but for both houses of Israel he will be a stone that causes men to stumble and a rock that makes them fall. And for the people of Jerusalem he will be a trap and a snare. Many of them will stumble; they will fall and be broken, they will be snared and captured.

Peter drives the lesson home in chapter 2:8, 'They stumble because they disobey the message – which is also what they were destined for.'

Recently a friend of mine, a missionary in Central

America, who had been pursuing doctoral studies in England, stopped in America on the way back to Costa Rica, to spend time doing a bit of deputation work in his home church, before he returned to teaching in Costa Rica. He sent me an e-mail of his impressions saying, 'The dominant feeling I get increasingly in Western churches, is of fear – people are afraid. They are afraid of what's going on in the culture, they are afraid of what's going on in society, they are afraid of the meaninglessness bound up with their young people, they are afraid of their own futures, and out of fear they lash out, they score points, they build empires. We are a frightened people, a frightened culture.'

Now of course that's not the only possible analysis, but it was insightful. In times of rapid transition it's not uncommon to find hearts of people failing them for fear. Then eventually, because we are afraid of what's going on, we start lashing out, we start trying to erect instant defences. We think we are speaking prophetically, when we may simply be expressing our anger, venting our spleen. And then we may need to hear again what God said to Isaiah in another time of massive change and threat. Do not call conspiracy what the current population views as conspiracy. Do not fear what they dread, the Lord shall be your fear. He Himself will be the stone that will crush the people where they reject Him. Yahweh will be that stone, God Himself. Fear Him.

And now Peter picks up these words and applies them to Jesus. He is 'A stone that causes men to stumble and a rock that makes them fall.' They stumble because, as in Isaiah's day, 'they disobey the message – which is also what they were destined for.'

Now it's important to keep both parts of the latter half of verse 8 in view. If you simply take the last clause and absolutise it, then you can't believe the first part. If they disbelieve, if they stumble, well it's what they were destined for, so you can scarcely blame them can you?

If you absolutise the first part, then it almost sounds as if God is asleep at the switch, so He let that one get by Him – they stumble because they disobey the message – whoops, hadn't thought of that! But in fact, in Scripture, the people of

God are compatibilists. Compatibilism is a convenient word for describing a certain kind of theological position. Compatibilism is the view that on the one hand God's sovereignty and on the other human accountability are mutually compatible – they are not mutually incoherent. If I could summarise two statements which are both biblically defensible, both true, I would put it this way. On the one hand, in Scripture God is absolutely sovereign, but His sovereignty never mitigates human accountability. On the other hand, in Scripture, human beings are morally accountable. We believe, we disbelieve, we choose, we disobey, we obey. But our moral accountability never renders God utterly contingent, it never makes Him entirely secondary, a mere reactor.

Now how those things are mutually compatible is a very complex issue. I think that it is easier to show that there are excellent biblical reasons for believing that they are not incompatible. And they are certainly both taught in Scripture, which for me makes them entirely compatible. So I believe in compatibilism! I can't prove them. I see some things I just don't know and I can't explain. I do see however in Scripture, that these things are utterly crucial for the Christian, they occur in many forms. Perhaps the most dramatic place is in Acts chapter 4. Here there is a whiff of persecution beginning to break out in the church. Peter and John then return to their 'own people', the text says, that is to Christians who have gathered together in prayer. The Christians in their prayer cite Psalm 2 which talks about the heathen nations gathering against the Lord and against His anointed. And then they say, in Acts chapter 4:27, 'Indeed Herod and Pontius Pilate' and the rulers of the Jews, '… conspired against your holy servant Jesus,' – in other words, they saw all of the events that led up to Calvary as a massive and evil conspiracy. And then they add, 'They did what your power and will had decided beforehand should happen.'

Now the fact of the matter is, if you don't believe both of those verses it's very difficult to be a Christian. You see, if you only believe the first part, that the cross was nothing more than the product of a human conspiracy, then from God's perspective it was a bit of an accident. It's now the case that

you cannot picture the cross as something planned in the
mind of God from eternity past, it happened simply because
Pontius Pilate was a corrupt and fearful governor, it happened because the Jewish leaders of the time were afraid of
political anarchism, it happened because Herod was a weak
and petty king up in the north and came from a bad line. It
happened for all the wrong reasons, but it wasn't something
which God designed – in which case you can't make sense of
the entire history of the Bible, which has all of those pictures
of a lamb being sacrificed and a priestly system and a temple
system, which the Bible insists find their ultimate fulfilment
in Jesus Christ.

On the other hand, if you just believe the second verse,
verse 28 and forget the first part, well you know, the cross
happened because God ordained it. And because God
ordained it therefore you can't very well blame Herod – it was
going to happen because it was going to happen, God
ordained it. God knew that Pilate was going to wash his
hands and God knew and planned in advance that the leaders were going to act this way. So you can't blame them, can
you, God did it. But if you can't blame any human beings for
the death of Jesus because God is sovereign, I don't see how
you can blame any human beings for anything because God
is sovereign.

Nobody is responsible, you don't need a Christ on the
cross.

So if you only accept the first verse, you destroy the cross
because God didn't plan it, it was an accident. And if you
accept only the second verse, you don't need the cross because
nobody's guilty – instead of being compatibilists, now we're
determinists – whatever will be will be, *qué sera, sera*!

But that's not the way the Christian thinks. The Christian
reads the Bible and, in passage after passage, learns that
human beings are responsible. I end up doing what, for all
kinds of corrupt and misguided reasons, I want to do, and I
am responsible for that. I am responsible for what I say, what
I do, what I think.

On the other hand, God is so sovereign that even in my
most obtuse wickedness I never escape the outermost bounds

of His sovereignty and in His wise purposes He brings good even out of evil. He brings good even out of the evil that drove Jesus to the cross, so that the human beings that broke Him there, not only Herod and Pontius Pilate and the Jewish leaders, but you and me in our sin, are still responsible for all that we do, even though God in His perfect wisdom was so shaping the events that even in the context of our massive rebellion and evil He was bringing triumph out of sheer grace. It's compatibilism.

Peter simply presupposes it. 'They stumble because they disobey the message – which is also what they were destined for.' Even when this happens you must not think that God was asleep at the switch. God still remains sovereign even in these matters – even in pronouncing judgement.

Here is the foundation of the temple: Jesus Christ Himself, as grounded in Scriptural authority. The temple is being built into an entire edifice with Christ as the chief cornerstone and ourselves as stones.

3) The significance of the temple (2:9-10)

'But you are a chosen people.' The 'But' at the beginning of the verse is over against those who have disobeyed the message, against them, 'you are a chosen people, a royal priesthood, a holy nation, a people belonging to God, that you may declare the praises of him who called you out of darkness into his wonderful light. Once you were not a people, but now you are the people of God; once you had not received mercy, but now you have received mercy.'

Here the primary Old Testament allusion is to Exodus 19:6, but it is worth reading 19:4-6. Moses, speaking for God, addresses the Israelites as they have emerged from slavery in Egypt and are about to receive the law. God says to them, 'You yourselves have seen what I did to Egypt, and how I carried you on eagles' wings and brought you to myself. Now if you obey me fully and keep my covenant, then out of all nations you will be my treasured possession. Although the whole earth is mine,' God is never a tribal God, 'you will be for me a kingdom of priests and a holy nation. These are the words,' He says to Moses, 'you are to speak to the Israelites.'

And now Peter, certainly aware of these words, speaks to the church, which in this case has a great number of Gentiles in it, and says, '… you are a chosen people, a royal priesthood …' Note the pattern in the Old Testament in Exodus 19:4-6: God redeemed the people; He claimed them as His people, distinct from all other nations, so that they would be His people. He commissions them as a kingdom, a body of priests, that is, the domain of this particular rule, a kingdominion – even though He is sovereign over everything. And of priests, that is, who offer up worship and praise to Him and in some ways mediate the glory of God to others. He dwells among them, He tells them to be holy as He is holy, and commissions them as a kingdom of priests. Yet we know what happened.

Eventually the declension is so bad that in the days of Hosea, which is still only 800 BC, they have become '*Lo-Ammi,*' (Hosea 1:9): 'Not my people, no longer the people of God.' But God in His mercy looks forward to the time when He will restore them as His people. Thus Isaiah says, 'And you will be called priests of the LORD, you will be named ministers of our God' (Is. 61:6). Indeed, some Old Testament prophets foresee an extension, even to the enemy nations, so that they too become part of God's people. In Isaiah 19:24 we read, 'In that day Israel will be the third, along with Egypt and Assyria,' proverbial enemies of God and enemies of the covenant community, 'a blessing on the earth. The LORD Almighty will bless them, saying, "Blessed be Egypt my people, Assyria my handiwork, and Israel my inheritance."' It is almost as if they are saying, in effect, that if God's grace can extend so far as to reach rebellious Israel, it can certainly extend so far as to reach pagan idolaters. This is the sort of fulfilment then that Peter here proclaims. Here there is a new covenant temple, a spiritual temple. The grace of God that could restore a disobedient and rebellious Israel could extend to wicked pagans like you and me.

And of course many of the elements bound up with the temple come across, do they not? A spiritual house we are told. What is the temple? It's the place that defines the peo-

ple of God, where God manifests Himself. That is what the
church is. The church as a whole defines us. And not only so,
it's the place where God manifests Himself in His glory and
His beauty. There are obvious changes of course. We are not
made of granite, this is spiritual house. Now there is one people made up of Jew and Gentile, a theme greatly celebrated
in Ephesians 2. Moreover, this temple is not built, this unity
is not achieved on the basis of the Old Testament covenant,
but by the coming of Jesus Christ and His cross' work – so
He is the cornerstone on which the entire new temple is
built. This is God's chosen people, a kingdom, a priesthood,
the particular domain of God's saving reign, a people given
over to praising God and to mediating God's glory to the
world. We are thus the people of God.

This symbolism is taken up in various ways throughout
the New Testament. In the last two chapters of the Bible we
are told that there is a new heaven and a new earth, and then
the metaphor changes. Instead the seer, John, sees the city,
the New Jerusalem coming down out of heaven, built like a
perfect cube. Now that's not the way you build a city. You're
not to think of this as a literal city. The only perfect cube in
Scripture is the Most Holy Place. You see, the whole New
Jerusalem is the Most Holy Place, which is why in Revelation
21 John says, 'I did not see a temple in that city, because the
Lord God Almighty and the Lamb are its temple.' You are
mixing your metaphors so as to say, the whole city is The
Most Holy Place, where God is in all of His glory. Or to
change it again, God Himself is the temple, He is the defining thing in the temple and we are in His presence all the
time – no more mediators, no more priests, no more sacrificial system, no more veil between – there is no mediation
necessary, we are forever in the presence of the King. And
already we, the church, are the temple of God, the locus
where God shows forth His glory, God's mediating agents in
this wicked world. That is how we are to view the church.

Moreover, this passage tells us not only what we are but
what we are to do: '… you are a chosen priesthood, a royal
priesthood, a holy nation, a people belonging to God, that
you may declare the praises of him who called you out of

darkness into his wonderful light.' It's a bit like Hebrews 13:15, 'Through Jesus, therefore, let us continually offer to God a sacrifice of praise – the fruit of lips that confess his name.' We do not offer sacrifices of lambs and bulls and goats, for the final sacrifice has come. We offer the sacrifice of praise.

Praise in Scripture is always secondary, as a response to God's primary activity. God acts and we offer praise. It's not as if we praise Him enough so that He can be coerced into doing something. Christians praise because of what God has done, and because of who He is. So we offer praise, we offer worship. Have you noticed how the worship language works in the New Testament? In the Old Testament, beside the private worship language of some psalms, most of the worship language of priests and of offering sacrifice is bound up, once the tabernacle is constructed, with the tabernacle and once the temple is constructed, with the temple. The people were to go up to the temple and offer praises and sacrifices at the temple, that's where they were to offer their animals. Sometimes it was done elsewhere, but that was the structure of things. So there were set times and set feasts, there were set songs and set praises. There were set priests and set sacrifices, it was constrained by ritual and structure and time and orderliness.

Now you come to the New Testament and you read a passage like this. 'I beseech you therefore brothers by the mercies of God, that you present your bodies as living sacrifices, which is your spiritual worship' (Rom.12:1). You see we don't offer bulls and goats anymore; we offer ourselves in gratitude to God, for what He is and who He is. It's not as if we have to go up to Jerusalem or up to Rome, or even up to Canterbury. Rather, what does Jesus say in John chapter 4? '… neither in Jerusalem, nor on Mount Gerizim and Mount Ebal', following the particular traditions of the Jews and the Samaritans, 'but a time is coming and has now come when true worshippers will worship the Father in spirit and in truth.' We are not constrained by place. I know that we like to think of our local churches or our cathedrals as peculiarly sanctified in some way – but, they are not! They may be sanctified in the sense that they have been devoted to God for a particular purpose, but they don't function in the Christian church the way the tabernacle or the temple functioned under the terms of the old covenant. Basically they are simply hunks of concrete. We are the temple of God, that's what the New Testament says.

Thus similarly I worry when we think of worship as something done between 10:00 and 11:00 on a Sunday morning, or still worse, between 10:00 and 10:30 on a Sunday morning before the preacher starts. There is a sense in which all of our life under the new covenant is worship offered up to God. We are not to return to some notion of worship that is merely cultic. So here we are always, constantly the people of God, 'declaring the praises of him who called you out of darkness into his wonderful light'. Thus Paul can go so far in Romans 15:16, as to see his evangelism as a priestly worshipping activity, because that too involves self-sacrifice, it involves mediation. And thus in our evangelism we are worshipping God. Our worship might well become evangelistic too, as we proclaim God to the people.

All of this is the fruit of sheer gratitude, '...for we declare the praises of Him who called us out of darkness into His wonderful light'. We have so much artificial light all around that we don't appreciate how dark darkness can be. But if you camp in the wilds of Scotland miles from any city, on a dark night when your torch batteries go out, then you begin to get a notion of what darkness can be! Our salvation has taken us out of darkness and into His most marvellous light. We celebrate it in our songs:

> Long my imprisoned spirit lay fast bound in sin
> and nature's night ...
> Thine eye diffused a quickening ray, I woke, the
> dungeon flamed with light.
> My chains fell off, my heart was free,
> I rose went forth and followed Thee.

> *(Charles Wesley, 'And can it be?')*

That is the view of redemption that Peter presupposes here.

4) The holiness of the temple (2:11-12)

Probably there is still some echo of the temple metaphor here, there is certainly an ongoing contrast between the people of God and the surrounding world, and the people of God mediating God's truth and God's glory and presence to the world, which is a priestly function. But now the practical entailments of what it means to be the people of God are briefly spelt out.

Note here the massive antithesis between the church on the one hand and the world on the other. It's hard for us to know exactly what it means to be an alien if we've never travelled abroad, but if we have, we know a bit of what it means. Christians will be alien in a broken rebellious world that pits things against God. In some sense the church is to see itself in that sort of way.

Note the parameters Peter stresses. Here we are strangers and aliens, so remember your heavenly citizenship; here we are warriors, so remember the nature of your warfare, '... as aliens and strangers in the world, abstain from sinful desires which war against your soul.' Here the world is right within us. It's not that we are the church, the goody goodies and out there are the baddies and we are the strangers and aliens and they may belong, but boy are they in trouble! The warfare in which we are involved is a warfare against sin within us. If we don't take this warfare seriously we won't fight sin seriously in our own minds, our own hearts, our own churches.

So, here we are strangers and aliens – remember your heavenly citizenship; here we are warriors but remember the nature of your warfare. Here we are to live good lives, so remember your calling. In the first century it wasn't long before Christians were suspected of all kinds of horrible things – treason against the empire and even cannibalism by the second century. How were Christians going to refute that? By the quality of their living. So that while the libels and the criticisms run through the empire, those who come to know Christians know them to be not like that. They are people of integrity, people of honour, people of service, people of self-sacrifice. The most important thing we can do in the whole world when the whole world seems to be against us, is to be people of integrity and Godliness and self-sacrifice and love, so that eventually, just by the quality of our living, in addition to all of our proclaiming, people see something of the glory of God in us. Here we are to be exemplary – remember your ultimate vindication.

Conclusion

Let me conclude with a couple of observations.

I was once asked to speak from this chapter and given the title *A peculiar people, the identity of the church in a neo-pagan world*. The word 'peculiar' comes from the Authorised Version verse 9, 'We are a peculiar people.' Some of us have thought Christians have been pretty peculiar (there are huge ways in which Christians must not be peculiar – odd, weird, bizarre), and there are some ways in which we ought to be peculiar. At least two domains from this passage. Firstly, in the domain of faith and gratitude. We are the temple of God, chosen in Christ, bought, constrained and shaped by the cornerstone, called of God to be God's kingdom and priests, to utter His praises to the nations.

And secondly in the domain of conduct, of lifestyle priorities, here too we must be peculiar to those who are outside. We are to abstain from sinful desires we are told, we are to watch our thoughts. We are to think differently about our vocation, about our families, about sexuality, about our pocketbooks. In all of those ways we belong to God – we are the people of God.

A new magazine is now widely circulating in North America, it's simply called, *Self.* The May edition, which I happened to have flipped through, has articles on eating, health, sex, the body, fitness, romance, money, love, Self! Self! Self! Self is the dominant god of this age, but God in His mercy calls us to die to self, for He knows full well that if you serve self you find nothing but the grave, you are crushed by the cornerstone. Jesus Himself insisted, the one who dies to self, lives, the one who loses himself, finds himself, the one who gives, receives. So we think differently. We are called to be a holy people, we are the temple of our God.

4. How Then Shall We Live?
1 Peter 2:13-3:12

Introduction: This world is not my home

Have you ever checked to see just how accurate those films are that claim to preserve at least the main thrust of some historical event? I confess I have not yet seen the film *Titanic*, but I note the shrewd observation of the *New York Times* book review for April 1998, page 17 – 'In the film, as the ship is sinking and all the first-class passengers turn out to be third-class human beings; all the first-class passenger men scramble to get into the limited number of lifeboats, and it is only hardy sailors equipped with guns who keep them out. But according to the actual eye-witness accounts, that is not what happened. The "women and children first" convention of the day was very strong. The male first-class passengers, without any recorded exception, stood back. True, John Jacob Astor, reputedly then the richest man in the world, fought his way to a boat, but it was in order to put his wife into it, and then he stepped back and waved her goodbye. Benjamin Guggenheim couldn't get to his wife, but he refused a seat saying, "Tell my wife I played the game out straight to the end, no woman shall be left aboard this ship because Ben Guggenheim was a coward."'

The New York reviewer concludes by saying, 'The movie makers altered the story for good reason, no one would believe it today. For this is the day of the self.'

A friend of mine has written, 'Me-firstism has come to feel so normal that we may have difficulty in believing that real people could live any other way. Having thrown off the yoke of duty and virtue through self-mastery, the modern world has swung into an orgy of pandering to the appetites of the masterful self. Advertisers promote selfism, psychotherapists and educators reinforce it and religion legitimates it. Self is the great idol standing at the centre of our conceptual world to which all bow down. We even have a duty-to-self ethic, as if self-denial were harmful, immoral and deviant.'

Add to this the amazing focus on the *now* in our culture, without any reference to eternity, the pressures of secularisation by which religious things are squeezed to the periphery of life. You can be ever so religious as long as it doesn't affect your business, your family, how you think, or what you spend your money on, it's just something you do occasionally on Sunday, like a nice decent middle-class citizen should. Grant also, post-modern sensibilities in which there can be no absolute truth, no truth that is binding, no truth that is trans-cultural. Add to this rising biblical illiteracy so that there are very few cultural moorings left, and we begin to see why sincere followers of Christ in many Western countries, may begin to feel they don't belong.

But of course in one sense this is how Christians felt in the first century too. At one level Caesar was their king, their ruler. On another only Jesus was their Lord, and if push came to shove you know which Lord was superior.

At one level there was so much pluralism in the day. In fact the government actually fostered religious pluralism as national policy. When the Romans went into some new turf, they insisted there would be a god-swap. The Romans would take on some of the local gods and the locals had to take on some of the Roman gods so that if any party were tempted to rebel it wouldn't be clear which side the gods were on, which thus diffused the dangerous political and nationalistic elements. In other words, in the name of empire peace, there was a push for religious pluralism.

And today of course, in our global village, in our multiculturalism, there are massive pushes also for many kinds of pluralism – not only the pluralism that recognises all kinds of distinctions and treats one another with respect, but the kind of pluralism that insists that all values and all religions and all perspectives are precisely equivalent, in value and worth, in moral sensibility. I don't know how many learned books I have read that insist that child sacrifice is a good thing to those societies that practise it, because in those societies it's very meaningful. I doubt if it is all that meaningful for the child!

There are of course many dangers to these sorts of situations, where the church feels out of sorts with the surrounding culture. On the one hand there is the danger of assimilation and on the other there is the danger of embattled holy-huddle thinking; we retreat into a little castle, lob out the odd grenade now and again and call it 'witness'. We don't engage with the world and live truly Christianly in the world. We don't think of ourselves as living in the world, but as living as pilgrims and strangers with integrity, in a world which in some respects is our own and in other respects is not our home, our citizenship is elsewhere.

1) Submission and authority (2:13-17)

Peter will not allow us to fall off on either side of those extremes. He begins in this text with some reflections on sub-mission to authority. Starting with verse 13, I had better admit right away that in recent years there have been two interpretations of this verse that affect how you read this entire section.

The first interpretation reads verse 13 like this – Submit yourselves for the Lord's sake to every human creature – that is, to every human being.

The notion of submission recurs in verse 18 with respect to slaves, in chapter 3 verse 1 with respect to wives, and although the word then is not used, in chapter 3 verse 7 with respect to husbands, it must then be assumed, because you still have that little phrase 'in the same way'. And this gov-erning verse in verse 13, if we take it this way, 'Submit your-selves for the Lord's sake to every human creature.'

The alternative is to read this more or less as the NIV does, 'Submit yourselves,' it's literally in Greek, 'to every human creation.' And the question is, what does that mean? 'Submit yourselves to every human creation.' There's no expression quite like that anywhere in the Bible. If every human creation means every human creature, then the first view is right. But it's a strange way of talking about human beings – 'Submit yourselves to every human creation' – why not say, 'Submit yourselves to every human,' or 'to every person'? It does seem a strange way of saying things.

I think it means, 'Submit yourselves to every creaturely structure.' The NIV tries to paraphrase it, 'Submit yourselves for the Lord's sake to every authority instituted among men…' I will list the reasons for this briefly.

First, the verb 'to submit', both in the New Testament and in all of its occurrences that I have traced in the first century and the surrounding centuries, means a submission to an authority in some sort of structure, in some sort of hierarchy, in some sort of recognition. It never ever is used in the sense of mutual reciprocity. 'Ah,' someone says, 'but what about Ephesians 5:21, where we are to submit to one another? Doesn't that disallow everything that you say?'

No, it does not. The pronoun 'one another' sometimes suggests full reciprocity and sometimes not. It depends on the context. For example, in the Apocalypse you sometimes get people killing one another off: 'they killed one another'. It doesn't mean that they all shot at exactly the same instant with a scatter gun so that each one managed to kill each of the others in a perfectly reciprocal way – it means there was general mayhem and slaughter. There are lots of instances of 'one another' that are not perfectly reciprocal. In the context of Ephesians 5:21 it is 'submit to one another,' then it turns out to be 'slaves to masters,' 'wives to husbands,' 'children to parents'. So if you want to make this perfectly reciprocal you've got to make all of those perfectly reciprocal too, including children to parents. Lexical facts are lexical facts and the verb 'to submit', both in the New Testament and in the surrounding Greek world, without exception means, 'to submit in some sort of ordered array.'

Moreover, the verb 'to submit' here is used in verses 13, 18 and 3:1, with respect to slaves, the submission to all authorities, specifically under governmental authority, and also wives. It is not used with respect to masters or to kings because they are not mentioned, nor is it used here with respect to husbands.

On the other hand, some of this discussion in current years, in my view, has got way out of hand with massive agendas. Lest you feel put upon, it is important to remember that the apostle Paul says to husbands, 'Love your wives as Christ loved the church and gave himself for her.' That is not sentimental twaddle! To love your wife as Christ loved the church cannot mean less than loving your wife self-sacrificially and for her good. Precisely what do you sacrifice for your wife for her good? Don't talk to me about your authority until you talk to me about your self-sacrifice for her good.

In short it seems to me that Peter lays out in 2:13-17, first of all the importance of showing proper respect to duly constituted authorities. 'Submit yourselves for the Lord's sake to every authority instituted among men: whether to the king, as the supreme authority, or to governors, who are sent by him to punish those who do wrong and to commend those who do right. For it is God's will that by doing good you should silence the ignorant talk of foolish men. Live as free men, but do not use your freedom as a cover-up for evil; live as' not servants, 'slaves of God.' There are several different words that could be rendered by 'servant' or 'slave' in the New Testament, this word must be rendered by 'slave' and the NIV has it wrong.

Now follow this important passage. Peter does not try to lay out a comprehensive pattern of relationships as some of the Pauline letters do that talk about both slaves and masters – or with respect to husbands, put more emphasis on what the husbands ought to do than what the wives ought to do, as in Ephesians 5. He picks up just two or three elements. The reason, I think, that he lays particular stress on how Christians ought to act and react is because he is interested in how Christians should act and react when they are being unjustly exploited – when they are feeling the pressure, whether they are in the home or in the culture that is attacking them, that is leaning in on them, that is trying to abuse them in some way. And we are to respond in a particular way we are told (verse 13), 'for the Lord's sake' – that is, we serve and honour the Lord with such submission.

Verse 14: one of the primary purposes of government is to punish those who do wrong. And Peter recognises that that is a legitimate function of government, even of the first-century Roman government which was often corrupt, which often had bribery in the courts. But nevertheless Peter can appeal to this as a principle even in a state as corrupt as that of ancient Rome.

It is important to reflect on this a little more. In some ways this may seem to be commonplace for us, Christians should be good citizens. But when Peter wrote this the issues were of burning importance. After all, the Old Testament saints had lived in a theocracy, that is a form of government in which ultimately God was the king mediated through a human king, or earlier through judges. Thus the religious dimension and the political and social dimensions were all bound up together, just as in a militant Muslim state today. Moreover, this was widely to be perceived as the right way of ordering cultures in the ancient world generally. Thus every culture had its associated gods, and if that particular culture went to war and won then the gods were winning, and if it went to war and lost then those gods were losing, and you had to offer sacrifices to those gods to try to please them. The social fabric, the religious fabric and loyalty to the government were all bound up with one belt around the whole thing. The locus of the covenant community in the Old Testament was tied to a nation, the Israelites. Along comes Jesus and establishes a locus that is not tied to a particular nation.

That is one of the reasons why His words, recorded in the synoptic gospels, are so important. 'Render unto Caesar the things that are Caesar's and to God the things that are God's' (cf Mt. 22:21). Shall we pay this to Caesar or not? After all it's got his impression on it. But if you have an impression of Caesar on it and the words over the top 'Our Lord and our God' in Latin, this is an exceedingly blasphemous piece, how can you touch it, let alone pay taxes with it? According to the Old Testament theocracy, surely what we should do is rebel against this usurper, only God is king. But of course, if Jesus says, 'Amen', then He's inciting the people not to pay taxes and they've got Him, He will be arrested. And Jesus ducks all of their pressures by simply saying, 'Render to Caesar what is Caesar's,' it's got his face on it, let him have it. 'And to God things that are God's.' It wasn't just a smart-mouthed response to get out of a tricky situation. It was an implicit recognition of the fact that the kingdom of God then dawning was not a theocracy in the sense that the old covenant community was a theocracy; it was a God-ruled realm, but it was not a God-ruled realm whose locus was a nation. It was a trans-national thing, which came to be the church.

Christians have not always recognised this point. It inevitably generates tensions because sometimes the demands of God and the demands of the state in which we also live may be at cross-purposes, and then you hear the Christians thinking their way through this dilemma – 'We must obey God rather than men!' (Acts 5:29). That is precisely what leads then to martyrdom – bearing witness all the way to death.

Verse 15: if we live Godly lives we will silence a lot of stupid accusations. I'll come back to that later.

Verse 16: 'Live as free men, but do not use your freedom as a cover-up for evil.' In other words, we are not to see such submission as a sign of our enslavement to human authorities, but as a mark of our freedom – we choose to do this, we choose to be obedient, we choose to deny ourselves, precisely in order that we may serve God by submitting to the authorities. This is a mark of our freedom, and of our enslavement to God – our freedom from those authorities precisely in that we choose to serve them. This is His will, you do this because you are His slave and you are aiming to please Him.

So the summary of this in practical form is spelt out in verse 17, 'Show proper respect to everyone: Love the brotherhood of believers, fear God, honour the king.' These are the apostle's preliminary reflections on submission and authority.

2) Hard cases (2:18-3:12)

(a) Slaves like Jesus (2:18-25)

The word for 'slave' in verse 18 is a different one. This one means 'a household servant'. But almost all first-century household servants were in fact also slaves. I think probably the best rendering here would be something like 'household slaves'. Here perhaps I should introduce a small excursus on slavery in the world and in the eighteenth, nineteenth and twentieth centuries in particular. I suspect that one of the reasons why the Authorised Version translated so many instances of the Greek word *doulos* which really does mean 'slave', by 'servant', is precisely because 'slave' had overtones and notions connected with it that we are not comfortable with. This side of the slavery that was put in place under the British Empire reached its fruition in America. We have a heritage of things about which we are embarrassed and we should probably think about these things.

A book that has helped me a great deal in this respect is one of the thick volumes of research by Thomas Sowell, an African-American scholar who so far as I know makes no pretence of being a Christian. He remarks rightly that virtually every culture until the nineteenth century had slaves. The Indians had slaves, the Chinese slaves. The Africans had slaves within Africa. Europeans often had slaves in the hinterland. The Assyrians, the Babylonians and the Israelites had slaves, everybody had slaves. Having slaves was not extraordinary, thus it was not in one sense on the historical scale of things all that extraordinary that we should have slaves in the Western world as well.

On the other hand, slavery in most of the ancient regimes had a variety of causes and inputs. Sometimes it was the product of military victory. But sometimes it was part of an economic system that didn't have any bankruptcy laws. If you went bankrupt you sold yourself into servitude to pay off your debt. If your business went bad you'd sell yourself and your family as slaves. If somehow your ship came in a little later you could buy yourself back, or maybe your family could buy yourself back. So in that sort of world it was part of an economic system and if you had a good master it might mean the difference between starving and not starving.

Moreover, not only was slavery endemic and tied in some cases to a different financial system, but it was cross-class and cross-race; that is, in the Roman Empire, there were African slaves, there were African middle-class people, and there were African nobility. There were British slaves and there were British ordinary workers. There were Italian slaves and there were also Roman free citizens. So slavery was not connected to a particular race.

Now, contrast slavery in the West. It was not really because of war, it was because of colonialism. We wanted workers for growing numbers of sugar-cane fields and the like, and only African workers; as far as the white experience was largely concerned, all Africans were slaves. Initially all blacks in the West were slaves, it was connected with a race. And it was impossible to think of slaves buying themselves out. But Thomas Sowell goes on to ask, what freed slaves in the West? Now you must understand Sowell is an historian, he's not a Christian. And he very carefully tracks out the influence of Whitefield and Wesley in the evangelical awakening and the rise of Wilberforce, ramming things through parliament that suddenly released not only the slaves in the West Indies, but the British Navy at a time when Britannia ruled the waves, which stopped the trade across the Atlantic.

Moreover, at a time when about eleven million Africans were transported to America, about thirteen million were transported up into the Arabic world. There the women usually became concubines and the men were not allowed to marry. They were treated far more brutally, but there is very little literature of shame in the Arabic world about that trade, unlike the literature of shame in our world, partly because of the rise of Christian conscience this side of the evangelical awakening. What largely stopped that trade for a long time was again British gunboats going into the Arabian Gulf; sensitised in fact by teaching that insisted human beings regardless of their colour are made in the image of God and you don't treat people like that.

Now what about the New Testament? Clearly on the one

hand the New Testament does not advocate the bloody overthrow of the Roman government. It doesn't insist on the
instant abolition of slavery. Yet on the other hand slave
traders in the pastoral epistles are condemned along with
murderers, adulterers and other public sinners – if you get rid
of all slave traders because they are sinners you sooner or later
don't have much slavery. Moreover, when there are instructions to masters, you get increasing emphasis on treating
slaves not only justly, but as brothers; until you come to
Philemon which is a spectacular epistle in this respect. There
is Onesimus, he has run away. Legally Philemon could have
him executed. He could certainly be flogged as much as
Philemon liked. There Paul writes (verses 17-19), 'but he's
become a brother, so receive him as a brother, indeed receive
him as you would receive me. And if he has robbed you of
anything then put it to my account, I will repay you. Though
of course I wouldn't want to mention that you owe me your
very soul. But nevertheless put it to my account, I will repay
you. Receive him in fact, as Jesus Christ.' You see, you don't
abolish slavery that is that deeply endemic in a culture simply by passing laws. We had the American Civil War, which
finally terminated in 1865, and we were still having bloody
riots in Mississippi in 1965! No, it takes changes of heart, it
takes the gospel.

Now here Peter does not venture a complete list of household duties for all sides, including Christian masters and
Christian rulers. This is less because he is not interested in
such things, than because he is focusing on providing strong
support for this utterly crucial truth for all Christians, that
true freedom is bound up with self-denial for the sake of others.

Now follow the flow in verses 18 to 20. The issue here is
not social stability or the perpetuation of slavery, as some
have charged Peter with; rather his focus is on the fact that
any unjust suffering slaves undergo, provides an opportunity
to show what is intrinsically Christian. He says, 'Slaves, submit yourselves to your masters with all respect, not only to
those who are good and considerate,' in which case in the
ancient world they are not much more than employers except

that you can't go to another job, 'but also to those who are harsh. For it is commendable if a man bears up under the pain of unjust suffering because he is conscious of God. But how is it to your credit if you receive a beating for doing wrong and endure it? But if you suffer for doing good and you endure it, this is commendable before God.' Isn't that astonishing? Let me tell you quite frankly, as we become a more litigious and a more secular society, we will witness in our jobs, in our homes and in our cultures, more and more unjust things. And we will often be the victims of them – sometimes directed against us because we are Christians, but sometimes just because this is an evil world.

If we get some sort of beating, whether literal or metaphorical or legal, because we have been corrupt; if we get thrown into jail because we have cheated the Inland Revenue, there's nothing particularly honourable about that, we are just getting what we deserve. If on the other hand we suffer unjustly and we handle it as Christians there is something distinctively noble and Godly and right and clean and testifying about that; it stamps us out as Christians, that's what Peter is saying. And it is finally tied to Jesus (verse 21), 'To this you were called,' that is to this kind of suffering, 'because Christ suffered for you, leaving you an example, that you should follow in his steps.'

This is in fact a common New Testament theme. The idea is, this is a gracious gift from God – 'For it has been granted to you on behalf of Christ not only to believe on him, but also to suffer for him ...' (Phil. 1:29). Do you know what God has graciously given to you? Faith and the privilege to get beaten up. Now is that how you think of your role as a Christian? And if not, why not? It is a constant New Testament theme.

This is not to show servility, despite the charges of Friedrich Nietzche, rather it is to demonstrate freedom, freedom to serve.

Let me tell you about Ruby, a little black girl in Mississippi in the mid-sixties, when the Civil Rights movement blew up in the United States. The Supreme Court ruled that segregated schools were unconstitutional and overnight in the Deep

South the schools had to integrate. In this particular school, when Ruby, a little black girl of about seven or eight, first showed up, there were riots. The parents pulled all their kids out of the school, and every day they showed up at the gates with placards, refusing to let their kids go in, and shouting hate epithets at little Ruby; she was the only black girl that showed up. It took a squadron of federal marshals to protect her as she went into school day after day – while she was surrounded by enraged, swearing, angry, bitter, white adults cursing at this little black girl. Day after day for a whole school year she was taught by one Christian teacher in the school who braved those shouts. The thing was so interesting in the press, that eventually a psychiatrist at Harvard University wanted to know more about what this was doing to that little girl. So he went south, watched her go in day after day, got to know the parents who were menial workers, semi-literate, Godly Christians. Then one day he noticed that as she was escorted in by the marshals she stopped, she seemed to say something for a couple of minutes, and then she walked on. Afterward the psychiatrist asked her,

> 'Ruby, what were you saying to those people?'
> 'I wasn't saying anything to them.'
> 'But I saw you stop and talk to them, what were you saying?'
> 'Oh I wasn't talking to them, I was talking to God.'
> 'Were you? What were you saying?'
> 'Oh, my parents have always taught me to pray for my enemies and this morning I left so quickly I forgot, so when I heard them screaming at me I stopped and I said, "Father forgive them they know not what they do."'

Let me tell you about a Korean pastor in 1948 on the 38th parallel of Korea. The communist party came south and took over the town where he lived and killed his two boys, Matthew and John. One of the murderers from the north was caught. The people were about to execute him, but the pastor stood in and insisted that he wanted to adopt him. His thirteen-year-old daughter Rebecca insisted that she wanted him as a brother.

How different from pagan aesthetes, even the best of them. Seneca, roughly the same vintage as Peter writes, 'What will the wise man do when he is buffeted? He will do as Cato did. He did not burst into a passion, he did not avenge himself, he did not even forgive it, but he denied its having been done.' There's stoicism, but it's not Christian faith.

Then it is as if Peter must say something more about the Lord Jesus (verses 22-25):

> 'He committed no sin, and no deceit was found in his mouth.' When they hurled their insults at him, he did not retaliate; when he suffered, he made no threats. Instead, he entrusted himself to him who judges justly. He himself bore our sins in his body on the tree, so that we might die to sins and live for righteousness; by his wounds you have been healed. For you were like sheep going astray, but now you have returned to the Shepherd and Overseer of your souls.

You see, the application burst the boundaries of Peter's treatment of the household and their conduct and now applies to all Christians.

There is an immensely deep connection between salvation and ethics. It is bound up with the cross. It's not just that we are saved by the cross, but this salvation by the cross shapes the foundation of Christian ethics. If you try to get Jesus as an example without seeing why Jesus went to the cross, then of course you end with a kind of empty sentimentalism. But if on the other hand you have Jesus dying for our sins and it doesn't affect the way you live, you have a kind of abstract theological truth and no self-denial – the two are massively linked.

It affects not only shepherds and overseers who are mentioned in verse 25, Jesus the Supreme Shepherd and Overseer (whose model then becomes important in our churches in chapter 5) but it also applies to all Christians.

(b) Women like matriarchs (3:1-6)

Women are likened to matriarchs, 'in the same way', this little phrase grounds what is said in Christ's self-denial – be submissive, yes. But the particular focus here is on Christian wives with non-Christian husbands who do not believe the word. That's the peculiar application of 2:12 where we are told, 'Live such good lives among the pagans that, though they accuse you of doing wrong, they may see your good deeds and glorify God on the day he visits us.' So also here, 'Wives, in the same way be submissive to your husbands so that, if any of them do not believe the word, they may be won over without words by the behaviour of their wives, when they see the purity and reverence of your lives.'

Indeed, what they ought to pursue is beauty of inner character – verses 3 and 4. Instead of trying to be beautiful in the same way that the pagans want to be beautiful, you want with all your heart first and foremost to be beautiful from within, to display a certain kind of character – what is here called in verse 4, the unfading beauty of a gentle and quiet spirit, presenting itself as an adornment, as it is in fact the fruit of the Spirit.

Now this does not mean that women shall be quiet and Godly while men shall be noisy and raucous. Gentleness is a Christian, Spirit-given fruit in all and 1 Thessalonians 4:11 urges a certain quietness on all Christians, as a Christian virtue. But this virtue is worked out, in this Christian wife, in this context in this way, as a particular quiet submission to her husband so as to extol the beauties of Christian character and gain him if at all possible. Sarah is called forth as an example in verses 5 and 6. Not because she and Abraham were righteous in every respect, but she is picked up on this particular point: she did address her husband as master.

(c) Husbands like fellow-heirs (3:7)

But then the husbands, in verse 7 we read, 'in the same way be considerate'. And 'the same way' takes you back to Jesus as our ultimate model, in the same way as Jesus absorbed things that were unjust and unfair in His pursuit of the good of others – '... in the same way be considerate as you live with your wives'. Be considerate means, live according to knowledge – that is, to a knowledge of the truth, to a knowledge of Christian witness, to a knowledge of your wife and her needs and her character.

'... And treat them with respect as the weaker partner.' Now this does not mean that every wife has an inferior IQ, or is morally weaker. What it does mean is, that by and large men are physically stronger and therefore it is more common for men to abuse their wives and beat up on them physically than the reverse. And you mustn't do that, you mustn't be abusive.

Ultimately I think this goes back to the Fall itself in Genesis 3 which is sometimes misinterpreted today. We read in the curse pronounced against the woman, verse 16, 'Your desire will be for your husband, and he will rule over you.' Those two verbs are found together in only one other passage in the Pentateuch. In the very next chapter, Cain, with the first instance of fratricide, is being confronted by God, 4:6, 'Why are you angry? Why is your face downcast?' God says to him. 'If you do what is right, will you not be accepted? But if you do not do what is right, sin is crouching at your door,' now the two verbs: 'it *desires* to have you, but you must *master* it.' And what happens this side of the Fall in the marriage, is that the woman desires to have her husband in exactly the same way – she wants to control things, and he for his part brutally controls her. Isn't that a description of what goes wrong in marriage? In other words, it's not all his fault and it's not all her fault. One tries to control things by a form of manipulation and the other tries to control things simply because he's stronger.

In the Christian way we walk instead with submission, with integrity, treating one another with respect and never ever a trace of brutality. Why not? '... so that nothing will hinder your prayers.' Not only your prayers individually, but also your prayers with your spouse.

I was speaking at a missionary convention not long ago and a Christian woman I had known for many years came up to me and said, 'I want you to tell me why my husband won't pray with me.' They had been on the mission field for about fifteen years. Now there can be many reasons for that. I am saying that before we talk too much about revival and ethics in the public sphere many of us have some reformation to do at home, with humility of mind, and repentance, and nurture and up-building and submission and love for Jesus' sake.

(d) Believers like brothers (3:8-12)

'Finally, all of you ... love as brothers ...' Here are the main characteristics of getting along with brothers – like-mindedness, live in harmony with one another. It does not simply mean that you agree to disagree, although there is an overtone of that. It means, ultimately you learn to think the same thing under the revelation of God, which takes time and communication, bowing your minds to the authority of what God has revealed. Sympathy, learning to rejoice with those who rejoice, to weep with those who weep. Have you ever noticed that an awful lot of churches have a very high percentage of social misfits? Do you know why? Because by and large the church for all its faults is still the most sympathetic society in Western culture, that's why – we should wear the misfits as a badge of honour. And then we are to love as brothers, we are to show compassion, we are to walk with humility with this wonderful conclusion in Psalm 34.

Conclusion

Do you see then how all of these ethical stances are tied to the cross? It is not an accident that chapter 2 verses 22 to 25 lies at the heart of this extended section. All of our ethics in the home, in the society, our culture, our approach to work, to one another, to our spouses, our conduct in the church, all of it finally comes from the cross. If you live in a particularly scrappy church, I want to know whether you and the other members of that church know anything about what it means to live in such a way as to absorb insult and pain and suffering. If you think only in terms of your rights, you will always find yourself on the end of bitterness.

Isn't that what Jesus Himself overcame? Isn't that what Paul says, agreeing perfectly here with Peter? 'Let this mind be in you, which was also in Christ Jesus, who, precisely because he was in the form of God' – that's a causal participle – because he was in the form of God, he didn't think of equality with God as something to be exploited, but emptied Himself, made Himself a nobody, took on human flesh, and then died the ignominious and odious death of the cross, wherefore God has highly exalted Him' (cf Phil. 2:5-9a).

> Astounding grace that God the Son
> Should choose to leave the Father's glory,
> And refuse to clutch His dignity, exploit His right,
> And make Himself a no one in our sight.
> The word made flesh, the Son of God, a man
> The timeless God clothed in a mortal span...

That's what redeems us. It is also what tells us how to live. This is a message all of us need to hear perennially and acutely, because it is exactly what we are contravening. And there is no way for us but repentance now, and tears and contrition; returning to that same cross to ask for forgiveness and to learn how to live.

5. Distinctively Christian Suffering
1 Peter 3:13-4:19

Introduction: What causes suffering?

I'd like to begin this last session* by thanking the organisers for the invitation to come, it is a privilege to be here and it is a privilege to think through the Word of God and to try resolve afresh by God's grace to live in its light.

There are lots of ways to suffer. You can hit your thumb with a hammer, fail an important exam, get jilted by a girl-friend or a boyfriend, or a husband or a wife after one year, or five years, or twenty years, you can die of leukaemia at the age of fifteen, as my daughter's best friend did – that'll make you suffer and all the people around you too. You can be bereaved after fifty years of marriage, you can have a stroke, you can ride in the shame of remembered guilt – that'll make you suffer. You can fuel the alienation of deep hurt, of having been abused and become an abuser yourself. In many parts of the world you can get killed for being a Christian; perhaps the most dangerous places statistically at the moment are places like Southern Sudan, but there are lots of other places – that'll make you suffer. You can lose your health, wealth, family and reputation like Job, you can suffer the ravages of

*Due to a misunderstanding there were five, not six, Bible Readings as had been anticipated by Don Carson. The outline for the talk he would have given in the extra session can be found at the end of the chapter. The robust among you can complete the study by yourselves!

war, famine, plague, you can have a land mine take off your legs, you could get gang-raped by soldiers when you yourself are a missionary, which happened to a daughter of a good friend – that'll make you suffer.

Of course the various categories of suffering in this broken sin-cursed world are all in the Bible, in general terms. But in this passage before us, we are focusing not so much on suffering in this global sense of all that belongs to a broken order, but rather on distinctively Christian suffering; not ordinary suffering that befalls all groups of people as it is borne by Christians, but the sufferings that may come to us precisely because we are Christians.

On first approach this subject may well be a bit offensive. It may sound a bit depressing to talk about Christianity and distinctively Christian suffering. Yet just a few moments' reflection remind us that we serve a master, the Lord Jesus, who was known as the Man of Sorrows and acquainted with grief. We remember the first Christians who actually rejoiced when they were counted worthy to suffer for the Name. And we remember the words of the apostle Paul, 'For it has been granted to you on behalf of Christ not only to believe on him, but also to suffer for him' (Phil.1:29).

It may help us to follow the flow of thought in the passage before us if we organise it into four sections.

1) Do not withdraw, for Christ is your example (3:13-22)

You will doubtless recall that Peter has earlier hinted at the topic of persecution of Christians, in chapter 1 verse 6, three times in chapter 2 and earlier in chapter 3. Now he treats it in an extended argument. He begins by saying that in many contexts Christians will of course not be harmed and should not expect to be harmed (verse 13). Probably he says this in part because some of the Christians may have already seen some outbreaks of persecution and be feeling a bit nervous, they are beginning to go round with a mopey attitude expecting to get clobbered. Still, Peter says it's very important to remember that ideally and often in practice, government is set up to order life for the better. Yes, the Roman government might be corrupt in many respects, but nevertheless it does stop a lot of thuggery and brigands and it holds down murder and corruption to some extent, and it does an awful lot of good. In fact if you take away the order of government very frequently what comes in as a result is much worse, mainly anarchism – just ask anybody who lives in the former Yugoslavia. We may not think that the old Yugoslav government was a paragon of righteousness, but would anybody want to suggest that anarchy and mayhem is much better? So there's a kind of practical realism. Government ideally tramps down evil; if you are doing good, why should you be afraid of the government all the time? The principle on a certain level is transparent enough; if you are not exceeding the speed limit you should not fear the traffic cop.

Yet there may be something more to verse 13. It begins with an 'and', not preserved in the NIV, with the force of 'then'. Thus verse 13 gets linked to the preceding passage, to verses 10 to 12. It is as if the text is saying in effect, '... the eyes of the Lord are on the righteous and his ears are attentive to their prayer, but the face of the Lord is against those who do evil.' So then, 'Who is going to harm you if you are eager to do good?' In other words, under God no ultimate evil can befall you even if you do face persecution and difficulty. It's akin to Paul's rhetorical question, 'If God is for us, who can be against us?' (Rom. 8:31). Also the psalmist saying in Psalm 56:4, '... in God I trust; I will not be afraid. What can mortal man do to me?' Well, on one level they can do quite a lot, but in any ultimate sense they cannot work outside the framework of God's sovereignty, and Him you can trust.

Of course some governments are corrupt, sometimes they are taken over by worldviews so alien to things Christian, that they persecute you for doing what is right, hence verse 14, 'But even if you should suffer for what is right, you are blessed.' This is of course according to the words of Jesus Himself in the Beatitudes (Mt. 5). In fact we align ourselves with the prophets, Jesus says, who were persecuted before us. You are blessed when you are persecuted. That's why Paul can write not only of the thorn in his flesh, but also of all the things that he suffered as a Christian and as an apostle. He says, 'That is why, for Christ's sake, I delight in weaknesses, in insults, in hardships, in persecutions, in difficulties. For when I am weak, then I am strong' (2 Cor. 12:10). In other words some of the promised blessing is right now, it's not as if we get only insults and weakness down here and then up there we get all our rewards. No, Paul is saying that even in his current experience, when he is weak he is strong.

That can be a tough thing for Christian leaders to absorb. There are all kinds of people who will try to undermine your ministry, or sometimes gossips will tear you apart behind your back and the damage in a local church might be quite severe before you discover how bad it is. And it is very easy to become self-pitying or even bitter. Or alternatively it's possible instead just to laugh it off and become hard and cynical, and all Christians can be tempted along these lines sooner or later.

That's not Paul or Peter's way. We suffer in only small ways compared to what our Master suffered and it is said of Him, who for the joy that was set before Him endured the cross, despising the shame. So Paul then, 'That is why for Christ's sake I delight in weakness, in insults, in hardships and persecutions and difficulties, for when I am weak then I am strong.' I am always nervous when everything is going well. Sometimes it takes real challenges to drive Christians to their knees. When a church is really going swimmingly sooner or later the prayer meetings start declining. Yet a first-class crisis comes along and people start wanting the power and release and sovereign sway of the Lord God.

In any case (verse 14b), do not fear what the world at large fears, '"... do not be frightened." But in your hearts set apart Christ as Lord.' Too often we withdraw and are defeated because we fear what people will say about us or do to us, we fear some fellow human being. This is after all what happened to Peter himself in the courtyard, he understands what he is talking about. He was afraid of what people would say. They had already arrested his Master and here is this young girl challenging him – 'Well we can tell by your accent, you are not from around here, you are from Galilee, you are also with Him.' And he collapses. The shame undoubtedly remained with him all his days. But the other side of the resurrection, the other side of Pentecost, you find him standing up to the High Court of the land and saying, 'We must obey God rather than men.'

So he writes, 'Do not fear what they fear, do not be frightened.' But it's not simply the prohibition; telling people not to be afraid is not usually very successful. He shows how you overcome your fear: 'But in your hearts set apart Christ as Lord.' Isn't that wonderful? He is re-recording Isaiah 8:12 and 13, '... do not fear what they fear, and do not dread it. The LORD Almighty is the one you are to regard as holy, he is the one you are to fear, he is the one you are to dread ...' That is the passage he quotes and applies it explicitly to Jesus. We are to set Jesus Christ apart as holy, we confess His Lordship, His transcendent deity, His unqualified sovereignty. This is more than mere mental assent, this is the heart of devotion; we are to set Him apart in our hearts, we are to stand before Him in the adoration of praise. The praising heart is immune to the fear of other people. We fear God and no one else. Did not Jesus Himself say, 'Do not be afraid of those who can kill the body. Rather, be afraid of the one who can destroy both soul and body in hell' (Mt.10:28). So in joyful recognition that God is God, we learn not to be afraid of what others will think or do.

We are to reverence Him in our hearts. After all, even now Christ is Lord and has all authority as Peter reminds us in the last verse of this paragraph. Jesus has gone into heaven and is at God's right hand (verse 22), 'with angels, authorities and powers in submission to him'. So strengthened then (verse 15b), we must 'Always be prepared to give an answer to everyone who asks you to give the reason for the hope that you have.'

Now on one level of course this does demand some development in study, some ability to give answers. Yet we must not think that this being ready to give an answer is primarily a question here of having sufficient courses on apologetics under our belts. I'm afraid to witness because somebody might ask me a question to which I do not have the answer, so I've got to take another course on presuppositional apologetics in order that I might have an answer and until then I am not ready, so I can keep my mouth shut. That's not quite the idea, but rather it is that we should not be afraid of people. We so sanctify Jesus in our hearts that we are emotionally, attitudinally ready, and then if somebody asks us a question about the hope that we have, we can at least answer, like the blind man who said, whether this or whether that I don't know, but I do know that once I was blind and now I see. The person who has sanctified Christ Jesus in the heart can at least say that. And then of course if they are responsible, they will also go home and speak to the pastor and get some books off the shelf and find out some answers so that next time they are not caught on that one. You see, you do not learn to do evangelism by taking courses on evangelism. They may be helpful, but you learn to do evangelism on the street; in a home Bible study; you learn to do it over the back fence. In the same way you don't learn to give answers to other people about the hope that lies within you by studying on indefinite numbers of courses. Ultimately you do it by doing it! And you develop an attitude toward doing it precisely by sanctifying Christ Jesus in your heart, fearing God. Be ready always to give an answer.

None of this of course should be coloured with a vicious anger or a smug condescension, as some witness is. Rather we are to do this (verse 15), 'with gentleness and respect, keeping a clear conscience, so that those who speak maliciously against your good behaviour in Christ may be ashamed of their slander.' In other words, we are to do this both so that we will keep a clear conscience and so that others, even if they disagree with us, cannot write us off as nasty hate-mongers; they may even be attracted to the gospel.

This is an important point in Christian witness. I know of a medical doctor serving in a Muslim country who has proved wonderfully effective in his Christian witness. A woman brought her son to him. He had a long gash in the calf of his leg and as the doctor cleaned it up, he explained how it was important to make sure that the wound was very clean before he bound it up. The woman listened, and then she suddenly volunteered, 'Sometimes I wish somebody could clean up my dirty heart.' Now what would you say? 'Well of course your problem Ma'am is that you are a Muslim. We Christians have an atonement theory that explains what to do with dirt. But while you believe in the sovereignty of God and the holiness of God you really don't have a kind of way of dealing with dirt adequately, do you? I'm not surprised the way you feel you do.' You just won an argument and you just lost a whole war!

Do you know what he said? 'I know exactly what you mean. My heart was so filthy-dirty, I was so ashamed of it, then one day somebody came and cleaned it up, just like I am doing with your son's leg. Do you want me to tell you how He did it?' Isn't that so much better? You see it's the personal testimony in a spirit of humility and brokenness, being ready always to give a reason for the hope that lies within us, both so that we maintain a clear conscience and so that others cannot write us off as hate-mongers.

In any case (verse 17), 'It is better, if it is God's will, to suffer for doing good than for doing evil.' After all, in this respect we follow the Lord Jesus whose unique death is the best possible model. One cannot be more righteous than He. One cannot imagine suffering more unjustly than He. 'For Christ died for sins once for all, the righteous for the unrighteous, to bring you to God.' Thus once again, that which lies at the heart of our salvation also lies at the heart of Christian ethics.

Now the next few verses, from 18b on, kicks off one of the most difficult passages in all the New Testament. Let me simply tell you what the three views are and then tell you why tentatively I hold to one of them and how I think it fits in the flow of the big argument here.

The three main views on 1 Peter 3:18b-22

1) After His death and before His resurrection, Jesus descended into Hell and preached to the spirits of those sinners who had perished in the flood at the time of Noah. Some say He was offering them a second chance, which is certainly against the vast sweep of biblical theology. Others say it was a kind of triumphalist proclamation of victory: 'You see the redemp-

tive plan of God did win.' One of the weaknesses of this view is the question why He should speak to this particular group as to other particular groups. But we'll let that pass. That is the first view. It is historically connected with the church father Origen.

2) Christ, through the Spirit, preached to the people who were alive in Noah's day when they were alive. Now obviously He didn't do it personally, but He did it by His Spirit perhaps through the preaching of Noah himself. They were either imprisoned then in the sense that they were in spiritual bondage, so says St Augustine (though I think he's wrong). Or better, they are in prison now, that is to say, Jesus by His Spirit preached to them in those days and they are in bondage now, in Hell, though not when Jesus preached to them. (Now that is the view I hold but I'll come back to it in a moment.)

3) The spirits in prison, some argue, are fallen angels not human beings. Jesus then proclaims to them His victory and their certain doom.

Let me tell you why I hold that the second view is most likely. I shall do so by laying out the turning points as I see them.

Verse 18b, Jesus Christ, we are told, was put to death in the body but made alive by the Spirit, the NIV has. Well strictly speaking it's not in the body and by the Spirit. The same preposition is used in the original. He was put to death in the body but made alive in the Spirit, in the realm of the Spirit. The reason why people don't like that translation is because it sounds as if His resurrection was immaterial – He was made alive in the Spirit but not in His body some might say. I don't think that's quite the issue. Do not forget that after all Paul speaks of Jesus Christ resurrecting with a spiritual body – He dies in the old domain of the body, but He resurrects in the domain brought alive by the Spirit – it is in the entire spiritual domain in which He is also given a spiritual body. This fits well then with Peter's emphasis on the relative unimportance of suffering in this transient world, compared with the eternality of all that is spiritual and the spiritual inheritance that is ours. Through Him, then, '… he went and preached to the spirits in prison'.

Who are the spirits in prison? The word 'spirits' occasion-ally refers to angels good or evil, but only occasionally. It also fairly often refers to human spirits of people who have died. (Mt. 27:50, Acts 7:59, 1 Cor. 5:5, Heb.12:23, and there are others.) But these spirits, we are told (verse 20), formerly dis-obeyed long ago.

Now there are very good reasons for taking the underlying Greek this way. Jesus went and preached to those who are now spirits in prison, when they disobeyed formerly, when God's patience was waiting in the days of Noah. What that means is that Jesus preached to them then by His Spirit; and now they are in prison, that is, in Hell itself. Remember in 2 Peter 2:5, Peter calls Noah a preacher of righteousness. Also in 1 Peter 1: 10-11 he says, 'Concerning this salvation, the prophets, who spoke of the grace that was to come to you, searched intently and with the greatest care, trying to find out the time and circumstances to which the Spirit of Christ in them was pointing when he predicted … such and such.' In other words, according to Peter, when the prophets preached in the Old Testament, it was the Spirit of Christ that was motivating them, impelling them, inspiring them, carrying them on, because after all the eternal Word is pre-existent, He is antecedent to the days of the human Jesus, so also here. In Peter's thinking Noah was the preacher of right-eousness, but he was the preacher of righteousness precisely because it was the Spirit of Christ in him who was impelling him to preach righteousness. In other words, Noah was preaching to his generation, he was insisting on the right-eousness of God and calling people to repent, because the Spirit of Christ was in him, empowering him to do so.

The parallels between Noah's day and Peter's day

1) Both were minorities in a hostile culture.

2) Noah was a righteous man in the midst of a great deal of wickedness, as Christians here are expected to be the same.

3) Both are to witness. Noah bore witness and became the preacher of righteousness to his generation. It was pretty hard to hide an ark that big in any case, wasn't it! So he had to give some sort of explanation and he gave an explanation that was

based on his faith and the word of God, for a long time until the flood actually came. So also Christians are to bear witness to the word of God for a long time, until the judgement finally comes.

4) Judgement in both cases was impending, sweeping judgement.

5) In this spiritual realm, Christ was preaching through the prophets in the Old Testament including Noah, and now He does so again here through us.

6) The righteous are saved, at the end they are vindicated. Hence 4:13, which makes this point abundantly clear. 'But rejoice that you participate in the sufferings of Christ, so that you may be overjoyed when his glory is revealed.'

7) Noah and his crew were saved through water, which he says is the anti-type, that's the word that is actually used (the NIV has 'symbolises') of Christian baptism.

Now what are we to say about this? In the 1930s in America there was a very famous preacher called Billy Sunday. He was a baseball player, rough-mouthed, crude and very gifted in his own sport, and he was wonderfully converted. He didn't have much theology, but he was passionate and he went around the country preaching an equal mixture of gospel and prohibition against alcohol. He set up a huge tent which unfortunately was not blessed with a concrete floor, in fact it had dust everywhere. If you pitched the tent on dry ground and people came forward at the invitation they would kick up clouds of dust. Alternatively, if he pitched the tent after rain, then when people came forward they slithered to the front in mud! So very soon he learned to put sawdust down in all the aisles. And out of this came the expression, 'to hit the sawdust trail'. You could ask somebody in America about 1934, 'When were you converted?' 'Oh I hit the sawdust trail in Cincinnati in '31.' In fact this expression became so endemic to the evangelical subculture that even if you got converted in a substantial cathedral you would still speak of hitting the sawdust trail.

Now baptism is a bit like that. You could ask a Christian in the first century 'When were you converted?' And they might well say, 'Oh I was baptised in '51 in Corinth' (except they didn't use that calendar then). Because in the first century baptism was so bound up with conversion, when you were converted you were baptised, and that is why Paul can say, for example, as many as have been baptised have put on Christ.

That's what's presupposed here. In the ark, only eight people, were saved through water, and this water symbolises baptism that now saves you also, it is bound up with the whole experience of conversion, it is the pledge of a good conscience toward God – not by the water itself, but by the resurrection of Jesus Christ who is gone into heaven and is at God's right hand with angels, authorities and powers in submission to Him. In other words, the chapter ends with the triumph of Christ.

So the point is, do not withdraw, for Christ is your example. Both in His sufferings as an innocent victim, and in His constant preaching to the most unpromising and in His final vindication – He's an example on all three fronts.

2) Do not be sinful, for Christ is your Saviour (4:1-6)

The willingness to suffer unjustly follows the example of Christ, and is committed not only to witness, but also to fighting evil, even if this means suffering. 'Therefore, since Christ suffered in his body, arm yourselves also with the same attitude, because he who has suffered in his body is done with sin.' The point of verse 1 is not that all physical suffering purifies people, it doesn't. A lot of physical suffering just makes people bitter. No, Peter's point here must be read in the context, note the 'therefore'. The idea is that the person who has suffered physically and/or personally, in his body, for righteousness' sake, for Jesus' sake, has made a clear break with sin – he or she ceased from sin in that sense. Let me give an illustration and you will see right away what I mean.

I know a good church with a very capable pastor, who took an elder on its staff, a medical doctor and a former missionary. We'll call him Charles. Charles was brought up in a Christian family with three older sisters; they doted on him and he turned out to be a really nice kid. He did all the right sorts of things; he made a profession of faith, went on to university, became president of the CU, qualified as a medical doctor, eventually married the right girl and went to work in a leper colony in Africa. After a number of years he came back and settled into this particular church. It was not long before he was asked to join the elders' board, where in fact he served very admirably for a number of years.

Then without any warning he told his wife he was divorcing her and was going to live with his nurse, and that's what happened. The senior pastor and others in the church spent a lot of time trying to counsel him and his wife but his mind was made up. In fact his attitude was, 'Why are you telling me what to do? I'm determined on this course, I'm not doing anything wrong, you don't have any right to tell me what to do.' In due course he married this other girl.

Months later I was talking with the pastor of that church and because I knew a little of the circumstances in this case, I asked him, 'What do think went wrong, what was the problem?' And he said, 'I don't think Charles was a Christian.' I said, 'Come on, give me a break! He was a missionary in Africa. He was exposed to the gospel all along, he made a profession of faith, he had followed the Lord for many years, led others to Christ, and you say you don't think he was a Christian?' And he said, 'No, don't misunderstand me. I'm not for a moment suggesting that Christians can't fall into adultery. All I'm saying is that I don't think he was a Christian.' I said, 'Why not?' He said, 'Because I cannot find any place in his life where he ever took a major decision simply because it was the right thing to do under the lordship of Jesus.' I said, 'What do you mean? There must have been some sort of self-sacrifice and principle of rightness going out as a missionary.' He said, 'No, not even then. He was brought up in a Christian family and everybody doted on him, he was everybody's idol and he did what everybody wanted, but he did what *he* wanted to do. He went to university and studied what *he* wanted to study. He was a natural leader and became head of the CU because everybody thought he was wonderful, so he did the wonderful thing and became head of the CU. He married the right girl and everybody applauded him.

He went and did public health because that's what *he* wanted to do. He went to Africa because that's what *he* wanted to do. At no point can I find any place where he took a decision against what he wanted to do for Jesus' sake. I cannot find any place in his life where there is an ounce of unambiguous self-denial. And so he eventually comes to the point where he finds a pretty skirt and he does what he always does, he does what *he* wants to do. And then he's offended that we challenge him, and he says in effect, "What right do you have to tell me what to do?" All along everybody's been telling him how wonderful he is for all that he does.' Do you see?

Biblically faithful Christianity turns on repentance and faith. It comes under the Lordship of Christ as a matter of principle – Oh God help us, we do sin. We do shake our puny fists in God's face in frustration, we who are Christians too sometimes. But there has to be a principal submission to the Lordship of Christ somewhere, or where is the repentance? What does it mean to confess Jesus as Saviour and Lord?

Now Peter says, '… since Christ suffered in his body, arm yourselves also with the same attitude, because he who has suffered in his body is done with sin.' On the night that he was betrayed Jesus cried in the garden, 'Not my will but yours be done.' Now I am not suggesting that Jesus was sinning, but He was tempted to. And the issue was whether He would do what He naturally wanted to do, namely walk away from this mess, or bow to His Father's will. In agony He cries, 'Not my will but yours be done.'

It is precisely when Christians begin to face suffering, for Jesus' sake, for Jesus' sake doing what is right, that you see that divide coming that reinforces all of what it means to bow to the Lordship of Jesus. It is not as if he is saying here, from now on because you had suffering you will never sin again. No, he's saying, when you face this sort of thing and then you do what is right there is a break, there is a turning point, there is an orientation that is fundamentally different. Besides, he goes on to say, judgement awaits those who abuse you, verses 4 and 5. And in any case, as for believers (verse 6), 'For this is the reason the gospel was preached even to those who are now dead,' so that first, 'they might be judged according to men in regard to the body,' that is the judgement of death common to all human beings still comes upon them, but that, second, they 'live according to God in regard to the spirit.' – that is, they live before God in the spiritual realm. Yes, the gospel absorbed into the life of the believer does not prevent us from dying, but we shall live in the heavenlies in the very presence of God – that's our orientation.

In various parts of the New Testament this kind of antithesis can become very sharp. There is a sense of course in which none of us is in any position whatsoever to gloat. We are never more than poor beggars telling others where there's bread, that's true. Yet, this antithesis becomes sharpest perhaps in the Book of Revelation where some people have the mark of the beast. If they have the mark of the beast then they are safe from the wrath of the beast, but they must face the wrath of the lamb. Others have the mark of the lamb. If they have the mark of the lamb then they are safe from the wrath of the lamb, but they must face the wrath of the beast. In the Book of the Revelation everybody's got something on their foreheads. So the question sooner or later becomes, what wrath do you want to face?

The fact of the matter is, Christ came and bore our curse, so that, although according to men we will be judged, we die – sin leads to death yet we live according to God in regard to the Spirit, we have escaped the wrath to come because Christ died for us. So do not be sinful because Christ is your saviour.

3) Do not be half-hearted, for Christ is your coming Sovereign (4:7-11)

The emphasis here on the end, on the ultimate judgement, and the ultimate vindication is very strong. Let me give you an outline for Sunday School classes and sermons:

    a) Pray unencumbered (verse 7).

    b) Love profoundly (verses 8 and 9).

    c) Deploy your gifts self-denyingly (verse 10).

    d) Speak for God, not yourself (verse 11a).

    e) Serve with God's strength, not your own (verse 11b).

    f) In all of this aim to glorify God (verse 11c).

That's the paragraph I decided I would skip over quickly, even though it is full of good things.

4) Do not be afraid of persecution, for Christ is your Patron (4:12-19)

Verse 12 at one level is simply repeating – don't be surprised when you face this sort of thing. But verse 13 offers a new perspective: we actually participate in the sufferings of Christ and this must be our cause of joy.

Do you remember what Jesus says on the Damascus Road to Saul who was persecuting the church? 'Saul, Saul, why are you persecuting me?' Not 'persecuting my church' but 'me'. After all the church is Jesus' body. What we suffer, He suffers. If we do something to hurt the church, we wound Christ. And thus we participate in the sufferings of Christ. This is such a strong theme in the New Testament that the apostle Paul can go so far in Colossians 1:24 as to suggest that, granted that the church must suffer, granted that there are the sufferings of Christ in this sense still to fill up, he would like to have more than his share so that others could have a little less. 'Now I rejoice in what was suffered for you,' he says, 'and I fill up in my flesh what is still lacking in regard of Christ's afflictions for the sake of his body, which is the church.'

A friend of mine, Doug Nichols, runs a large mission devoted to working with street children in the poorest cities around the world. He came down with cancer and was still trying to maintain a very busy schedule while the chemotherapy was making him so weak. Blood was seeping out from under his fingernails as his twenty-one-year-old son was driving him to his next speaking engagement. And this son said, 'Dad, I wish I could take some of this suffering for you.' The father smiled and said, 'Oh no you can't do that. Jesus has given this to me, this suffering is mine and I rejoice to serve Him.'

It's such a different stance from the self-pity that characterises most of us, isn't it? I'm not suggesting for a moment that there are no tears in these things, of course there are; sometimes just tears of exhaustion. I remember when I got typhoid in Africa. I was so debilitated I couldn't stop crying.

I know that's true, we are in the body; and yet, sufferings endured for Jesus' sake? Rejoice that you participate in the sufferings of Christ so that you may be overjoyed when His glory is revealed.

This is not masochism, it's living with eternity's values in view. 'If you are insulted because of the name of Christ, you are blessed...' Did you get that? Then why are we so afraid of insults that we hardly ever open our mouths to witness? Think of all the blessing you're not getting. What's the matter, don't you want blessing? '... you are blessed, for the Spirit of glory and of God rests on you. If you suffer, it should not be as a murderer or thief or any other kind of criminal, or even as a meddler.' Some of us suffer from that, yes. 'However, if you suffer as a Christian, do not be ashamed, but praise God that you bear that name.' Then were the apostles glad that they were counted worthy to suffer for the name. The fact of the matter is that suffering is coming at the end. If it is time for judgement to begin with the family of God, what will the end be for those who do not know God. If it is hard for the righteous to be saved, what will become of the ungodly and the sinner? 'So then, those who suffer according to God's will should commit themselves to their faithful Creator and continue to do good' (verse 19).

Conclusion

This twentieth century has seen more Christian martyrs than the previous nineteen combined. It has also seen more gospel outreach than the previous nineteen combined. I'm neither a prophet, nor the son of a prophet (and I work for a non-profit organisation!) but let me tell you what is going to happen. Jesus says in the parable of the wheat and the tares, 'Let both grow until the end' (cf Mt. 13:24-30). And unless Jesus comes back first, what will happen in this next century about to open up on us, is that both will grow some more. There will be more outreach and there will be more tares. If you think that in this bloodiest of centuries we have managed to abolish war, wait until you see the twenty-first century. There will be more struggle, more fighting between good and evil. And there will be more Christian witness – that's what's going to happen. And it is quite possible that in the West there will be more persecution than there is, although there is more here than some people realise. Oh I can imagine a thousand scenarios in which it will become much more difficult to be a Christian. Some of you became Christians, went home to tell your parents and they just treated you like a pariah because they just think you are a self-righteous prig.

> If they persecuted me they will persecute you.
> For the slave is not above the Lord he serves.
> My assignment was the cross,
> You my slave will bear some loss.
> My disciple takes his cross
> And daily nerves his heart and mind to follow me.

We must take up the challenge of taking on the hard jobs, reaching the hardest places in our cities, going to the hardest places around the world; asking not, what job, what form of ministry will fulfil me? But, can I take on my share of the sufferings of Christ's body? How can I bear witness to those who ask me for a reason for the hope that is within me? For Christ is our example and we know that Christ's strength is made perfect in us in our weakness. Our joy is both for this world and the next, and the over-joy comes in the life to come. We follow the Saviour.

I think that one of the most beautiful hymns written in this last decade is that of Stuart Townsend, 'How deep the father's love for us, how vast beyond all measure,' which contains these words:

> I will not boast in anything,
> > no gifts, no power, no wisdom,
> But I will boast in Jesus Christ,
> > his death and resurrection.
> Why should I gain from his reward?
> > I cannot give an answer.
> But this I know with all my heart,
> > his wounds have paid my ransom.

Let us be disciples of Christ, in the light of His ransom.

Outline for 6: Going to Glory
1 Peter 5: 1-14

(see note on p. 82)

Introduction: Glory! Glory! Glory!

1) **Christian leadership on the way to Glory (5:1-4)**

2) **Christian humility on the way to Glory (5:5-7)**

3) **Christian warfare on the way to Glory (5:8-9)**

4) **The Christian's God holding out the Glory (5:10-11)**

Conclusion

Studies in Revelation

by Nigel Lee

1. A Revelation of Jesus
Revelation 1:1-8

When I said to my friends that I was going to take passages from Revelation this week they looked at me in absolute horror. Ron Dunn said, 'If the committee had given me Revelation, I'd have given it them back!'

Revelation is a strange book, it's a book that we're not familiar with, the kind of literature that we're not used to reading. We enter a very strange world when we get into Revelation – locusts the size of horses. You get kept awake at night by some tiny little mosquito, imagine if it was the size of a horse! We are going to see bowls upon bowls of divine judgement poured out on the world and terrifying beasts coming out of the sea and out of the land, trying to control our lives. We don't know how to handle this kind of literature.

Also, the book has been a honey pot, for swarms of cranks and heresy peddlers and date setters, down through the years. People with all kinds of private, personal and political agendas dive into Revelation in order to find what it is that they want to say to you. It reminds us a little bit of the Book of Daniel and we are not very sure that we understand that, so we stay away from it.

Another reason it has been avoided and not often been

preached on, is that where the church is fighting for its life and witness against the encroaching hostility, we sometimes suspect that we have better things to do than to study eschatology. It would only lead to fighting each other wouldn't it? What does '6 6 6' actually mean? Do you think that we will reign with Christ on earth for one thousand years or not?

And so there has crept up on the church the view that Revelation is a book that is difficult, it's dangerous, it's best avoided, there is a big sign up which says 'Keep off the grass', just stay away from it. But that won't do, will it? Not for Christians. It's God's word. How will you defend yourself when the Lord Jesus asks you, 'What did you think of what I put in that book?'

Why study the Apocalypse? (verses 1-3)

1) 'I sent it to you, my servants, for your help and encouragement. Did you find it so?'

2) We notice in the very first verse, that it is a book that is addressed to you personally, to everybody who thinks of themselves as a servant of God. The revelation of Jesus which God gave to show His servants what must soon take place. The Father gave it to His Son who passed it to an angel, who transmitted it to John, who wrote it down, and now I am trying to preach it to you. It's a very long conveyor belt but it is God's Word at the end of it. This book is the climax to the whole sweep of Scripture that started in Genesis, and if we disregard it it's like tearing out the last act of a play. We need it.

3) Why should we take it seriously? God has promised to bless us if we read it. Isn't that wonderful? Just read it, and pay attention. If you are finding things difficult by verse 3, God says, 'Come on, keep going. I am going to help you if you read and study and pay attention to this book.' This is the first of seven pronouncements of blessing that we get through Revelation. 'Blessed are you if you die in the Lord', chapter14; 'Blessed are those who are eager for the Lord's return', chapter 16; 'Blessed are those that are invited to the wedding supper of the Lamb', chapter 19. I'm stacking up some of those blessings already. God has said, 'You come to

this book, refuse to be scared off by some of the rumours and stories and reactions and I promise that I'm going to bless you. Read it and take to heart what is written.'

4) Some people regard Revelation as a little bit mystical and they ask, 'Well, is it practical? If I read all this symbolism and all about the tabernacle and all about these judgements, is it going to help me love my wife more? Is it going to help me be a better witness in the community?' What do you mean by practical? True, it doesn't say very much about winning your neighbours to Christ. But if we start to doubt the extraordinary love of God for sinners like us, and His justice in a world that has torment and judgement and pain and disaster, if we stop believing that He really does care for us, we will soon stop evangelising. We'll stop bothering about our witness in our neighbourhood, and these judgements and these persecutions are precisely the things that can sometimes destabilise us and make us question whether God really is there caring and loving, or not.

This book was given to John in prison to pass on to the churches in Asia Minor, part of what we now call Turkey, an area at the end of the first century that was renowned for its worship of the Roman emperor and for its brutal punishments of those who refused. John has been locked away on the island of Patmos in order to snuff out his bold witness to the Lord Jesus. And the Lord knows where he is and has come to the island of Patmos and given John such a revelation of His glory that the ripples spread out right to the ends of the earth to this day. God's doing. It's a book that's always found to be immensely practical, helping the suffering church to still believe in the love of God.

5) But my final reason for studying the Apocalypse, as it's called, is the simplest and the best. The book is what it claims to be: the revelation of Jesus Christ. Isn't that why you've come? Because in your heart and soul, you need a revelation of the Lord Jesus Christ. Some are very conscious of the difficulties that they've been going through lately, some have come in dryness and pain, some in overwork, some from churches that almost seem like a persecution, some carrying undealt with areas of guilt, and what you long for more than

anything else is a revelation of Jesus for your own soul and for your condition.

The word 'apocalypse' can seem faintly menacing. We start to think of four horsemen riding around dealing out famine and death and persecution and so on. To John the word simply meant an unveiling, a lifting off of the cover. It is the revelation of Jesus Christ. This book isn't intended to obscure Him in fresh clouds of mystery and difficulty, but to reveal Him more carefully so that we may love Him more. It's very hard to love someone that you don't really know. We love in response to what we know. 'Let Me show you more about My Son,' says God, because what you will find happening is that your heart will slowly start to love Him more. That's the purpose. He's the Lion of Judah, He's the Lamb of God, He's the Judge of all the earth; He's got power, He's got such gentleness and accessibility; He is the one who is going to deal with injustice and unrighteousness. He is the Bridegroom who comes loving and wooing. 'Let Me show you this so that you may love Him more.'

Preliminary questions

1) What is prophecy?

In verse 3 this book is also called not only a revelation, it's called a prophecy, 'Blessed is the one who reads the words of this prophecy'. In 2 Peter chapter 1 the apostle Peter likened prophecy to the morning star. A few weeks ago I and a few friends were sailing a yacht out to the island of St Kilda in the Atlantic. I was on watch from twelve to four as we were approaching the island. It was pitch black with birds flying around (sea birds keep flying even through the night). Before dawn breaks you get the morning star in the sky. It starts to gleam and shine as an evidence that dawn is coming; it hasn't broken yet, there's a great deal more light that you need, more that's going to come, but there's something to steer by, it's a kind of encouragement, it's a gleam in the night. We were heading for that island which began to appear as a sort of ghostly black shape on the horizon, sailing by the morning star.

Prophecy, says Peter, can arise in your heart just like that. It starts to gleam there, it's a promise, it's something to steer by. It's not the full dawn but it's an evidence that the dawn is going to very soon break upon you; it's a prophecy.

2) How soon is soon?

Notice also these first three verses in the prologue, the emphasis that John brings on the nearness of all the things that he's going to talk about. Verse 1, this book is given to show you what must soon take place. Verse 3, the time is near. In Revelation, the things seem rather distant and far-off, like some science-fiction film or *Star Wars* movie or something. They are not. The Lord Jesus is exactly like we read of Him in the book: *now*, with glory and power and majesty and gentleness and that deft touch to wipe every tear from every eye. This book is lifting the curtain which hides the unseen world, the battles and the struggles and the conflicts as God sees them, which are going on now. It's happening around us.

Have you also noticed, glancing through the book perhaps, how the flow is constantly interrupted by singing – all heaven breaks loose in praise every now and again.

My life was touched many years ago when as a teenager I went out to East Africa and got involved in what has come to be known historically as the East African Revival. I can remember sitting on hillsides in South West Uganda in a huge crowd of ten thousand people, listening to the preaching of the gospel. And whenever the preacher somehow touched their hearts especially – we don't do this in Britain – they would erupt in singing. You remember the European Cup Final between Manchester United and Bayern Munich? The Manchester United supporters were getting quieter and quieter as we got to the end of the match – two minutes from time, yes! One goal, two goals and we'd won and the singing erupted.

It isn't just confined to the end of Revelation, but at the end of every section, whenever the Lord has a victory, there is a great outbreak of singing. The book is designed to arouse that same kind of response in you and me. How many of our songs have lines that you recognise from the verses we read? We get caught up in the praises of heaven as we read through the book.

Look up! God himself is coming (verses 4 and 7)

From verse 4 onwards John is passing God's greetings on to the seven churches in the province of Asia – 'Grace and peace to you from him who is, and who was, and', you might expect he would then say, 'whoever more shall be'. But what he actually says is, 'Grace and peace to you from him who is, and who was, and who is to come.' He's coming. In verse 7, 'Look, he is coming…' The one that they pierced, He's on the way. In verse 8 it's repeated, '… the Lord God, who is, and who was, and who is to come, the Almighty.' Three times at the very start of this book we are reminded that God is going to come back to the planet.

Also chapter 22 verses 7 and 12, 'I am coming soon.' And right at the end of the book John himself has a little interjection, 'Lord, please come. If it's going to be like all we've seen, oh Lord, please come soon' (cf verse 20). People will look and will see those wounds that our sins caused. He's coming.

Three things to remember about Jesus (verse 5a)

In verse 5, God suddenly starts telling us a few things about His Son. It's almost as if He gets excited. There's a pause and He says, 'I've got three things I want to tell you about Jesus before we go any further.' You see, the revelation of Jesus is actually beginning right away:

a) He is the 'faithful witness.'

John had been imprisoned on Patmos for his faithful witness. And I can imagine that questions had arisen in his heart, 'Why is this happening to me? I am the only apostle left living and here I am locked up in this island prison camp. Why can't He get me out? Why do I have to go through this day after day?' The Lord knows what it feels like to suffer for faithful witness.

In Mark's gospel chapter 14:61 we read this, 'Again the high priest asked him, "Are you the Christ, the Son of the

Blessed One?" "I am," said Jesus. "And you will see the Son of Man sitting at the right hand of the Mighty One and coming on the clouds of heaven." The high priest tore his clothes. "Why do we need any more witnesses?" he asked, "You have heard the blasphemy. What do you think?"'

A few hours later Jesus was standing in front of Pontius Pilate, the Gentile governor and He said to him, 'There is another world, you know. There is another kingdom; it isn't simply yours that matters. This Roman one isn't all that there is. There's another power, it's far superior, it is God's power.' And of course they condemned Him to death for it. He never ducked it. He told the truth. He was the faithful witness. And one day the position will be reversed, that Roman governor will stand before Jesus. One day those chief priests and those accusers will stand before the Judge, the Lord of all the earth. He had been the faithful witness.

b) He is the 'first born from the dead'.

There is a reminder immediately of what faithful witness can lead to in the short term. All over the world our brothers and sisters are suffering rejection, backlash, the knock on the door at night, possible death sentence. What an encouragement it is to Christians trying to witness around the world to be told that not everybody fell down with conviction when Jesus was the faithful witness. In fact they turned on Him, they blocked their ears, they put their hands over their eyes, they rushed upon Him, they tried to stone Him because of His faithful witness. God raised Him up from the dead, the first of a great army of people.

Just a couple of days ago I was involved in the funeral in our church of an elderly lady of a hundred and one. She had laid in hospital and said, 'I want to go. I've been praying. Why doesn't the Lord take me?' When she died it was quite extraordinary, I have never seen the news of anyone's death lead to such an outbreak of happiness and rejoicing and thanksgiving! She had been praying for years and years – she'd become a Christian at the age of eight, she'd followed the Lord for ninety-three years and now she'd gone to be with Him. And we were rejoicing in her funeral service, not just that her prayers had now been answered, she could see Him face to face, but the Lord's prayer had been answered – in John 17 verse 24 Jesus prays, 'Father, I want those you have given me to be with me where I am, and to see my glory.'

c) He is the 'ruler of the kings of the earth'.

What an astonishing claim. Put these three together. Even if our witness leads to us being thrown to the lions or crushed under the chariot wheels or under the tank tracks of some modern godless dictator, God is still in control. God was in control when His Son was sentenced to death by Pontius Pilate. Jesus, and Jesus alone, is the ruler of the kings of the entire world and always will be.

John responds in praise (verses 5b-7)

The immediate reaction of John is to break into excited praise and thanksgiving himself. 'To him who loves us and has freed us from our sins by his blood, and has made us to be a kingdom and priests to serve his God and Father – to him be glory and power for ever and ever! Amen.' In his doxology, he gets excited about three things himself:

a) He loves us.

I heard recently about a church somewhere near Copenhagen, that has been built entirely out of broken things. They decided not to use anything that is not cracked or broken in the building of that church. They've gone to the brickyards and said, 'Please give us the chipped, cracked, broken bits.' Broken planks, broken bits of glass. Broken tiles. And they've fitted everything together. Can you imagine sitting in a church like that and looking around? Wouldn't you think, 'This is the place for me, this is where I belong, because I too have been broken, chipped and cracked.' And yet He loves us. The ruler of the kings of the earth loves us. Most rulers don't even know their own subjects. But, your King knows you. He knows you and He loves you in a way that no monarch ever can, ever did. Never forget this.

We are going to find these studies quite heart-searching at times. His eyes are like blazing fire and He will look into things in our lives and our churches, driving us to repentance and tears at times. We are going to see awesome judgements poured out upon the world. Never forget, whatever emotions you go through – He loves you. Yes, He disciplines those He loves, Hebrews 12:6 says so, and discipline isn't an easy thing. It isn't an easy thing in families. Well it wasn't in mine anyway. I was always doing something wrong. I stand before you as one thoroughly and frequently spanked. One day I was over my father's knee, waiting for the blow to fall and it didn't! My parents are quite different in personality. My father is actually very gentle and soft-hearted. Nothing happened and I looked round. My father was hesitating, my mother was gesturing and at the sight of this little parental struggle I went, 'Eheheheh.' That made us all laugh and I got out of it. It's not easy. Not easy in school, not easy in home. But the Lord knows how to discipline those He loves.

b) He has freed us from our sins by His blood.

This is wonderful. This is the gospel according to Revelation. Jesus never hid His scars from His disciples. When He came back from the dead the one thing He seemed anxious to show them were the scars in His hand and sides, to prove who He was, the Lamb of God slain before the foundation of the world, to show where He was put to death for our sin. I've often thought this – when I see the Lord face to face I'm going to look into His eyes, but then I want to see those nail prints in His hands, those wounds 'still visible above, in beauty glorified'. I want to see them.

He showed His disciples His wounds in order to win realists to true discipleship. He's freed us from our sins. The forgiveness, the acceptance, the relief, the joy, He's done it, it's over. This is gospel according to Revelation right at the beginning. We are free, from the accusation, the guilt, the drag, the weight of sin, if we will only respond to His grace.

c) We are made to be a kingdom and priests to serve God for ever.

We have a job to do. We are in a kingdom. Not just in a sense of being the people that He rules, but we are being prepared ourselves for government. Paul says we shall reign with Him. We are priests, every single one of us, being taught how to make our offerings, our gifts, our lives, our service, over to Him, and receiving so much back in return.

'To Him, the Lord Jesus, be glory and power for ever and ever! Amen,' says John.

We saw six things about Jesus. 1. He is the faithful witness – He stood for the truth unflinchingly. 2. He is the first born from the dead and many will follow Him. 3. He is the ruler of the kings of the earth. 4. He loves us. 5. He has loosed us from our sins. 6. He has made us into a kingdom and priests. And then in verse 7 John gets excited and slips in another little doxology, 'Look He is coming, every eye will see Him.'

Finally in verse 8 Jesus Himself speaks His first words in the whole book. 'I am,' He says, taking the name of God, 'I am the Alpha and the Omega,' the beginning and end of the Greek alphabet. 'I am the beginning of your story. I am your Alpha and Omega.' The Lord watched over the forming of each of us in the womb, the genetic pattern. He knew what was going to happen. 'I am the one who was there at the start.' And whatever you've gone through, divorce, adoption, these things that sometimes fall like shadows across our lives if we are not careful; the biggest shadow in the whole world is the shadow of the cross. It falls both ways, all the way back to Genesis chapter 3 and all the way on to now and right into eternity. 'I am your Alpha, and I will be there for you at the end. I am the one that spells out the whole meaning of life, I was there at the beginning of the foundation of the universe, I've created it, I know all about it.' The Lord created the world with a word. And at the end of time He will speak another word and the whole thing will be rolled up like a garment, no longer needed (cf Heb 1:11). 'I am the Alpha and the Omega.' All the meaning of everything that comes in between is wrapped up in His purposes. He's coming, He's coming. I'm so excited at this thought sometimes.

Last December my wife and I were in Nepal where you see many little boys playing with kites. There we heard the story of a blind boy who was asked as he flew his kite, 'Why do you play with a kite? You can't see it.' And his answer was, 'I can't see it but I love to feel the pull.'

In Revelation you start to feel something of the pull of the Lord Jesus, on your heart, on your life, the One who loves you, has freed you from sin, given you a job to do. It's heart tugging stuff.

2. The Lord among the Lampstands
Revelation 1:9-20, 2:1-7, 2:18-29, 3:14-22

This is rather a long reading, isn't it!

We obviously can't cover the whole of Revelation in five mornings, we haven't got the time and in any case I haven't got the ability; there's a great deal I don't understand in the book. I chuckled when reading chapter 7:13-14, where John says '... one of the elders asked me, "These in white robes – who are they, and where did they come from?"' 'Haven't a clue,' said the apostle John, 'you tell me.' I think we can identify with that quite a lot!

We have seen that the book is written in order to give us a revelation of Jesus – in His character, in His ways, in His future work. And we have seen in chapter 1, at the beginning of the book, something showing us a little of the Lord's glory and splendour, that great vision, it's sometimes read out in communion services – the One who was dressed like this, with eyes like that and feet like that, and so on. It's right at the start of the book. It's not kept for us till the great climax at the very end, this is the beginning.

Now why does God do that?

Preliminary observations

God's tactics – how does He start?
Why does He show us something of the glory of Jesus right at the start? Remember firstly, the churches to which he is writing are about to face bitter persecution. Some, perhaps many will be thrown into prison, there will be martyrdoms, torture, death; these churches before very long will be under enormous pressure.

And remember secondly, there are various things already wrong with them before the pressure begins. Some of these churches are in real trouble. One is said to have the reputation of being alive, but actually it is already dead. Another is apparently allowing compromise right in the heart of its leadership. The last one that we read of, Jesus Himself says is wretched, pitiful, poor, blind and naked. The lamps in some of these churches, who are about to face great difficulty, are burning very low.

And remember thirdly, John, when receiving this vision, was himself in prison on Patmos. He says in verses 9 and 10, I am your brother, companion; in the suffering of the kingdom, the patient endurance is ours in Christ Jesus. That's actually all he says about himself and his circumstances in the whole book – nothing about the trial, nothing about the arrest, nothing about his feelings, just, I am copying what Christians so often do.

Now God's method of beginning to put these churches right, preparing them to face what may be coming, God's method of sustaining His servants when they are in trouble, is to show them something of Christ and His glory in a way that they can see, so that their hearts are softened, so that they begin to say, 'Oh wow, there's the one I follow.' They begin to melt and turn and fall in love with Him again. That's what God is up to in this first chapter at the beginning of the book.

And there's another reason why He does it. The rest of the book is going to be full of judgements of one sort or another: seven seals broken open and things escaping; seven trumpets that initiate great judgements; seven bowls poured out to the destruction of the entire planet. None of these things is the final judgement at the great white throne – that's where the books are finally said to be opened; these are preliminary judgements, they are warnings, they are the consequences of rebellion, they are God trumpeting to us if you like, of what will eventually come if we don't pay attention and respond. It's rather like the plagues in Egypt, plague after plague as evidence to Pharaoh and God's own people, culminating eventually in the death of the first born, the final judgement. Now we need to be shown at the very start of the book, who is in charge, what is He like. Is the one running this someone that we can, in the midst of it, respond to and worship and love? Or is this person just a monster and a tyrant?

So what God is doing in the first chapter is showing us at the beginning something of the glory of Jesus, in order to prepare those who first received the letters and us who read the book, for what's coming.

In the pivotal verses 12 to 18 we are introduced to the judge of all the earth. John in verse 10 has heard a voice that was behind him, clear and ringing like a trumpet. He turns round and there, facing him, is this extraordinary person. He is described with all kinds of symbolism. This judge is wearing a judge's robe, His hair is said to be white and snowy like wool. We see a symbolic description of His eyes and His feet and His mouth – symbolic; He wasn't actually standing there with a dirty great sword sticking out, you know you couldn't imagine a person like that, but this is a description of someone who speaks like that.

Symbolism – how does it work?

The book is full of symbolism and you can easily get tricked into regarding it as some kind of Bible code which you try and work out. Whenever it uses that word does it really mean this? Symbolism is not actually very difficult, we use it all the time. If you visit the Old Bailey and glance up as you enter gates, there is a blindfolded figure with a sword and scales. Now you don't immediately say, 'Who is that person? What is that person's name?' No, this person is a symbol of the justice that is supposed to be available in the British courts: fair, even-handed, weighing evidence, able to punish wrongdoing. It's a symbol. You see it and immediately your imagination works and you know what you could expect, it is hoped, if you had to stand in the dock there.

Or take the Old Testament phrase, 'a land flowing with milk and honey'. Does that actually mean that when Israel crossed the border they were immediately up to their knees in a soggy mess of milk and sticky stuff, like children's unfinished breakfast cereals? No, the key word is 'flowing'. The symbol is simply saying, in this country there is going to be an abundant provision of whatever you need: it's a land flowing with milk and honey.

Or take another example: in Revelation 5:5 we are introduced to 'the lion of the tribe of Judah'. Who's that we say. Well that's Jesus of course, like a lion, like Aslan in the Narnia chronicles. And in the very next verse, verse 6, we are introduced to 'the Lamb of God'. Who's that? Well, it's Jesus of course. But I thought you just said Jesus was like a lion, majestic and fierce, and now you are telling me that He's like a little lamb, somehow gentle and feeble and accessible. Yes, and one picture is placed on top of the other so that you begin to understand not just who is being spoken about, but something of this person's character – majestic and yet gentle. You are be helped in your imagination to understand things about the way in which God exercises power, what He's really like. It's been said that your mind is not a debating chamber so much as a picture gallery. And so this book Revelation, is rich in these pictorial ways of getting us to respond.

Sometimes, for instance in chapter 1 verse 20, we are given a pointer to help us. We are told that the seven lampstands are churches. That doesn't mean to say that every time you read the word lampstand you think, ah that equals church. No, you are being helped in your imagination to begin to think perhaps of your own church – is it shining brightly, does its oil need replenishing, does it need a clean-up, is much light going out into the community? How is the lamp in your church? That's the way symbols work.

Meet the judge of all the earth (1:12-18)

We are introduced to the judge here in the first chapter, a glorious figure symbolically described. He's dressed, verse 13, in a judge's long robes with the sash of office across his breast. He is someone like a son of man and yet pulsating with light. His eyes blaze like fire, His feet glow like molten bronze. His face was like the midday sun – this is the light of the world in person. No longer veiled in flesh, we are seeing the Godhead and He is coming to sort out His churches, His lampstand. He has spoken to John as He approaches him, John turns and sees Him, John hears His voice which is like the sound of a large tumbling waterfall; it's not feeble, this is a strong and decisive voice, His words are pictured as coming out sharp like a razor-edged sword.

What is He doing? He's just called out to John on the Lord's Day, He has summoned him, in verse 10, He is coming to inspect the churches. Are any of you school teachers? Does the word 'OFSTED'* make you shudder? My eldest daughter is a teacher and you only have to whisper the word 'OFSTED' and she goes white and pale and can't talk to you for half an hour! This is going to be far more serious than any OFSTED report.

First is going to come the examination and scrutiny of the churches in chapters 2 and 3 and then, from chapter 6 onward, the judge begins to inspect the world. And that is the right moral order in the Book of Revelation. Peter the apostle says, in his first epistle, chapter 4 verse 17, '… it is time for judgement to begin with the family of God…' If God is going to gather His people around Him and reign with them for all eternity, He must begin with judgement there. And then, says Peter, if it begins with us, what will be the outcome for those who do not obey the gospel of God? So in Revelation itself the judge comes first to His own people – they are this representative seven churches, and then judgement ripples out beyond them into the rest of the world in the rest of the book. I wonder what effect it would have on you to meet this particular person? His eyes, which see all

*Office for Standards in Education

there is to see about you. There's nothing feeble or short-sighted about this judge and you hear his voice saying, 'There are certain things about you and your church that I hate.' I believe it would shake you to the core, as it has shaken me pondering over these passages. In verse 17 John falls flat to the ground, just as he did the last time he saw this person in glory on the mountain of transfiguration, where again that veil of flesh was gone and he saw the inner reality. John and his brother James and Peter, the other two now dead, put to death by wicked and evil men, all three of them had seen the Lord like this.

John sees Jesus and goes down as if pole-axed. John is one who, as Isaiah 66:26 puts it, '... I esteem: one who is humble and contrite in spirit, and, trembles at my word.' But the judge is so aware, he's lively, he's not a statue like something from Madame Tussaud's. Immediately He reaches out His hand, raises John up from the ground and says, 'Now, John, start to take dictation. Write down the things that you are seeing, for others, of what is and what's to come.'

And then come these letters to these seven very real churches in Asia. We are not going to study each in detail (I think you are probably more familiar with this part of the book of Revelation than any other part), but I want to begin by drawing out four features that are common to each of the seven letters.

What the Lord thinks of the church

a) The Lord knows our situation.

Seven times He says, 'I know. I really know.' Five times He says, 'I know your deeds, I know about your service.' Sometimes Christians can imagine that the Lord doesn't really know all that we do and that somehow He is more concerned for the people we are trying to serve than He is for us, perhaps getting weary and dried up in our service. 'I know your service, I know your hard work, I know what's really happening.' Once He says to one of the churches, 'I know your afflictions, I know your poverty, I know your poor state, I know about you.' Once He says, 'I know the very tough area that you live in, where it seems that Satan just hangs out.' And some of you work in very tough areas and the Lord knows that. You'd love to work in a more fruitful area, you'd love to be able to have some of the stories of people week after week turning to Christ, but it isn't like that, it's bricks through the window, it's barbed wire round the buildings, it's few numbers, it's discouragement, and the Lord knows that. He knows exactly where you live, where He's put you, where you battle.

b) Each church is under attack.

There is not one of them that's having an easy ride. There are dangers from the outside: persecutions. There are dangers from the inside: it could be heresies, in some cases it's immorality. And we have to acknowledge that some of these churches are in great danger, that the Lord Himself will close them down.

Let's look at three of them, Ephesus, Sardis and Laodicea. The Lord Himself says to Ephesus, 'Look, if things aren't sorted out I will come and personally remove the lampstand.' To Sardis He says, 'You've gone to sleep. If you don't wake up I will come like a thief in the night.' To Laodicea, who were so pleased with themselves, He says, 'You make me want to throw up.' The ones that could be closed down by the Lord are not actually the ones facing persecution, nor are they the ones battling with immorality even in the leadership. They are the ones that have simply cooled down and become switched off and lost the plot – that is an awesome thing for us to face: the loss of passion, of joy in His presence, of that inner part commitment. You lose your first love, you cool down, you become Laodicean, you are more in danger of having the lampstand removed, than some of those others that are in a fiercer fire-fight.

c) Are we listening to the Spirit?

All the churches are told to listen and learn from what is being said to each of the others. To every one He says, 'He that has an ear, let him hear what the Spirit is saying to the churches.' No one church is told to go and sort out any of the others. He doesn't say to Smyrna, 'Well you got a pretty good

OFSTED report, would you mind going over to Pergamum and sort them out please, they're in a right mess.' No, the leader of each church is responsible to the Lord for their own church and not for any other. But the message is, are you listening to what's being said to other churches? Take heed, lest you fall.

d) Solutions.

The fourth and perhaps the most important thing I want you to notice is that the solution to each church's problems is found in something of the Lord Himself. In each church there is reference back to that great vision that we saw, of the judge in chapter 1. For instance, look at the letter to the church in Pergamum. 'These are the words', says the Lord, 'of him who has the sharp two-edged sword.' Immorality has crept into the church when no one was looking. There's idolatry in the church and what is needed is a sharp word from God, perhaps a sharp word regularly preached to cut out those things that have come in. That's what they need and the Lord sees it and says so.

In His letter to the church in Smyrna, he says, 'These are the words of him who is the First and the Last, who died and came to life again.' Why does He say that to that particular church? Because some in poor Smyrna will need to know exactly that. He is the resurrection and the life, He died and came to life. That's the thing they need to be told at that point.

The first time I was ever asked to preach on the book of Revelation, was a few years ago on board the OM ship *Doulos* for one of their Sabbath weeks, when they close down and simply spend a week with an invited teacher in Bible ministry. We had a wonderful time and it was as if the glory of the Lord seemed to draw near and people's eyes were opened and they were quietly touched.

They were rejoicing and they went away with food to chew on, and their hearts cleansed and refreshed – they were motivated again. Ten days later in the Philippines Muslim terrorists threw a bomb into the middle of a meeting. Two of that ship's company who had been listening only days before went to be with the Lord. A number of them were injured. Some still carry shrapnel in their bodies.

The Lord has spoken so that we may pay attention. So often we just let things fly over the top of our heads and say, well I know that's true, I don't need that. They needed that. I'm not saying this because I think there are going to be any great accidents or crises necessarily in any of our lives. But we live in the real world where this kind of thing happens, and the Lord speaks because that is what you need to hear. The Lord gets through to you in different ways, sometimes it can be a remark that somebody makes that they don't even know quite what they are touching on in your life, but the Lord says, 'Did you hear that? Just take time out on that.'

The solution to each of these churches' problems is the sword, it's the promise, it's the rebuke, it's the vision, it's the glory of Jesus from one aspect or another. If I go and preach in a church my prayer would be, 'Lord, help me to help them see the things about You that they most need to see.'

Ephesus: the good that isn't good enough (2:1-7)

And so we come to Ephesus 'the good that isn't good enough'. Hard work, perseverance, enduring hardship; they've even learned to hate the things God hates; God hates some things very fiercely. If we are going to be His children and walk in His steps, we need to learn to hate some things. This particular church was expert at sniffing out false apostles, but somehow with all this effort and this admirable doctrinal correctness, they let slip the one thing that mattered to the Lord most of all: their first love. You could meet with them and they would listen to you very carefully to see whether your doctrine was off, they would sing all the songs that had been chosen so that every single line was absolutely accurate and in line with the truth; but somehow there was something missing – that love, that joy and that spontaneous commitment to Jesus. All they had was good, but it wasn't good enough. They had lost their first love.

How does this kind of thing happen to us? Because it does; it happened to me. It could be a question of disobedience; something which when you pause before the Lord with anything like a prayer that goes beyond the early morning, 'God bless this mess please and help me get to work quickly Lord', something the Lord would put His finger on – that can cause you to lose your first love. Or maybe it's just overwork: men and women, worn down, the meat grinder of modern life. Or maybe it's bitterness about something that happened in the church or in the family, or just no investment in your relationship with the Lord at all. You know there can be a build-up in our lives of little, deadening things; it's no great crisis, it's just that you gradually get overgrown with the ivy of those kind of things, little unhappinesses at home, with your partner, with your children – that's a way in which you can lose your first love.

What's to be done? The judge is also qualified as a physician. He will give three instructions – we're not to muddle them, we are to take the pills in the right order.

1. Remember what it used to be like. Take time; are you walking with the Lord as you used to? You ought to be, you ought not to be any less, remember.

2. Repent, honestly turn back in unconcealed confession if that is what is needed.

3. Repeat what you used to do at first, that time for His Word or that hunger for prayer.

A friend of mine was asked to speak to a student group on prayer. He has been asked to do this on a number of occasions and has finally boiled down his whole philosophy of prayer. He's gone through 'Do this, remember that' and now he says (along with Nike), 'Just do it.' He told them that on the phone and declined to come to the seminar.

The good that isn't good enough. Does this touch you? Is there need for reflection and repentance, that your first love might be refreshed and restored.

Thyatira: the love that isn't loving enough (2:18-29)

Thyatira seems to have gone to the opposite extreme of Ephesus. It is loving, in fact it is the only one out of these seven that is actually commended for its love. It is full of faith and service and perseverance; and growth apparently – the Lord says, 'You are doing now more than you used to.' A most loving church. But it's the church that also has the longest list of faults. They love but have forgotten how to hate. Do you see the balance? The Ephesians, oh they knew how to hate false doctrines, but somehow in the process they had lost their love. The Thyatirans, they were loving, you'd get a good hug and a cuddle if you went there, but they had forgotten how to hate. They apparently tolerate a woman named Jezebel. 'Tolerate' in the original means 'let go';` it's exactly the same word that was used among the Ephesians for 'let go' their first love. The parallelism is deliberate. And she calls herself a prophetess, she's very sure she knows the mind of God, but her teaching is actually false and there's no one in the church bold enough to say so. And this regular injection from this person, of little bits of false teaching, is quietly sliding open the door to sexual immorality in the church, and a number of people are being drawn through it.

Now you imagine this church. They are loving, affectionate, warm, active, they are growing, but they won't stand against anything; they don't seem to have any convictions against anything. 'You just tolerate her,' says the judge, holding this whole church guilty of being accessories to the crime. He is charging them with criminal negligence, because they don't stand against things that are false or dangerous. They have somehow lost that inner moral fibre or backbone and they just drift along with a Christianity that is floppy and nice but doesn't actually believe anything very much, that won't last to the next generation. You can't love the Lord if you are not prepared to hate what the Lord hates. So He calls for repentance again. 'You listen to what I am saying,' He says, 'and you acknowledge that it is true and you take ownership of that which I am charging you with, and once you've owned it, then you can give it to Me and have your guilt taken away.'

I do believe that the church in our country does need a wake-up call to be loving and not just dutiful, not just correct in doctrine, with all the furniture of our minds arranged nicely; to be a loving, risk-taking, passionate, sacrificial church, yes. But not just loving, to care about what is being taught in our midst – in our conventions, in our schools, in our churches. What are you actually listening to? Do you challenge rubbish that comes from prophets who ought to know better, who are in danger of destroying other people's faith? That is what the Lord charges Thyatira with. We need both, we need a balance.

So what is the balance? One is maybe too loving and the other is too hating. I suppose the balance is to be somewhere moderately in the middle, isn't it? Kind of lukewarm, not very extreme about anything. And the Lord says to a nearby angel, 'Will you pass the heavenly spittoon please.' Modern British society pushes us this way – be non-judgemental, be relativistic, stay cool, don't have any convictions that will bump into other people or cause difficulties at home. And so we gradually, as the modern British evangelical church gets squeezed by our society, stop being caring about what is true doctrine, what is social rebellion, what is passionate service, we don't get stirred up about anything at all. On top of that we, like the Laodiceans, think we are the bee's knees – nothing to learn, loads of good conferences, Christian publishing like we've got books coming out of our ears – we are wonderful! And the Lord comes to the Laodiceans and says, 'My dear friends, you are naked.' The emperor has not only lost his empire, he hasn't got any clothes on. 'You are pitiful. You don't know how to pray like the Africans or the Koreans. You don't know how to witness like the Nepalese or the South Americans. You don't know how to suffer like the Russians or the Chinese and you think you are so wonderful.' Who are we? We are the Laodiceans. And the judge has come and gently pointed it out to us. What's the answer? Again, it's something in the Lord Himself.

Laodicea: can I eat with you? (3:14-22)

He starts to talk in verse 19 about His own love. 'My love involves rebuke and it involves discipline.' It involves the Lord Jesus Himself coming and knocking again at the door of our hearts; it's astonishing the way this vision to the seven churches ends. Here is the sovereign Lord of the entire universe, with thousands of angels at His command and He comes to knock at the door of the Laodiceans because He wants a little bit of fellowship. He wants to be let in, in order to sit and have some intimacy. So keen is He on friendship and intimacy He will knock first and He wants to sit at table with you and feed you things from His Word. Do you ever let anyone into your home and into your kitchen and you sit back and they say, 'Just leave it to me I'll…' You sit and they feed you. The Lord says, 'Let Me in, I want to feed you. Let Me at the sewing-machine, I want to make you some new clothes. Let Me come into your home and bring you back from poverty and blindness and feebleness, you need Me again.' There's a great deal more to our judge than just sitting up on the bench and looking down with rather fearsome eyes.

Do you ever ask yourself why does the Lord bother? In all His beauty and glory and majesty and purity, all His intelligence, all His power, dressed there in His judge's robes – why does He come and spend time lingering, loitering almost, amongst a group of churches whose love can grow cold, whose behaviour can be so disappointing at times? Why does He bother? It's because He has one eye on the future. He is the bridegroom and at the end of time, these ordinary repentant people, in all these various different churches, who've gone through different things, they are going to be His bride. And through the process of time and trouble the Lord will have so dealt with our lives that anything that is inappropriate in a bride, particularly the bride of the Son of God – any unfaithfulness in our hearts, any lack of affection – that will all have been faced and dealt with and repented of and will be gone. That's why He bothers, that's why He speaks to us. He's loving us towards that great day at the end of time.

Revelation 19:11-16 is a magnificent climax. You stand and watch, and over the horizon comes a white horse cantering towards you. And on that horse is the Lord. This is His wedding day. Here comes the bridegroom and His name is Faithful. He's been faithful to you, through all the ups and downs, through all the tears and all the hassles of an engagement, He has been utterly faithful to you. And eternity is going to start with the wedding – a wedding in purity, a wedding with new prospects, new home, new beginnings, that's how the book of Revelation ends and how eternity begins.

Why did He bother? Because He loves you, because He's God.

3. The Lamb upon His Throne
Revelation 4:1-11, 5:1-14, 6:12-17, 7:9-17

May God help us to understand this great portion of His word.

The throne of God (Chapter 4)

The scene at the beginning of chapter 4 has now shifted dramatically for John. There's a door standing wide open into heaven, a door that has always been shut up until this point; and John suddenly hears a voice like a trumpet – the same voice that he heard in chapter 1. It's now inviting him to look into heaven. So John steps up and peers in. And the very first thing he sees is a throne.

The throne itself

It is very rare in Scripture to see anything like this. This is the throne of heaven, the most important place in the entire universe, this is the control room of heaven and earth and everything that there is. This involves some fantastic claims. There is a place you know, from which everything else is ordered and planned. And this throne has someone sitting on it. There is someone in charge, someone who is taking responsibility ultimately for this world and what happens. This someone sitting on the throne is looking at John as John starts to peer into heaven.

We are not the playthings of chance or blind fate – there is a throne. There are millions of people in our own country who don't believe this. They don't believe there's a heaven, they don't believe that there is anyone out there taking charge or responsibility – there is no ultimate throne of authority. How could you believe such a thing after having lived through Kosovo, the Omagh bomb, innocents slaughtered in the street, blood running in the gutters in country after country? How can you believe in a God like that with all the horrors and killings and famines and injustices? In my work with university students this is the most weighty argument against Christian belief that one ever comes across.

The novelist, Somerset Maugham, had made a Christian profession at school, as a young lad. He had a 'clubfoot' (as it used to be called in older, cruel days) and he suffered the jibes of other lads because he couldn't play sport so well. He believed that God could answer prayer, God could heal. So one night in his boarding school he prayed earnestly to God, believing that in the morning his foot would be healed. He could feel it down under the bedclothes, twisted. He went to sleep, confident that God would heal that foot. When he woke in the morning it was exactly the same as the night before and Somerset Maugham turned into an implacably anti-Christian novelist because of that experience at boarding school. And maybe you have those kind of questions as well – what can God be like actually if, in spite of all my prayers, He lets my church fall apart, and my prayers don't seem to be answered?

In this book we are going to come across some huge judgements let loose on the world. Does God enjoy doing that sort of thing? Why does He do it? I am piling up rhetorical questions because the sight of this throne in heaven demands it. Is there really a throne and what sort of government emanates from it?

The throne of God is mentioned about fifty times in the New Testament. Nearly forty of those are in the book of Revelation and most of those forty come in the chapters we have just read from. So if you want to get your thinking straightened out this is the place to come, because we need our thinking founded on Scripture. The throne is standing there in blazing glory, by itself. By the end of chapter 7 verse 9, you see exactly the same throne, but now surrounded by so many beings, human beings and angels, that it is impossible to count them, a vast multitude. And they are all there willingly and they are all waving their palm branches and pressing to get close and thrilled at what they see. How did God do that? How does God manage, through the famine and injustices, the terrors and judgements that we can read of in chapter 6, the martyrdoms and the earthquakes, how does He manage to have an uncountable number of people at the end, who love Him so much?

We are going to see in these chapters something of the quality of the throne and government of God, the character and achievements of the Lamb, so that we may understand how all these people can say, in spite of all that's happened, 'Lord, we love You, You are worthy, You are wonderful, we want to be with You for the rest of eternity.' We won't be able to linger on every detail, but we are going to follow the drama. Revelation is a very dramatic book, and if we do sense something of the thought-flow of this, please God it may open a doorway for us too, to see something we need to as Christians.

Quickly through some of these details then. There is a person on the throne, apparently a very real person. John saw the throne and says immediately, it had someone sitting on it. But John found this person so difficult to describe that he could only talk of him in terms of flashing jewellery, jasper and carnelian. What are they like? Haven't a clue.

The rainbow

Then there's a rainbow all around that throne, resembling an emerald, and immediately we remember that cataclysmic judgement of God back in Genesis chapters 6 and 7 – a time when every imagination of people's hearts was only evil continually. God poured out a flood and afterwards He put a rainbow in the sky as a sign of His covenant promise, 'I will never do that to you again.' That little rainbow at the time of

Noah was only a small picture of the rainbow that is permanently around the very throne of God. Everything that comes out from the throne of God has passed out through that rainbow, reminding us that God is one who is slow to anger and quick to have mercy.

The twenty-four elders

Then around the throne were seated twenty-four elders. Apparently God has another collection of thrones snuggled up quite close to His own throne. Who are these elders? Haven't a clue. I have read many suggestions, we are simply not told in the book. What we are told is that they are elders, in other words they are creatures. God Himself is not an elder. God is beyond all time, God can't be described as senior, God is outside time and beyond it.

What is God doing? Apparently sharing the government of things with some of His creatures, He has delegated some authority to these others sitting on thrones. Here is something colossal about God Himself: He believes in delegation. He loves to trust people. He did it with Adam and Eve. He trusts us with our children. He doesn't give us children and then bring them up for us. He gives us an eternal being to do our best with. God isn't a power-hungry autocrat.

In chapter 13 of this book we will meet a beast who wishes to control everything about you, control your economy, your buying and selling, control your worship. God is one who wishes to delegate authority. He will even be prepared to allow Laodiceans, as we saw earlier, to sit on thrones with Him.

The lamps

Then we see in verse 5, in front of the throne are seven blazing lamps. In the ancient world, what you had in front of your throne was a very important symbol about you. King Solomon had two lines of twelve chained living lions. You would approach his throne to present your requests very carefully, wouldn't you?

God governs by means of light, truth, openness, showing us things, inviting us to come and walk in the light as He is in the light. There are so many governments in this world that are kept in place by darkness, secrecy, fear, intimidation, by not letting people in the know. And sometimes even churches can be like that. It's not God's way. God's government consists of bringing people into the light, showing us our sin, pointing to Calvary, banishing fear, getting us to walk upright in the light with Him. In front of His throne there is this mass of light.

The crystal sea

In front of the throne there is also what is called a glass, crystal sea, absolutely still, can you imagine? The Hebrews weren't very fond of the sea, they didn't trust it, it was restless, it couldn't be contained or controlled. Maybe John remembered nights on Galilee when storms had whipped up, nearly swamping the boat, and the Lord Jesus would walk through the waves to them, get into the boat and turn the sea into something flat, crystal glass – there's only one person in the universe that could do that, Jesus Himself, the creator.

The living creatures

Then there are the four living creatures said to be in the midst, in the centre, and around the throne. Who are they? I haven't a clue, we are not told. What we are told is that they are living, they are full of life. This throne of God is not some dusty old museum piece which you have to tiptoe around lest you disturb the woodworm. This is brim-full of life. I won't go into the significance of lion, ox and man, but I want you to get the core point. This is a picture of the throne of God, it's expressive of God's government, it is vibrant with life. God invented life, God has given you life, God knows how to sustain life, God loves life – 'I came that you may have life, that you might have it more abundantly' (cf Jn.10:10).

One of the biggest lies we ever meet, which subtly creeps into people's hearts and minds, is that if you get too closely involved with God He will spoil your life. In order to spice up your life you need a bit of late-night TV pornography. These living creatures around the throne are so excited because of the holiness of God; there is no real life unless we

are in open, light-filled relationship with the holy one of
God, allowing Him to speak to us, the one who shines light
into our lives, the one who has designed a colossal future for
us, and where we are excited about sharing His nature. Holy
is the Lord and He will forgive and transform and make you
like Him. That is real life. The lie of the devil is to suggest
anything else.

A song of praise

Suddenly at the end of chapter 4, the living creatures, then
the twenty-four elders start to sing, all around the throne.
'What a Creator,' they are singing. 'He gave life, He's merci-
ful, He draws His created creatures into leadership and government with Him, it's just so wonderful to be able to be so
close and to worship Him.' That's what they are singing
about. Does it fit your emotions? Are there times when you
don't feel this? You wonder about the government of God in
your own life. Why am I as I am? Why am I damaged the way
I am? Why has life turned out for me the way it has? And I
simply want to say, look at that throne. You can talk to the
one who sits on it yourself. He willed us all to be – by His
will, you were created, you have your being. He loves you as
you are, He wants fellowship with you, that's the way He is.

The Lamb of God (Chapter 5)

Chapter 5 will tell us some more things about Him which
will get you praising. It's almost as if you are making a televi-
sion programme of this. You have been standing back looking at a wide screen with rainbows and glass seas and the big
picture and suddenly you zoom into the right hand of the
one who is sitting on the throne, a single detail in this vast
picture; he holds a sealed scroll held in his right hand. What's
in it? We don't know yet. Later when those seals are opened
we face a series of awesome judgements.

But first there is a little drama. An angel, a very big angel
(did you know that angels come in different sizes?) this great
big angel asked a question. And it's not, 'When do you think
all these judgements are going to begin?' or 'What is going to
happen now to the human race?' The question is much more

profound. 'Who is worthy, who has the quality of life, the authority, the moral right to begin to release these things from the throne of God upon the planet, upon the human race? Who is actually worthy to pronounce and execute the judgements of God?' Not, 'Who can cause suffering?' Any old fool can cause suffering in the world. But, 'Who is qualified to start cleaning up, start putting things right? Who is actually worthy to punish evil in society and not be himself involved?' The angel throws out the big question, and at first it seems as if he's going to be met with silence; no one was found. No one worthy to bring God's judgements while upholding God's moral reputation.

John starts crying, weeping and weeping and I'm sure you understand why. Can you imagine the injustice and the cruelty and the pain and the misery of this world just going on and on and there being no one to bring an end, no one to clear it up, no possible hope of release or rescue? Can you imagine living in a world where opening the scroll and discovering the meaning of your life is now impossible? Your achievements, God's evaluation of you? John is racked with sobs at this awful prospect. I guess for many of us, part of our appreciation of the Lamb of God depends upon how much we have really given our minds to imagining what life would be like if there were no such Lamb upon the throne.

One of the elders, pastorally very kind, sees John crying there in the doorway of heaven, goes forward and says, 'John, don't weep, look. The Lion of the tribe of Judah has triumphed, He was not defeated by sin, He remained without sin, He triumphed over temptation, over sin, over death – the Lion of the tribe of Judah has triumphed.' John turns to see this person like a lion, with all the characteristics of a lion, and yet apparently a human being born of the tribe of Judah and as we said earlier, he sees a lamb, rather small and weak and with its throat obviously cut. And yet, a lamb now, standing there in the midst of the throne of God at the very epicentre of Heaven. The Lamb of God. It is the commonest term used in Revelation to describe the Lord Jesus, it comes twenty-eight times. God is obviously saying, 'If you get nothing else, remember this about My Son: He died that you might be forgiven.'

This Lamb looks so weak, but the elder wants you to look a little closer. Can you see seven horns sticking out? Very un-lamb like actually. Symbols biblically of power. And then seven eyes, seeing everything. In 1 Corinthians chapter 1 Paul is describing the impact of the Gospel of the crucified Saviour on the Corinthians themselves. 'Many of you thought it was a weak, poor, wretched, foolish thing, what an absurd Gospel, talking about a crucified person, a man, a Jew. The Gospel looks a picture of weakness and foolishness, but it turns out to be the power of God,' says Paul. Paul often had to say to the Corinthians, 'Stop looking merely at the surface of things.'

He alone is worthy

And the Lamb comes forward, He's the only one worthy, and He takes the scroll from the right hand of Him who sits on the throne, and immediately the pace quickens. Things now start to happen. All heaven rises to its feet, or perhaps more strictly (verse 8), they all fall down! Actually there's pande-monium because they're all holding harps – the Greek word for harp is *kithara*, we get the word guitar from it. They all go flying. They've also got golden bowls full of incense, they all crash on the floor. This incense is the prayers of the saints, your own prayers influencing the atmosphere of heaven. Down go the guitars, there's incense wafting around, the Lamb has come to take hold of the scroll and He's about to begin breaking off the seals one after another when surprise, surprise, singing breaks out. Through verses 9 to 13 we get one song after another, singing like you've never heard. (In my wildest megalomaniac imaginations I would like to con-duct that!)

First the twenty-four elders and the living creatures start to sing, verses 9 and 10. And then angels, a hundred million – ten thousand times ten thousand, can you imagine it? And then it says, every creature in heaven and earth – beautiful, pure, heavenly voices singing, and you're in there as well. This is a moment I have been looking forward to – other people singing and my little voice somewhere in this fantastic choir.

Singing in the tent here is great but can you imagine this? What are they singing about? The cross at Calvary. They surround the throne and the Lamb and they sing, 'You, You were slain. With Your blood You purchased people from every single tribe and language.' Later in this book of Revelation we are going to see those days when the beast has come and is seeking to prevent anybody buying and selling without his express permission. And right under his nose God has been going around purchasing people, it is fantastic! These angels are singing to the Lord, 'You bought people for God. You knew that God would like people and so You went out and bought loads of them, to offer them, that they might serve God.' He has made you to be a kingdom and priest. Oh the grace of God and the wonder of it. I hope your imagination can stretch around it.

This is going to be an extraordinary day, these lengths to which God in His government will go; from the throne He decided to make you, to make a world which is entirely temporary, which will one day be done away with when God has secured what He wanted from it, which is your love – to turn creatures into children, to put His Spirit in them, to make them like Himself, to share His great home and purposes with them. They praise Him because He is the creator, and then they praise Him because He redeemed us, He purchased, He made us to be a kingdom and priests to serve God.

The judgement of God (Chapter 6)

Six seals

Now watch. The Lamb starts to break open the seals. Things start to move, judgements begin. (We didn't read through every detail of that.) There are going to be wars and rumours of other wars. There are going to be all kinds of horrible things. Jesus Himself said, these things are not the sign of the end, these will always happen, they are just the beginning of pains. There will always be persecutions, hatred of Christians, martyrdom going on and then as we get nearer to the end, the picture seems to include a proliferation of false prophecies, false signs and wonders designed says Jesus, to deceive, if it be possible, even the elect. Christians are now finding that they are coping, not just with persecution from outside, but with a tidal wave of false teaching and gullibility inside. The synoptic gospels have given you that picture – now this is John's version, these four horsemen, these seals that are broken. But John is showing you the Lamb of God in control and answering the ultimate moral problems behind this whole process.

Why did the Lord spend time with the disciples, spelling out these details and outlining future events? I suggest that if He hadn't done so, we would have been dismayed and shattered when they finally happen – earthquakes, ethnic cleansing, churches wrecked by false teaching. These are the things that shake people's faith.

The Climax

The end of this process in chapter 6 shows us the wrath of the Lamb. This is an extraordinary concept – have you ever seen a lamb get massively angry? I think we find the whole idea of God's wrath difficult. We don't like to talk about it and sometimes we have problems even thinking about it. I guess it is because when we get angry and wrathful we tend to get ugly, we tend to lose our glory. We slam doors, we give people whiplash answers, we go silent, we leave them, we go out of control. The Lamb of God does not do any of those things. He is always in control, always wise in His judgement. But be very assured of this, though He is moderated and self-controlled, this day is coming.

What would you think of a God of love who never expressed moral outrage at all, against those who do wrong or against those who attack those whom He loves? This day will come. And the kings and the generals, and the rich and the ruthless and the poor and often equally rebellious, will see the heavens roll aside, they will see Him coming, and they will plead with God's own creation to fall on them and hide them from God. And it won't. The throne of God, the Lamb of God, the judgement of God, no escape, even though they seek caves in the bottom of the mountains. One day this sorting out and cleansing process, handled superbly, impeccably, by the only person in the universe who is qualified to do it, bringing about justice, harmony, and all the cleansing that this world now needs, He will come and He will do it.

The church of God (Chapter 7)

Let me quickly point out three things from chapter 7.

1) This wrath does not fall on believers. There's a very clear distinction between those in chapter 6:16 who are wanting to hide from the Lamb, and those in chapter 7:9 who can't get close enough because they want to see Him, they want to sing to Him.

2) There is a clear distinction between the 144,000 from the tribes of Israel in the first half of chapter 7, and the great multitude in the second half of that chapter. The first group has been counted. Twelve times twelve thousand, may be a symbolic number, but they have certainly been counted. The second group is deliberately said to be impossible to count. (We've run out of mathematics, hallelujah! A great multitude and no one could count!)

The first group is said to be from Israel, the second group from all the other tribes and languages and nations, a much larger group by definition, not just from Israel. Make of that what you will. I am persuaded that we haven't heard the last of the Jews in the plan of God. I do believe that the great Shepherd of the sheep has further surprises in store for us.

3) They are worshipping the Lamb for being such a great Shepherd. They break into song again. Let's read again chapter 7:16-17, 'Never again will they hunger; never again will they thirst. The sun will not beat upon them, nor any scorching heat. For the Lamb at the centre of the throne will be their shepherd; he will lead them to springs of living water. And God will wipe away every tear from their eyes.'

My sister died of cancer just eighteen months ago. I was asked to preach at her funeral and I took those verses. 'Surely goodness and mercy will follow us all the days of our life, and we will dwell in the house of the Lord forever.'

The Lord is with us even through the dark valley of shadow. He's prepared a table before us, goodness and mercy all the days of our life, and we will dwell in His house forever. You may be thinking, well it ain't always so. And I understand. Life isn't always very easy and I get sad too sometimes, and broken up inside and full of tears. Right at the end of this great section on the throne of God, it says that God Himself will wipe away every tear from your eyes. It requires a very steady hand to wipe away someone else's tears. Very often we give them a tissue and they do it themselves. This says, 'He will wipe away every tear.' Trust Him for that? Every tear. What a God, what a throne, what a Lamb!

4. The Beauty of the Bride
Revelation 15:5-19:10

I want to offer you an overview of the whole book of Revelation, a skeleton if you like – it might get a bit chewy (like some kangaroo meat I had recently in a Yorkshire pub!) but in sharing something which is structural, I hope to give you an idea of the thought-flow of the whole of Revelation; otherwise I think we can easily set off plodding through the book, examining it very dutifully verse by verse, without really knowing where we are. The small details can blow up like sand in your eyes and spoil the whole panorama; we don't see the whole thrust of the thing because we are worrying about this bit or that bit that we are trying to get out of our eyes. Some of the earlier explorers of Australia did just that, they wouldn't take any advice, they wouldn't look at the big picture, they wouldn't talk to the Aboriginals, they just went off into the desert, got lost, and died there. And I'd hate for you to die in the study of the book!

A short overview of the Book of Revelation

We have looked at something of the Lord's glory in chapter 1. And then in chapters 2 and 3 at His own not so glorious churches. We saw that judgement must begin at the house of God and there was a message for each of these churches.

Then from chapter 4 onwards there follows a series of sections, each following the same pattern. Something in heaven is said to be opened.

4:1 John looked and there before him was a door standing open in heaven.

8:1 The seventh and last seal was opened.

11:19 God's temple in heaven was opened.

15:5 The tabernacle of the testimony was opened.

19:11 Heaven itself opened.

These verse references are key division markers in the material.

Each time there is an opening in heaven our attention is immediately drawn to a piece of furniture from the tabernacle or the temple and each one of these pieces of furniture is rich in significance and meaning.

4:1 a door was opened and at once we saw a throne.

8:1 the seventh seal is cracked open and at once we can see the altar of incense, where the prayers of God's people ascend to the throne of God.

11:19 God's temple is opened, and you see the Ark of the Covenant.

15:5 the tabernacle of the Testimony is opened and immediately our attention is drawn to seven golden bowls used in temple service.

Now what is God saying by this literary device?

Firstly, there is a throne in heaven and it's not empty. God is sitting on it – God is sovereign and He must reign, He must judge because He is God; this is ultimately a moral universe. And that is the reason for everything that then flows in that section. We see that the Lamb alone is qualified to begin opening those seals and pouring out those judgements. God must do it because there is a throne – that's the reason why He must act and intervene as He does.

Secondly, there at once is the altar of incense – God's people pray. And that is another reason why God must act, because God is a prayer-answering God, He will vindicate His people, He responds to their prayers. And that is a reason why there are judgements in this world.

Thirdly, we see the Ark of the Covenant. And we are

reminded there is another reason why God must intervene and act and judge as He does, because He has a covenant with His people and He will keep it. That is the section containing the beast, who tries to enforce idolatry on all the peoples of the world, through intimidation and threat and economic squeeze, but some are loyal to God and to His covenant and God will step in to protect and preserve those in the face of totalitarian oppression. He will come to their rescue, He will raise them up to eternal life, because He is a covenant-keeping God. Another reason, do you see what's happening? God is opening His heart up to us, He is showing us why He acts as He does.

Sometimes the things that happen in our lives are hard to bear, but they become a little easier when we can see a reason why. And I believe what we are seeing is God covering the same events, but from different perspectives. The same punishments, the same judgements, the same cleansing process from a different point of view.

God must intervene and judge because He is God on the throne. He must intervene and judge because His people cry out to Him, 'How long, O Lord, when will we be vindicated? Oh God, come and bring justice.' This longing in their hearts is because they are His children, it is reflective of His own character. And then He must judge and intervene because He keeps His covenant, He has set out its terms and He will be bound by it.

Each of these sections, starting in chapters 4, 8, 11, 15, and eventually in the middle of 19, ends with a great outbreak of singing and praise in heaven as we have already seen. It's wonderful to behold. But when you look at each of those songs you see that they reflect the things that have just been shown to us in the preceding section. The people around the throne are starting to say, 'Yes, I've got it, I see now why You have intervened and done as You did. Oh that's wonderful, let's sing.' And as we read through the book I believe it is intended that we should, section by section, say, 'Ah yes, now I see.' We join in with the singing of heaven because we've seen the point, we've seen the why. Helpful? I hope so.

An overview of chapter 15:5-19:10

Now to put some meat on the bones. We are not going to have time to cover every single detail, but I want you to see the main purpose of this particular section.

In chapter 15 verse 5 we read that the tabernacle of the Testimony was opened, the Testimony to God's glory. The tabernacle in the wilderness contained not only the Ark, it was also a testimony to God's glory, what God is actually like, what it would take for us to come to His home and to be welcomed there.

God had come down in glory to speak to Moses in the thorn bush in Exodus chapter 3. Generally in Scripture God isn't very complimentary about thorns. He says that their end is to be burnt (cf Heb. 6:8). God had come down into thorns in order to talk to His servant Moses and set him going. Of course God will come later into thorns in order to speak to us. God came down to that tabernacle in the wilderness and filled it with His glory. It became His dwelling place, His second home if you like. God said, 'You are my people and I want to be with you. You are camping in the wilderness, let Me join your campsite. Build Me a tent in the middle of the camp and I'll go camping with you.' And so they made Him a magnificent tent and He came and lived in it as His second home and His glory filled it. We are going to be asked to think in this section, about glory. What does it mean to be glorious, to live near the glory of God, to begin to reflect that glory?

Out of this tabernacle come these angels in procession carrying golden bowls, and each angel is dressed in clean, shining linen with bright golden sashes across their chests. We are not normally told in the book of Revelation what angels wear. For all I know they could be in jeans and T-shirts, even the very big ones! However, in this section there is great stress on clothing, on appearance, on beauty, on ugliness. And so here come these particularly well-dressed angels carrying bowls containing the wrath of God.

At the end of this particular section the marriage of the Lamb is soon to start. And we read that the bride has made herself ready. How many of the people here who have been brides, were told on their wedding day, as the clock was ticking, to hurry up? And how many of you were late? I was late for my own wedding. I overslept and my wife drove round the block a few times till I finally made it. The bride in chapter 19 is said to be wearing fine linen, bright and clean, exactly the same as the angels were wearing at the start of this section. She is ready, she has developed the same values as the bridegroom and she looks wonderful.

But in the middle of this section, in chapter 17, there is the revelation of another woman. She is a prostitute, she is beautiful and seductive, she is used to mixing easily with kings, with the well-to-do. But she is also treacherous; underneath the glossy and gaudy appearance there is a heart of faithlessness. By the end of chapter 17, she will be exposed, stripped naked and disgraced. You can see the contrast emerging, can't you? Her name is Babylon. And that leads us in the next chapter to thinking of the city of the same name, the community that was built up from Genesis chapter 11 onwards. Its values and foundation, as we see in chapter 18, will eventually be destroyed.

From this summary, one thing is clear. This section in the Book of Revelation is asking us to think about true and false glory. What is it, in God's sight, in the bridegroom's sight, that makes you truly beautiful and glorious? What is it that attracts Him? What is it that is merely temporary in life, shallow and easily peeled off? How can you be the kind of person that would satisfy the heart of the eternal bridegroom? What is glory, how do we display it? We are going to be asked, in this section of the book, to contrast the faithlessness and seductiveness and the treachery of the world, with a love from heaven that has lasted, surmounting impossible obstacles, that has come through the difficulties of the engagement, a love that is really worth responding to. Now you see where we are going, let us look at some of the details, from chapter 15 onwards.

The procession of beautiful angels (Chapter 15:6-8)

They are magnificent as they come out of the temple, each one carrying a golden bowl filled to the brim with the wrath of God. Extraordinary. If we'd been writing the book we might have dressed these angels in black, covered them in sackcloth and ashes because of what they are about to do. We don't normally associate wrath with attractiveness do we? We tend to think that wrath and anger are always in themselves wrong because when we get angry we tend to become ugly. But anger is a part of God's nature, it's a part of His glory – this is a picture of beautiful anger, of righteous wrath. God knows how to be angry and we may be glad of it. Angry against those who abuse children, who break their marital vows, who destroy the planet, who exploit the weak. God knows righteous wrath in heaven.

The bowls of wrath (Chapter 16)

We see a successive outpouring of these bowls and we can't help noticing that as every single one is poured out, it does something to disfigure, de-glorify, all human dignity and light. Let me take you quickly through chapter 16.

The *first* bowl is poured out, in verse 2, and at once ugly and painful sores break out on people's faces. Is there anything more ugly, more sad in this world, than a human face covered with boils and scabs? People made in the image of God and yet de-glorifying themselves by turning their back on the Creator and worshipping the beast instead. And the judgements begin to happen. The major theological statement in the whole of Scripture on the wrath of God, I believe, is in Romans chapter 1, where it is connected to the concept of the glory of God. Romans 1 verse 18, the wrath of God is being revealed from heaven – why? Because people have turned their backs on the glory of God, they refuse to glorify Him, neither will they give Him thanks. Instead they exchange His glory for the images of created things, birds and beasts and so on. And so what happens through the rest of Romans chapter 1? They become de-glorified, they are given up successively to things that disfigure them in mind and body and spirit. It's inevitable. You turn your back on the light and darkness begins to fall on you.

The *second* and *third* bowls, verses 3 to 7, God now starts to disfigure the environment. The seas and rivers turn to blood, the only thing left to drink is blood, because they have shed the blood of saints, the blood of the prophets. Let them drink it then, says God.

The *fourth* bowl is poured out, between verses 8 and 9. And now the sun starts to go out of balance, it starts to scorch people. At the moment in this universe God has placed the sun in exactly the right place, we are neither too hot nor too cold. But now God is beginning to dismantle the creation that He had so carefully put together at the beginning of time. He is unravelling the work of Genesis chapter 1 and people have nowhere else to escape to. The folly of created beings who try to live on this created planet as if there were no Creator, they want nothing to do with Him. And in verse 9 we read that they refuse to glorify Him, they refuse to repent, even though He is now speaking to them very, very loudly.

And then the *fifth* bowl is poured out, in verses 10 and 11. Now the whole of creation is plunged back into darkness; we are now right back to Genesis chapter 1 verse 2 and the human beings are still refusing to repent, covered in sores, gnawing their tongues in pain, it says. God's government has been based on light. Men actually prefer darkness because their own deeds are evil (cf Jn. 3:19). This was the Lord's verdict on the human race. You prefer darkness? You shall have it. And God puts the light out.

The *sixth* bowl is poured out, in verses 12 to 16. The sixth angel causes evil spirits to assemble for a great battle against God.

And the *seventh* bowl is poured out, between verses 17 and 19. Now there is a loud cry – It is finished! It is done! There is a final convulsive earthquake that ruins what's left of creation. The end of verse 21: 'And they cursed God on account of the plague of hail, because the plague was so terrible.' There is an implacable evil and rebellion in the heart of the human being, even when God takes apart everything in their world, strips away hope and the very planet we stand on. God will have so worked through these judgements which are warnings, which are a trumpet call, that at the end, the last thing left standing is the rebellion and the defiance of human beings against their creator. And it will be plain that God has acted in justice and truth, available every step of the way. And the last thing they do to God is that.

Now why does God pour out His severity on creation, on the rivers, lakes and hills, in this way, what's going on? Why does God demonstrate in this section, so clearly and so finally, how fragile and temporary the world actually is? What follows in chapter 17 will answer the question for us. We begin to be introduced to the great prostitute.

The great prostitute exposed (Chapter 17)

Look at verses 1 to 6. She is beautifully dressed in purple and scarlet, the finest you could buy, glittering with gold and jewellery – this isn't some cheap tart you know, this is someone that the kings of the earth fall in love with. This is someone who is world-renowned for her appearance. But her beauty is deceptive, it's just on the surface; come and have a look a little closer.

Look at what she's drinking first of all. Can you get up close enough to look inside the cup, the golden cup and see there the blood of the saints – every now and then she's knocking back another draught of the blood of the saints. Get close enough to her to smell her breath, she's intoxicated; she's hooked on adultery, she's a deceiver. The big difference between a prostitute and a bride is this question of faithfulness. This woman is a seducer, she will say the nice things you want to hear and she doesn't mean a word of them.

God cares most deeply about our affection. He watches how you listen to His word day by day, because He is a jealous God and He loves you dearly. Paul would say to the Corinthians, 'I betrothed you Corinthians to one Lord. Oh what's happened to you? I'm afraid that the enticing one, the deceiver may have started to draw away your heart' (cf 2 Cor. 11:3). It can happen, I know. The world around us is very beautiful and seductive – it's a wonderful place that God has made. Though we have spoiled it in many ways, it is still beautiful, and Satan will use it to entice people away from God. So God in this section demonstrates how temporary and superficial the world really is.

John says, 'Don't love the world or anything in it. If you love the world the love of the Father is not in you. Everything in the world, the cravings of sinful people, the lust of their eyes, the boasting of what they have or do, comes not from the Father but from the world, and the world, is passing away. God is a jealous God, jealous for our own heart loyalty and affection and He's jealous for our own good' (cf 1 Jn. 2:15-17).

How foolish it is for us to give the love of our hearts – we only have so much, but to give it away to something that will vanish, that cannot last. You see someone else's pretty body, or someone's sense of humour and charm, and you begin to go after that person. Inappropriate. Or an easy bit of popularity or wealth, or something that you just like doing in this wonderful playground-planet that God has created. Any of these temporary possessions or relationships – guard your heart because from it come the issues of life (cf Prov. 4:23). Satan will use the stuff around and the people you know, and especially those that get close, if you are not careful, to draw away your heart from that loyalty to God. And under the surface image of sophistication and glitter in the world there is, says God, violence and betrayal and revenge and a blindness to the glory of God. Brilliantly put together isn't it?

God wants us to learn to care about the things that He cares about, to hate what He hates, to be able to reach the end of a section in which bowls of wrath are poured out and to say, 'Yes, that is right, I love Him more than anything else around.' Look at His glory instead, look at His beauty, look at His plans. Chapter 17 makes plain for us that the world is at enmity with God and will eventually be exposed. Am I talking to somebody here – are you teetering on the brink of foolishness in your life? I know how easy it is to be at the edge of that precipice. Draw back, draw back.

The great city brought to ruin (Chapter 18)

As we move into chapter 18, the picture changes to a great city named Babylon. Now we are looking at a great community, and it's a clear reference back to Genesis chapter 11, the first city, Babel. That city was built so that people, as they say, 'could make a name for themselves'. They weren't content to have the name that God was going to give. They also built a tower to reach up to heaven. I'm not quite sure whether it means it was simply very, very big, or it perhaps means that it was designed as an observatory, or whether it was simply designed to elevate people so that they could escape from any future flood, which God had said He would never pour out on the world anyway. Eventually Babylon became a wealthy, powerful, sophisticated place, outwardly very impressive; some of the water systems, the sewage systems, the heating systems there in that ancient city, were better than in many places in the world today. But there was no place for God there. And eventually Abraham was called out of a city that was part of that city culture – called away from the sophistication, from the central heating and the water supplies and the gardens and the fruit markets and so on – called to live in tents, wander around in the desert, no fine buildings, no place of his own.

Now, we must ask this question: what caused a man like Abraham to leave the city and live the rest of his life like that? Acts 7:2 simply says that the God of glory appeared to him in Haran – a magnificent city with every luxury and convenience. We don't know how, God showed Abraham a greater glory and it is only seeing that glory in life that gets your heart and mine started on pilgrimage, to start moving away from the Babylon that's in us, indeed enough to analyse the problems of our modern Babylonian society, the lack of moral and spiritual foundations. Abraham went looking for a city that had better foundations.

We can analyse the surface image and the lack of substance underneath, but how do you get people to want to leave? God gave Abraham a vision, a revelation. And in John chapter 1 verse 18, the author simply says his testimony, 'We saw His glory, He came and we saw in what He was doing and saying and promising and living, something that would cause us to leave our nets and leave Galilee and eventually give up our lives – we saw His glory.'

In chapter 18 we see a song of triumph – 'Babylon is fallen' say the angels, and they start to be so pleased about this.

We see the kings, the merchants, the stockbrokers and the entrepreneurs, all those people who have invested everything in this world and nothing in the next, they start to become terrified; they are out of their minds as they watch everything going up in smoke.

This has happened before you know. Come with me back to Daniel chapter 5. There was king Belshazzar, feasting and drinking from those bowls that had been dedicated to the Lord, when suddenly the finger of God appears, the finger that had written the ten commandments, the finger that was one day going to write in the sand when a woman was caught in adultery, the finger writes on the wall – 'MENE, MENE, TEKEL, PARSIN', which means simply, 'You have been weighed in the scales, you're a lightweight.'

In our English language the word 'glory' carries overtones of light, of shining brightness, 'the effulgence of His glory' says the old version. But actually in Hebrew the overtones are much more to do with weight. If you look at old paintings of English monarchs, particularly Henry VIII, he was very weighty and large. And what God is saying, in the middle of this celebration in Babylon, 'You are actually lightweight, it's superficial.' And the Babylonian kingdom collapsed that night, it came down like a pack of cards.

This section in the book of Revelation is starting to ask you questions – which kingdom do you serve in? I know what your answer is supposed to be, but is it true? As the One looks at you with blazing eyes, which king do you really love? Really? What are you heading for in life? Glory or exposure? Are you allowing yourself to be diverted from that engagement, that commitment, are you heading for the marriage supper of the Lamb?

The procession of the beautiful bride (Chapter 19:1-10)

I think the first five verses of chapter 19 are looking back to all they have come through up to this point, and just now at the wedding day, on the brink of the actual marriage – the struggles, the efforts of the prostitute to entice. We read in verse 2 that He has condemned the great prostitute who corrupted the earth by her adulteries. He has avenged on her the blood of His servants, verses 1 to 5. And verses 6 to 9 are then looking forward to the wedding itself – it's come, she's ready. And it's not just appearances, it isn't simply that she has dressed up fine. Verse 8 says the fine linen stands for what she does, it's the righteous acts, it's deeper than just a bit of make-up and a new hairdo – it's who she is in character. Through all these struggles and all these difficulties, being brought one day to that day when you stand and you look into His eyes.

She's ready, she's come, He's brought her. This is the beginning of a whole new eternity. And when John was writing his gospel, John pictures the story starting with a wedding (cf Jn. 2:1-11). He's just been introduced as the Lamb of God. John the Baptist said, 'He's the one that has come.' All these sacrifices, thousands of them, over the years, but you know, God has a Lamb Himself, and the Lamb has now come and been tethered there within Israel, to be watched over for three years, and then will be the sacrificial Passover Lamb. He's the Lamb of God.

And the Lamb goes to an ordinary small-town wedding in Cana of Galilee – all the relatives, all in their best. It was the responsibility of the bridegroom to arrange for the wine and the poor lad didn't know he had so many uncles and aunts; after a glass and a half they've run out and the people are looking at him and thinking, 'What sort of a character is this that we are giving our girl to? Can't even get enough to drink at his own wedding.' There's a bit of a flap and Mary comes running to Jesus – 'Run out of wine, do something.' And Jesus makes a very strange reply. 'Why do you involve Me, it's not My wedding day you know. My time isn't yet, it's his responsibility.' Then the Lord steps in and helps the chap out, and as you know changes those big stone jars full of water, into wine, the best wine they'd ever tasted in that region.

One day it will be the Lord's wedding, He will take responsibility on a vast scale, for the supply and the provision. And you and I will be there. God will have brought suffering into our lives on the way, and frustration and impatience, engagement feelings, feelings of separation, difficulties, wonderings, doubts, and through it all we will have been brought finally, one day, to this day. John 2 verse 11, the writer simply records, 'On that day we saw His glory, we saw how He cared for them, we saw how He rescued that poor man, how He actually gave them the very best. We saw His power, we saw His attention to detail.' And John and the other disciples start to take their first steps on this long journey towards this wedding day. And eventually we come streaming in – Abraham will be there, 'Yes I saw His glory,' and Moses and David and all the rest – these disciples all streaming to where Jesus Himself is the bridegroom. By that time God will have so dealt with our hearts that we love Him, with loyalty, with deep affection. We've come to love the things that He loves and hate the things that He hates – nothing left in our hearts that could dissatisfy the Son of God Himself. And the world? Gone. Good while it lasted, burnt up, temporary thing, as the bride leaves her earlier home, she leaves it behind. Maybe she takes the odd teddy bear or little things with her, but she's looking forward to the new beginning, the new start, the new relationship, the new bond. This is the point to which the book has brought us.

We've skipped over various sections in Revelation – I'm sorry I have to do that – what the Lord would have told us between chapters 11 and 15, about the perversion of power. But we've been looking here at true and false beauty, glory. May the Lord use His Word to make us more like Him.

5. Our Eternal Home
Revelation 19:11-22: 21

Introductory overview: Journey's end
(Chapter 19:11-20:15)

There's a special feeling when you come to the very last chapters of the Bible. Today's reading wraps up the whole story. Do some of you remember reading books like *Swallows and Amazons* or The Chronicles of Narnia to the kids, cuddled up before they went to sleep at night, and you'd get to the end and they'd say, 'Daddy, can you start all over again?' Because it's been so wonderful they want to go through the whole thing again. This is the end of the journey, this is where we are heading. I remember as a kid, going on long journeys to Ireland for the summer holidays. We'd be driving down to Fishguard, and I would be saying, 'Is it much further?' when there was still about fifteen hours of the journey ahead of us.

The Lord began this journey with people in the Garden of Eden, coming and looking and searching and calling, 'Adam, where are you?' They heard His voice and then He clothed them. It took the shedding of blood, a simple illustration at the start of the story – out of death could come acceptable life. They went out into a hostile world, and the Lord would come and walk with them and visit them. Abraham, we read earlier, saw His glory and started to walk before the Lord; down through the story, one after another, began to move towards this day. Psalm 84:5-7 says, 'Blessed are those whose

151

strength is in you, who have set their hearts on pilgrimage. As they pass through the Valley of Baca, they make it a place of springs; the autumn rains also cover it with pools. They go from strength to strength, till each appears before God in Zion.' The threads of the whole book and the whole of history, are being drawn together finally in the chapters we've read. The sovereignty of God, the beauty and glory of God, His power, His love, His sacrifice, all coming into this point.

Colossians 1:16-17, 'By him' – by the Lord, by the one who has been revealed to us, a little bit more day by day '... by him all things were created: things in heaven and on earth, visible and invisible, whether thrones or powers or rulers or authorities; all things were created by him and for him' – to be offered up for Him. 'He is before all things, and in him all things hold together.'

The bridegroom is approaching the earth

Again in these chapters we won't cover every detail but don't miss the big picture. In chapter 19:11-16, the bridegroom is now approaching the earth. And we read before, something is standing open. But this time it isn't just heaven or some piece of furniture that you see – the whole of heaven is standing open and there's no furniture, but the one is coming of whom all those pieces of furniture had previously spoken. Symbol is now giving way to reality. The bridegroom is coming; after giving all these reasons why He must do the things He's done and why He will ultimately come, because there is a throne, because He answers prayer, because there is a covenant, He is now actually coming.

What's He like? We see Him first of all, the bridegroom, faithful and true. He's been faithful and true all along. And He's coming on a white horse galloping closer and closer, riding, for you.

We read that He is the Judge. With justice He judges and makes war. We saw those eyes like flashing fire, at the beginning of the book in chapter 1 verse 14 – John had seen them and written down what he saw. And now we are being promised that you will see them too, every believer here will see what John saw, the one coming with those flashing eyes.

He is not only the bridegroom and the judge, He's apparently a conqueror – He has been absolutely victorious already out there in battle, and He's coming home. They used sing of David when he came back from fighting Israel's battles, 'David has slain ten thousand.' He would come home from one battle after another for these victory parades. This is going to be some victory parade, when He comes, having defeated sin and death, every last enemy of the human race put down, and He will come in triumph, His robes dipped in blood.

In Isaiah 63, remember that great vision, 'Who is this coming from Edom, from Bozrah, with his garments stained crimson? Who is this, robed in splendour, striding forward in the greatness of his strength? "It is I, speaking in righteousness, mighty to save." Why are your garments red, like those of one treading the winepress? "I have trodden the winepress alone,"' says Jesus. We'll see Him coming, with red stains on His garments, He's confronted God's enemies, poured out God's wrath, worked a mighty victory in a bloody battle, and He's now returning home for His beautiful bride. Have you got the imagination for it? It is a huge heart-expanding vision.

His name is The Word of God, it's Jesus coming, one of the three names that He has earned the right to bear. He is Faithful and True (verse 11), He is the Word of God (verse 13), He is the King of Kings and Lord of Lords, and out of His mouth still comes that sharp sword as we saw in chapter 1. He's the ruler, He's the ultimate, He's the one for whom it all is, He's the one that has saved and redeemed and He's coming, and we will bow before Him, welcome Him back, King of Kings and Lord of Lords.

Friends of mine were involved some years ago in attempts at Christian witness in the mountainous areas of the Sudan. As darkness fell they would show the Jesus film on the side of baked mud houses. Big Sudanese warriors with their guns and their spears would come and would watch and when they saw Him die they would be just heart-broken and would weep and murmur. Then the film would carry on and they'd see the resurrection, and you'd hear these deep-voiced war-

riors say, 'Oh yes!' And then you'd start to hear Kalashnikovs
going off, 'Bababababa!' The sound of gunfire – a very Middle-
Eastern way of celebrating a victory – this is a real gun-firing
occasion in the Scriptures – Bababababa! – Yes, He's the Lord
of Lords!

The devil, the beast and the false prophet are destroyed!

What has He accomplished? Very quickly, from verse 19
down to the beginning of chapter 20:3 you can see what He's
done – Satan is now defeated – that evil trinity, the beast, the
false prophet, and Satan the serpent himself, defeated. The
first two are captured with hardly a fight being recorded and
they are put in the lake of fire, by the end of chapter 19. And
then Satan, at the beginning of chapter 20, is said to be
bound, thrown into the abyss, and that then locked and
sealed for a thousand years.

At this point our attention is drawn to a great number of
time words. In verse 3 of chapter 20, Satan is confined to the
abyss for a thousand years. After that he must be set free, but
only for a short time. And the believers are raised to reign
during those thousand years apparently. Is it literally going to
be a thousand years? Haven't a clue. (I'm determined to get
one or two more of those in before the end!) It may well be,
I don't see why not. Or it could be a symbolic expression for
'a very long time'. Either way it'll be good and I'm looking
forward to it and it will be just right whatever it is.

In verse 5 we read that the unbelievers are not raised yet.
There's a clear distinction, as there has been all along,
between the believer and the unbeliever; there are going to be
two resurrections.

God's final judgement

In verse 11 we come to the great white throne, the final
judgement. And if it is objected that this Second Coming
and final sorting out all appears to be taking quite a long time
in Revelation, all I can say is that salvation wasn't achieved in
a day either – thirty-three years. I know you want to ask me,
'Are you pre- or post-millennial?' I have a friend who says he's
pan-millennial, 'It'll all pan out in the end,' he says. I incline

towards pre, with a lot of questions. Oh the feeling of shock around the room! Don't worry about it, I've been trying to avoid saying that all week, keep your eyes on the big picture.

Ron Dunn was telling me that someone asked Graham Scroggie, the great Bible teacher, who I think came here, whether he was pre- or post-millennial. He thought for a moment and he said, 'Madam, that is a pre-post-erous question.' Get the big picture? Whatever happens, it's going to be great, get ready for it.

Chapter 21, the end of all things now begins to give way to a new beginning. 'I saw a new heaven', interesting, a new heaven, 'and a new earth' – the first one finished, not needed any more, God's going to make a new one. God hasn't used up all His ideas about physics and chemistry, you know. (I bet that pleases the examiners!) He's going to make a whole new lot. He has never been short of ideas and here is a new city to live in.

This is the city, the new Jerusalem, that Abraham had set off looking for. He was a perceptive old character and he had looked at Ur of the Chaldees. He knew enough about the city culture in which he lived and he wanted a community whose architect and builder was God. You can get a very fine architect and a cowboy builder, or you can get a very decent builder but he's not really working to any plans. And Abraham wanted a community that had been both planned and designed by God and then God had done the actual building, one with proper moral and spiritual foundations. Imagine Abraham at the end of his journey, watching this thing coming down – 'That's it! It's all worth it. All those long years in tents, the sand in the sleeping bags and in the sandwiches; and the years we had with that twit Ishmael, the only man in the Bible to be called a wild donkey of a young man and I had to be his father.' And he kept looking and he never saw what he was searching for. He died in faith in the promise, and here it is, emerging right there in these opening verses of chapter 21.

The wedding day (Chapter 21:1-11a)

A new community

Who's going to be here in this great new community, this city? Continuing the idea of the wedding, who's on the guest list? If you go to a wedding, after you've put your present on the table, or at least stuck your card on someone else's present, you go down the line and you kiss these poor, smiling people, then you check the board to see where you are supposed to sit. Oh no, they've stuck me with that relative! Who on earth are these people, why did they get an invitation?'

We are introduced to some of the folks who are going to be there, and then verse 3, this is a wonderful verse, 'And I heard a loud voice from the throne saying, "Now the dwelling of God is with men."' God is going to be there – the dwelling of God is with men, He will live with them, they will be His people and He will be their God, that's the whole point of heaven, God is there. If you are not that interested in God, don't go there, there won't be any point. I hope during this week, you are starting to get more interested in the character of God – what's He like, what can you talk to Him about, what are His resources that you can avail yourself of? This whole planet is temporary, at the end of time the Lord will speak again, as He did at creation and it will all be rolled up, put away, done with, because God wants to make a new one, better. The world has been created as a temporary place from which God may have people, That's what matters to Him.

Relationships are at the very heart of who God is, Father, Son, Spirit, in relationship. There is love and communication and trust and delegation and partnership within who God is. This is why these things are so important; our capacity for friendship, for relating intimately, honestly with other people, is one of the most profound human things about us. But the thing about God is that He wants to draw others in to this relationship, this friendship, this is what God has always wanted. This is why He came to Eden, this is why He accepted Abraham's hospitality, this is why He came down to the tabernacle to camp amongst His people in the wilderness;

this is why Jesus came. God has such a heart for people to relate to them.

In John chapter 14 verse 23, we read these words: Jesus says, 'If anyone loves me, he will obey my teaching. My Father will love him,' get this, 'and we will come to him and make our home with him.' An extraordinary thing. Jesus has just said, 'I am going to heaven, I'm going to prepare a place for you, I'm going to get it ready. I will come again and take you to be with me because I want you to be with me, I want my servants to be where I am. But while you are on the journey we will come and live with you in your home and be the resources that you need and the deliverance from insecurity and fear and so on.' God is going to be there and that's the point. Get to know Him now as well as you can, you'll have much to talk about.

Can you imagine walking down those streets and walking around the corner and there's Jesus, 'Oh hello, I was looking forward to seeing you.' And what will you want to talk about? The things that you did perhaps, the things that you bore, the mistakes. 'Can I see those nail prints in Your hands?' And Jesus will show you. He will know why they are there. I don't believe that we are going to be absolutely unconscious of sin committed in the past. We will just know that in His grace and His love it has all been covered and forgiven and not held against us. If you said to Jesus, 'Those holes in Your hands, why are they there?' And He says, 'Holes, who gave Me holes? I don't know why they are there. I can't for the life of Me think how they got there.' No, He will know why they are there and so will you, but it won't be held against you.

All the redeemed are going to be there with God, from all over the world, every cross-cultural situation. That vision of the uncountable multitude in chapter 7 verse 9 will be fulfilled. We read again that He will be wiping away every tear from people's eyes and there will be no more death. Oh the sadness of sorrow, parting, of funerals, of loss.

Since I was last at Keswick my sister died in her forties, of cancer. And my parents, especially my mother, are in many ways heart-broken. I know that some of you are in exactly the same situation. We are looking forward to a day when the one who is faithful and true and trustworthy has said, 'Never ever again.' Bear it, be strong, be faithful, be true like Him. There's coming a day, no more death. No crying, no mourning. You look back at things in your life, there's real sadness; some of you I suspect have had difficulties that you can barely talk about. Perhaps your sexual orientation, perhaps things in your health, or your upbringing, stuff that's happened to you when you were kids. You think, 'I wish it hadn't worked out like this.' But it has. The Faithful and True one has been with you, has loved you, has brought you to this point, and as you step across the threshold and into the place that's been prepared for you – no more mourning, no more pain, no more crying, no more death, not ever again, it's all finished and done with; I can hardly believe it, but it's true.

There are people who will not be there. Verse 8 speaks of the cowardly, the unbelieving, sexually immoral, idolaters, people who practise lies and so on.

The new home (Chapter 22:1-7)

What will our new home be like? We've said that God is going to be there, we are going to be there. Just recently we decorated our lounge and we worked and worked. Finally there was nothing more to do and we sat down with a cup of tea in the middle of this transformed room and said, 'Yes.' And it looked beautiful. It's all over, we did it. The sweat and the tears and the paint in my hair ... And there is going to be that strong feeling when you will say, 'Hey, isn't it good?'

Refreshment

What's it going to be like? Well apparently there's a river of the water of life, clean, cool, beautiful, sweet, fresh, unpolluted water, flowing out from the throne of God. God has been providing water for His people all the way through Scripture – water out of the rock in Exodus; Psalm 46 verse 4, 'There is a river whose streams make glad the city of God.' Jesus said, 'Thirsty? Come to Me.' And all these images and pictures and events work like thought models for something that is actually true about God's own home. God scatters through life things that help us understand the great climax of the journey – we start to understand why He talks in these terms and does these things. God's home has a source of never-failing refreshment and you will never have tasted water like it.

On each side of the river stood a tree of life. I don't quite understand the grammar of that – is it one great tree and the water flows through, or is a lot of trees down either side? Haven't a clue. But the point is there is food to eat and there are no restrictions like Eden. Every month fresh fruit, different fruit.

Home has been defined in many ways. One of my definitions of home is, 'Home is the place where you can raid the fruit bowl without asking.' You are home, there is food to eat, refreshment after the long journey.

Atmosphere

Then there are a few more details, particularly about the atmosphere and things to look forward to. No longer any curse, says verse 3 – not on the ground, not on the process of childbirth, no curse of the law, no death, all completely overcome through Christ, His cross and His coming. Imagine the freedom and the security of that. His servants shall serve Him. One of the problems with the cartoon picture of heaven is that it shows people sitting around idly with harps – I cannot imagine anything less to look forward to than sitting around for a thousand years with a harp — pointless, for me total boredom. I'm very encouraged to think that we shall be able to serve Him – there will be stuff to do no doubt. And we, the sons and daughters of Eve and Adam, will have learnt to do these things better.

Verse 4, 'They shall see his face…' What a great promise: we shall see His face. All the instincts to hide that started to arise within the human race in the Garden of Eden, gone. We shall see His face 'and his name will be on their foreheads'. He will have written His name there. When kids are growing up they learn to write their name and they like doing it here and there. I can remember coming home from work one day and seeing mysterious crayon lines up and down the wall beside our stairs – orange, green, blue, red. I said,

'Johnny, have you been writing on the walls?'
'No, no.'
'Johnny I think you were writing on the wall.'
'No, no.'
'Johnny those are your crayons.'
'Yes I know, but Shiona did it.'
'Johnny, you've signed it at the bottom!'

He was just getting into writing his name everywhere – it's a little sign of possession, identity.

The Lord will have written His name of ownership, the expression of His character, in us and on us. The high priest under the Jewish economy used to bear God's name on his forehead – he alone could enter the presence of God; no woman could ever go there, none of eleven of the tribes could go there, only one man from one tribe, on one day, once a year. But we are going to be able to have access to the Lord all the time, all of us whoever we are, with the name of God written on our forehead.

Lighting

And the lighting system of our new home – no more night, no need for lamps, or even the sun, because the Light of the World is in that city. In chapter 21 verse 23 we read, 'The city does not need the sun or the moon to shine on it, for the glory of God gives it light, and the Lamb is its lamp.' Another symbol giving way to reality. In one sense we know the sun and moon are temporary, but they are also symbols of a greater reality – they will one day give way to the glory of the Lord and we shall inhabit that place and the light will be from Him.

Security

We read that all this will never end. Look at the end of verse 5, 'They will reign for ever and ever.' They can never be thrown out like they were out of Eden, naked and covered by those animal skins, slinking off into a hostile world. This security is one of the deepest gifts that a bridegroom can give to his bride. It doesn't always work out that way in life, does it? Till death us do part, and God is never going to die. Safe at home. Isn't God gracious? And you do feel blessed just by reading it don't you? And reassured. He's coming with you, He's making His home with you, He's preparing a place.

God's final appeal (Chapter 22:8-21)

And then what does God do right at the end? We've come all the way through the story, Genesis, Exodus, Leviticus, Numbers, the people have been gathered, evil has been dealt with and put down, justice maintained, we are almost at the final full stop of the word of God, and God gives another last appeal to you. Is there anybody here still thirsty, still hanging back, still not opened up their lives to Christ? Anybody? Please come to Jesus, please don't hang back any more. Please come (verse 17), 'the Spirit and the bride...' – everyone else here in this tent would say the same to you – 'Please come.' And the Holy Spirit says, '"Come!" Whoever is thirsty, let him come; and whoever wishes, let him take the free gift of the water of life.'

F.F. Bruce, writing of these words at the end of Revelation says, 'The blindest idolater, the fiercest persecutor, were he even Nero himself, might we add the most abject apostate, may come if he will and accept the full and free benefits which the gospel provides.' There could be somebody here, and you've seen others stand up to commit themselves, volunteer in response to the Lord for missionary service and you knew that wasn't for you. You've heard of seminars going on for those who are Christian workers and you know that's not for you, because deep down you know that you are not a Christian yet. The last thing God will say to you is, 'Come! Come while there is yet time.' You've sat all the way through this book and God knows you are there. He knows the seat you are sitting in. And before He puts the pen down, 'It's you I'm talking to, I want to bless you as well.' Don't go home in the car, maybe with a partner who's a Christian, without having come.

Some of you remember the disaster at the football ground at Hillsborough, when many young Liverpool football fans were crushed to death. The bodies of those suffering were carried to a local hospital in Sheffield and there was a surgeon working there that evening who was a Christian. After long hours, he was drained and exhausted and he took a short break and went down to the canteen for a coffee. One of his colleagues, who knew he was a Christian, came to him and said, 'You are a Christian, surely you've got something to say to these people, there's hundreds of them up there. Can't you go and offer them some comfort or something?' So wearily this Christian went back up the stairs, went up to the first man he saw, a big strapping Liverpool dad and said, 'I am so sorry for what's happened here this afternoon. But I am a Christian and I'll pray for you, it's all I can do.' And this big dad said, 'Huh, what does God know?'

What does God know about losing His Son? God knows all there is to know. There isn't anything that God doesn't know about losing His Son for us and our salvation. And He has raised Him up to life to be our Lord and Saviour. This has been our focus. May it have a deep impact upon our lives as we say, 'Lord you bought me for the price and I'm so glad. You've come for me, You've spoken to me, and even right at the end of the book I've heard again Your wonderful word "Come!" Lord, I'm coming.' That's the response. We can join in with John, 'Lord, if you are like that, if You are like all that we've seen in this Revelation of Jesus, come please, quickly. We long to see you.' Amen.

The Addresses

If any Man is Thirsty
by Derick Bingham

John 7

I don't know what kind of a day you've had today. It makes me think of the minister, on a day it was raining cats and dogs who said, 'Lord, thank you that every day is not like today.' There's always something to thank the Lord for!

The Feast of Tabernacles

Traditions and the way they build up are very interesting, aren't they? If you had been in Israel during the week of the Feast of the Tabernacles, you'd have seen thousands of little children, under booths that their parents had erected, having a ball. Hundreds and thousands of Jews came from all over Israel and all over the world. Where did this tradition come from? This feast happened at the end of the vine and the olive harvest, at the end of a series of feasts and it lasted for a whole week. God had commanded that people make these temporary booths of tree branches, to live in during the feast. Plenty of food, reaping the full harvest of their inheritance.

But what was the point of all this? Well, it was all to help the people of God remember how they got to where they were. They were to remember that they had once been slaves in Egypt, they had been redeemed and had made a long pilgrimage across the desert to reach their inheritance and they had had to live in tents for forty years. Now that they were settled, they were being reminded that they had once been pilgrims. It made them appreciate what they had once been; fascinating that God would say, 'Live with your families outside under tree branches, for seven days.'

It's very easy, isn't it, to forget where you've come from, once you've settled and got the job and the home you were looking for, it's very easy to forget. As our dear friend Arthur was telling us this evening, how easy it is in the comfort of our homes to forget those in Kosovo and many parts of the world whose homes have been wrecked and who have gone through this desperate refugee situation.*

Well, over the years the Jews began to add their own tradition to the ceremony. Not only did they live in tents, but they now daily filled a golden pitcher with water, and ceremoniously poured the water out at the base of the altar. On the last day of the feast it was done twice; it was a very dramatic moment in the ceremony, with thousands of people in the temple courts and around who would then wave their branches and shout 'Hosanna! Lord save us now!'

Of course the tradition had something behind it. God had miraculously brought water to them twice on that journey across the wilderness, when they were very thirsty, and now they were remembering that God had given them this water. Their crops still needed rain, so really they were praying for rain to soften the ground for ploughing, as well as celebrating that God had given them this miracle of water. Sometimes God chastened His people by withholding water from them and the pouring out of the water was an unspoken prayer for more rain. And of course it also had some other deep teaching.

Look at a few texts for a moment with me. As the prophets pondered Israel's needs they began to talk about a day when God would pour out not just water, but His mighty Holy Spirit on all flesh. Not only that, but there was much more that God had for His people. Let's look at Isaiah 60:1-3:

*Arthur Prescott had just given a moving account of his recent visit to Kosovo.

> Arise, shine, for your light
> has come,
> and the glory of the LORD
> rises upon you.
> See, darkness covers the earth
> and thick darkness is over
> the peoples,
> but the LORD rises upon you
> and his glory appears over you.
> Nations will come to your light,
> and kings to the brightness
> of your dawn…

That's a wonderful promise. Look also at Isaiah 25:6-8, where we get more of God's amazing promise for His people and also Zechariah 14:4, 8, 'On that day his feet will stand on the Mount of Olives ... On that day living water will flow out from Jerusalem...' That was the Feast of Tabernacles. There was promise, nostalgia and memory in it, and it was good. Even the tradition that they added was excellent.

Jesus comes to the feast

Notice that John 7:2 states categorically it was when the Jewish Feast of Tabernacles was near, that Jesus starts the journey towards Jerusalem. When they came to this great climax on the last day of the feast, and poured out the water from the golden pitcher, suddenly there is standing over in the corner a man dressed in peasant garb, and He cries with a loud voice, 'If anyone's thirsty let him come to me and drink.' For a Galilean to suggest that after such a spectacle people would still be thirsty, was for many of them an effrontery they were so angry that they wanted to take Him. 'Who is he, who does he think he is, standing there crying this to us in the middle of all our tradition and all of our wonderful ceremony with its spiritual teaching – who's he?' 'If anyone is thirsty, let him come to me and drink. Whoever believes in me, as the Scripture has said, streams of living water will flow from within him' (verses 37-8).

If a peasant stood up in the middle of a similar situation

today and claimed that, I'm sure CNN would arrive asking what on earth was happening? Here is someone who claims that if you believe in Him, then streams of living water will flow from within. What on earth is going on here? It's incredible, what drama. I want just for a moment to dig into the background here. Something of great importance is happening.

The major problems that run from chapter 7 to chapter 10 are problems relating to the way that God has chosen to reveal Himself in Jesus.

In chapter 7, the problem is, how is Christ to make Himself known when His testimony provokes prejudice, and even hatred? How do you reveal Christ to people who respond in this way? If you were prejudiced against me it really wouldn't matter much what I said to you, you wouldn't be interested. I have discovered in life the greatest enemy of truth is prejudice.

In chapter 8, the Father is seeking to expose man's sin without condemning man. How do you expose a person's sin and yet love the sinner? It's very hard. In the story of the woman taken in adultery we see how Christ handled the problem — loved her as well as opposing the sin.

In chapter 9, the question is, how do you offer light to someone who doesn't have the faculty of sight? So you have the story of the blind man.

In chapter 10, how can the true shepherd be distinguished from the false shepherd? So you have this amazing chapter in John about the good shepherd and false shepherds.

How on earth are we to communicate this wonderful message to our generation at this time of great moral crisis? It's a problem, and you can learn a lot from how this is done in this section of Scripture.

Now this is the problem we face in chapter 7. As the Father moves the Saviour, His Son, towards the Feast of Tabernacles and eventually to the cross itself, notice how the chapter begins. God is going to reveal Himself in Christ, to prejudiced people, who hate the very sight of Him and would kill Him, given half a chance. How does He do it? It's intriguing. Christ's brothers come along and they say what they think He should do to reveal Himself. Let's put it into the NIV, the Northern Ireland Version – 'This is a one-horse town, you'll never impress the world from here. You've got to move out of here, you've got to go up to Jerusalem and reveal yourself in the great centre of religion, you'll never do it from Nazareth. Can any good thing come out of Nazareth?'

A couple were once in Nazareth and when the wife saw an open sewer running down the middle of the street, she started to cry. 'What's wrong with you dear?' her husband asked. 'To think that my Lord lived here,' she replied. He opened his coat and pointed in and said, 'But look where He's living now.'

I've been to Nazareth and a member of the local church took me down to his carpenter's shop; with such gentle and loving proper pride he showed me his planes: he was a carpenter in Nazareth. When Jesus was there His brothers said, 'You'll never do it from here. If You want to reveal Yourself show Yourself to the world' (cf Jn. 7:4). Even His brothers did not believe in Him, the Scripture says. And Jesus gives an amazing answer, 'My hour hasn't come yet.' These brothers had no awareness that our perfect, lovely Saviour on His way to Calvary was living from moment to moment in sensitive rapport, with God's directing will.

Notice what He says to them – this text has been burning in my soul all day – 'The right time for me has not yet come; for you any time is right' (verse 6). Have you thought about that? If I can paraphrase it into a modern situation, young people would say, 'Do your own thing.' Jesus is saying, 'You can do your own thing, you can go where you like, think what you like, chase what you like, drink what you like, say what you like. The way you live, for you any time is right. But that's not the way I live. I don't live according to My own will, for Me any time is not right, it's what My Father says is so.'

Just a few days ago I was on the Isle of Man and I was taken on a tour round the workshop of one of the greatest watchmakers in the world. He makes one watch a year and it costs £1,000. His name is George Daniels, he's a very famous writer on chronology. I met George, he's an older man, a very interesting character and I asked one of the world's greatest watchmakers, who has a medal for his brilliance from the Swiss,

'How long have you been interested in chronology?'

'Since I was a little boy of five.'

'George, what have you learned about time in all of those years of study of time?'

'I have learned that human beings know they are going to die, so they measure time. But God lives in an eternal now, He doesn't know anything about time.' Well, with due respect, Mr Daniels, you're wrong. From the sixth hour to the ninth hour, says the Scripture, there was darkness. Why was there darkness? As the Saviour went into the very heart of His suffering for our sins. And the Scripture actually states the very hour that it happened. George Daniels, the great chronologist said, 'God doesn't know anything about time.' Oh friends, with all our hearts we believe He does. He stepped into time, He sent His Son to bleed and die at Calvary and when the hour was come He bowed His head and gave up the Spirit. I've seen people die and they die and their head drops. But our Saviour bowed His head first, and then gave up the Spirit. They did not take His life from Him, He gave His life a ransom for many. Hallelujah what a Saviour!

The cost of being a disciple

And you love Him, yes? You seek to follow Him in your college, in your university, in the office, in the bank, in the hospital where you work, in the classroom where you teach, in the farming community, in that business which you run, in that factory, on those computer programs that you set up? You seek to serve the Lord. I think of all these dear young people who have come here this week, giving their time and their energy to teach little children the Word of God. How we honour them, bless God for them. How many a Sunday you could give to lots of other things, but you don't because you want to teach that Bible Class, you want to worship the Lord, you want to set aside time.

The other day after I had preached in a Baptist church in Stirling, a couple took me round the corner to their shop.

They said, 'We don't open on Sunday and because of that we are going to have to close our business. But we'd like to give you a gift, we'd like to give you a pair of shoes.' And I've been preaching in them this week, what a gift. I was so moved.

Maybe someone here knows the cost of not following your own will and not following the agenda that your heart and flesh and the world and the devil would tell you to follow. How many of you ministers, pastors, leaders are finding how frighteningly difficult it is in the tide of evil that is sweeping against you? You have given up your own time and said, 'Lord, not my will but Yours be done.' Is it worth it? 'For you any time is right. My hour hasn't yet come.'

Yesterday Margaret and I were in Ambleside. I'm so glad to have Margaret with me, when I think of what she's given up in order that I might do this, and many of us who teach God's word can testify to that, without our wives we couldn't do it – what a cost. Yesterday in Ambleside we went into the glassblower's shop and we were awesomely struck by what the young man there was doing. I came home so moved by what I saw that I wrote a poem relating to this verse.

'For you any time is right but the right time for me has not yet come' – doing God's will as opposed to doing my own. Is there someone who is struggling with this? Maybe you are thinking of quitting service for the Lord. You are so weary and tired and beaten and bruised by the enemy, broken almost, and you say, 'Derick, if you only knew where I am and what I have to do, how difficult it is…' Just a moment, let me tell you of the craftsman of Ambleside.

> I watched him at work in Ambleside,
> As he made that sand into glass.
> And what I learned that afternoon,
> I feel I must not let pass.
> The molten liquid he stretched and pulled,
> His measuring rule he applied;
> He cut and smoothed and rolled it along,
> Its natural shape he defied.
> As slowly, so slowly its new shape emerged,
> He frequently left his seat,

And took his creation to the furnace door
And moved it into the heat.
It was at one thousand four hundred degrees
They said, and I am sure they had not lied.
And he did not spare that white-hot heat,
That craftsman of Ambleside.

As I quietly watched that master at work,
My Master gently said to me,
'There are things I do now that you don't
     understand,
That one day you'll eventually see.'

Do you know what that craftsman is truly about?
Do you know what he'll finally make?
And how useful it will be in palace or home,
For a king or a mother to take.
A beautiful plate on which to place food,
A vase to put flowers in place,
A lampshade to focus an evening glow,
An entrance table to grace.

A chalice to drink from, a paper-weight,
An anniversary piece of true pride,
A figurine or sculpted face
And many other creations besides.
So now from the heat may I turn not away,
Though against it I have often cried.
May I cry no more because of what I've learned,
From the craftsman of Ambleside.

Are you in the heat of the furnace? You say, 'Derick, I'm crying against it, I don't know where it's going.' Well I hadn't a
clue where that craftsman was going yesterday, I thought he
was making this but I was wrong, he brought out something
totally different. Come on, it's not over yet. The Lord knows
what He's doing in your life, in your home, in your church,
in your ministry. If the heat has been turned up it's for your
good. I know that all things that happen to you are not good,

but they all work together for good. I know that all my life doesn't seem to add up, but I can tell you something: it adds up in Christ eventually, according to Ephesians 1.

They would have shoved Him, cajoled Him to reveal Himself in Jerusalem, but He wouldn't go. He was regulated by His Father's will. Wouldn't you want your life to be like that? Isn't this a beautiful verse? There was a man sent from – where? – from God, whose name was John (cf Jn. 1:6). Wouldn't you like to be sent by God? Didn't the Holy Spirit first call Paul and Barnabas to their ministry, and then the church had fellowship with them in it? It was the Holy Spirit who first called them.

Is the Spirit of God speaking to you tonight? Maybe calling you to service that you are fighting against? Don't fight it; God, if you will obey, will do a beautiful thing. I recently interviewed Elisabeth Elliot for a secular newspaper in Northern Ireland. I talked to her for two hours. When you think of what that woman has suffered. She talked about the trials and difficulties and do you know what she said to me? She said, 'I am the most contented woman in the world.' I never had any woman say that to me before, that way – or any man.

Recently, I don't do this very often, I stayed in a forty-roomed castle in Scotland. In the evening we gathered in the beautiful drawing room. This dear American Christian was asked to speak and I was asked to follow him, and it was difficult. He had been a multimillionaire who found his Saviour and gave away his fortune. He had discovered that in America when pharmaceutical companies put 'New! Improved!' on toothpaste or some other product, the rest of their stocks are then finished; so millions of pills for example were being put in landfill sites because they had new improved ones. My friend decided, 'I'm going to try and get these pills and other pharmaceutical products and send them to the Third World where they are so needed.' Now his life consisted of saving a thousand lives everyday. And then he said this – it's haunted me for days – the words of that man who gave away a fortune and gave his life to working in the Third World: 'I gave up affluence for influence and I gave up success for significance.'

When I think of C.S. Lewis, passed by for a professorship twice at Oxford because he was a Christian. He was winning little children for Christ and writing for them by the million across the world, and jealousy rose against him in academia and he was passed over twice for what he deserved. When I think of what that dear man took, of all the money he gave away and the kindness of his life, when at times he lived virtually in poverty – I've researched his life and it's true. When I think that just recently the Domino Pizza Man gave away £350 million because he read something out of *Mere Christianity*, by C.S. Lewis, on pride and said, 'I am that proud man.' If Lewis had ever thought, 'When I write that paragraph somebody's going to give away three hundred and fifty million,' when that money would have been so useful to him! What am I saying? I'm saying what Lewis said, 'Everything that isn't buried won't be resurrected.'

Was I shouting there? I don't mean to shout at you, but it overwhelms me. We need to hear it. 'He who saves his life shall lose it, and he who loses his life for My sake and the gospel's shall find it' (cf Mt. 16:25). Give up affluence for influence and success for significance. He is no fool who gives what he cannot keep, to gain what he cannot lose (Jim Elliot). Why are you holding back? What's wrong? Has the devil got us by the throat? We should be a mighty army, as Charles Price once said, 'The gates of hell are not offensive weapons, they are defensive weapons. They *can* be driven back.'

Oh that God would use the convention at Keswick this year to bring a great spiritual revival amongst His people. You can't revive the lost but you can revive the saved. We need a revival, we need passion for these things. We need to have our hearts on fire for the Lord Jesus. It may be expressed in the gentlest of ways, in the kindest of actions, as with my dear friend Dr Jackson out there in the Third World with his millions of pharmaceutical products. Who can tell what God will do with these three thousand people before me tonight if you were to yield to the leading of the Spirit, if you were to yield your home, your gifts, your talents and everything you

have to the living Saviour? Let Him have it. What have you
to lose? Nothing.

I once interviewed the Duke of Westminster, one of the
richest men in this nation. He's an Ulsterman who lived in
Northern Ireland for nineteen years, and he told me, 'Money
cannot buy you happiness.' I said to him and maybe I
shouldn't have, 'Your Grace, what would be a luxury to you?'
He said, 'That question annoys me.' I repeated the question.
He said, 'Three healthy children are a luxury. I'm the president of SCOPE which deals with children with great disabil-
ity and I see horrendously difficult and heart-breaking things.
To have three healthy children is a luxury.' And I could have
crawled under the table, I felt so spoken to. I found him to
be a very great man, and in fact he's been helping Franklin
Graham and other Christian organisations recently. Pray for
that dear man. Of all the public figures I've ever met he's one
of the people who has impressed me most, and his dedication
to his wife and to his family, he said, 'When I said to my wife
that I would love her until death,' he said, 'I meant it, I
meant it.'

It isn't to be found in money. If God has given you a lot of
money and given you business prowess, don't be ashamed of
it, God can use that. I'm not saying that you have to give up
your business and take the next bus for Belfast. I'm saying,
just do what the Lord tells you to do. Do it, just obey Him.
You say, 'How will I know?' You'll know. I remember saying
to a fellow once, 'How do you know you're in love?' And he
said, 'You'll know.' If the Lord wants to guide you to do
something you, you'll know. That's the burden of the message
this evening that I have on my heart. It's a very powerful message.

Letting Jesus loose

How did God reveal Himself in Christ? When Jesus went up
to the temple you'll notice that He taught incognito. I reck-
on from studying this passage, and it was Professor David
Gooding who pointed this out to me, the crowd didn't know
who He was when He taught in the temple on this occasion.
He went up in the Father's time, not in His brothers' time,

and He stood up and He started to teach. And they didn't know it was Jesus. You say, what's significant about that? Well, after He had finished, the Jews were amazed and asked, 'How did this man get such learning without having studied?' This peasant standing here is not a rabbi as we know rabbis, who on earth is he, where did he get this from, this Galilean with this Galilean accent? You say, 'How does that apply to us?' Well it applies beautifully. Even though they didn't know who He was, I'll tell you something, they knew that His teaching was different.

Many of you young people are facing comparative religion in your schools. It is now a policy, you've got to teach all kinds of religions in schools and you bring in Christianity and you also teach it along with all the rest, and people are panicking all over the place. What are you panicking about? I don't care where you take this truth and place it. It will rise head and shoulders above everything else. There's no need to be afraid of it. The great Spurgeon said, 'You don't need to defend a lion, all you need to do is let him loose.'

I talked to a professor from China recently, a great academic who is an expert in the comparison of cultures and I asked him, 'How did you become a Christian?' And he said, 'I was listening to Transworld Radio in China and somebody was teaching the Sermon on the Mount. I thought, this is different.' And I said, 'Are you going to write about it?' His head went down and he said, 'I can't, I'm not allowed.' And I was spoken to, I thought, Lord Jesus here I am and I can write books, I can go anywhere in freedom around the Western World and preach the word and testify for the Lord with nobody stopping me, and there's that poor man, he's not allowed to do it, he would lose his job, he would have all kinds of problems. Do we appreciate the freedoms we've got? And the fact that the government and our nation give us these freedoms – we should appreciate it and tell them sometimes that we do, rather than always criticising them.

The Prime Minister recently (and I'm not trying to draw attention to myself) gave me backing for a book on the life of Wilberforce that I wrote for little children. He wrote and he said it was a story deserving to be told to a new generation. You think of Wilberforce, five foot four inches high. Boswell on one occasion went into the yard at York Castle where there was a crowd, and he said, 'A little shrimp jumped up on the table to speak and as he went on the shrimp became a whale.' Wilberforce who stood in front of the British House of Commons for three hours and pled with the British government to allow the gospel into India. The East India Company wouldn't let it in, it caused riots amongst Hindus or Sikhs and they didn't want the disturbance. And Wilberforce said, 'The gospel is the law of liberty. Widows will no longer throw themselves on their husbands' funeral pyres if they become Christians, the gospel will set them free.' And the little man stood there, with ulcerated colitis and his nervous disposition – the little Cambridge graduate became a mighty flame for God. And what happened? The government passed it and the gospel came into India.

He set out, with King George, to campaign against blasphemy, drunkenness, and child prostitution. He introduced family Bible study, his was one of the very first families to do it; he wrote a book translated into five languages, and he was converted basically through reading one of Philip Dodderidge's amazing books (the man who wrote 'Oh happy day that fixed my choice on Thee my Saviour and my God.') Apart from that he also bust the slave trade. A hundred and fifty thousand slaves were freed in the West Indies because of that little man's witness and you say, 'Oh Derick, it's awful hard where we are and it's very difficult and there are just a few of us.' Well, just try to be like Wilberforce, and excuse the language, but the great Lord Nelson said, 'Wilberforce and his damned followers.' The vested interest of great English houses was against him because many of them were built on the slave trade, on money that came from plantations in the West Indies. But he kept going. And the nation was turned around.

Could there be another Wilberforce in here tonight? God knows we could do with a few! What are you scared of? What's holding you back? Why are you diffident? Why don't we go back to our homes, our hotels, our caravans, go back, maybe you're under a tree branch like these people, if you are it'll be a wet one! Let's go back and say, 'Lord, this week, tell me what you want me to do.' Let's make this a great altar of dedication to the Lord.

Come to Me

And you say 'What is the message?' 'If anyone thirsts let them come to me and drink.' Who's the speaker? Christ. What are we going to call people in this nation and across the world to? Christ. When Sadhu Sundar Singh became a Christian, his professor asked him, 'What's different about Christianity? What principle did you learn in Christianity that you didn't have in your former religion?' He said, 'I found Christ, sir.' 'Come on,' he said, 'there must be some principle, there must be some philosophical thought or other that's different. What have you found philosophically that's different?' 'I found Christ, sir.' That's the centre of our message – 'All one in Christ Jesus'. I'm in Christ, the body of Christ and that's enough. He stood and said, 'If anyone is thirsty come to me.' Not to a denomination, not to a sect, not to a philosophical thought, not to a group of this, that or the other – 'Come to me.' It's almost audacious if it weren't true. 'Is there anyone out there who's thirsty? Come to me.'

Well, who's the invitation for? Anyone. I'm glad it doesn't say, 'If Philip, or Tom, or Mary is thirsty,' because I would think it's just Tom's and Mary's and Philip's and that's it. It says, if *anyone* is thirsty. The only qualification you need is to be thirsty. Is there someone here tonight on the verge of conversion? Wouldn't it be wonderful if hundreds found Christ in these coming days through our witness, and even here tonight people found Christ? Anyone? Are you thirsty? You say, 'Derick, am I thirsty.' Well, what's the supply? The supply is of course the gift of the Holy Spirit. When we think of what He did and what He accomplished. He turned those twelve disciples into men who turned the world upside down when He filled them. And I tell you, we need to be filled with the Holy Spirit.

It's beautiful, isn't it? You get the thrust of the message. You come to the Lord and get to know the Lord. As you let it loose His very teaching will stand up. I write in secular newspapers and work in the media quite often because I desperately want to get this out into the traffic lanes, as the Gideons put it, of humanity. We need to get it out where the people are. What's the point of sitting in a bath with your fishing rod and waders and tweed hat, looking lovely, but not catching anything. Let's get out there into the waterways of the world, spiritually speaking, and tell them of Jesus.

I stand here tonight in God's presence and I feel the Lord at work. Let's go back as we close, to the craftsman of Ambleside and watch him take the glass and put it into the heat, then bring it out and into the heat, then bring it out and into the heat, then bring it out and put it away for service after it's fixed right and moulded right and prepared right. There's no telling what'll happen. You've been listening so well on such a cold rainy night. Respond and there's no telling. The tide could turn if you and I say, 'Lord, Your will, not mine.' May that be so, for Jesus' sake.

I am the Light of the World
by Ajith Fernando

John 9

The emphasis this evening is on the call of God to service and we are going to have a time when people will have an opportunity to respond to that call, if such a call comes from God.* I'm going to take this passage and apply it to the call that God gives for us to serve Him.

The cause of suffering

You know the background to this situation. Jesus is with His disciples, probably in Jerusalem. Verse 1, 'As he went along, he saw a man blind from birth. His disciples asked him, "Rabbi, who sinned, this man or his parents, that he was born blind?"' The Bible of course teaches that suffering is in this world because of sin. Often people do suffer because of their own sin but some people thought that all suffering is always directly because of sins committed by the suffering person, or that person's family – this is what Job's friends told him, he was suffering because of his sins. With that idea in mind this question is a very real question. Here's a person who has been born blind – who has sinned? Is it the parents?

* At the end of the message an appeal was made for people to stand, in response to a specific call from God for full-time service at home or abroad.

181

The Jewish rabbis had the idea that if the pregnant mother sinned, there may be some deformity in the child. There was also the idea, from Genesis 25:22, that the child could sin in the mother's womb. Jacob and Esau jostled with each other in Rebekah's womb. So they are asking, what caused the suffering of this person? They ask for the cause, but Jesus gave them the purpose of suffering. Look at verse 3. '"Neither this man nor his parents sinned," said Jesus, "but this happened so that the work of God might be displayed in his life."'

This is often the biblical response to the problem of suffering. It gives some hints on why there is suffering, but that is not a major concern of the Bible. It doesn't clearly tell us who is responsible: God, Satan, humans, nature, or just chance? Rather, what it says is that God can turn suffering into good, God can use it for a purpose and He calls us to participate in His plan to alleviate the suffering in this world. This is a practical approach to the problem of suffering. God did not cause the blindness, but He can use the blindness to do good, to display His work.

There is a very positive message that we take into the world. The idea of reincarnation is growing, with people saying that it gives a better understanding of the problem of suffering; people are suffering for the things they have done in their past rather than this life. I think that is not at all just. If we are suffering for things we have done, but we have absolutely no memory of this past person that we were, I think it's rather unfair that we should be suffering for things we don't know anything about.

There was a Japanese man, who lost his sight in the middle of his career. Being a Buddhist he was taught that he was suffering this blindness because of some wrong he had done, either in this life or in a previous life. Unable to accept that, he looked for an answer. Someone suggested to him the Christian answer to this problem. He started reading the New Testament and when he came to John 9, particularly verse 3, he asked the question, 'Could the works of God be manifested through my blindness? Then that is the answer,' he said, 'I'll use this blindness.' He became a Christian, then an evangelist, eventually coming to Scotland to study theology and returning to Japan as a professor of theology. 'I will use this blindness.' That's the way the Bible looks at this.

God's fellow workers

Verse 4 talks about how God is going to change this situation, 'As long as it is day, we must do the work of him who sent me.' It is very interesting that Jesus says, '*we* must do...' – Jesus was going to perform this miracle, but he says, 'As long as it is day, we must do the work of him who sent me.' Now some of the scribes who transcribed this felt that there was a mistake here. It talks about 'he who sent me,' so Jesus must have said, 'I must do the work of him who sent me.' So they seem to have changed it, and we see in some translations, 'as long as it is day I must do the work that he sent me.' But that's not what Jesus said. What He seems to have said is, something that isn't obvious at the start – 'We must do the work that he sent me.' In other words, Jesus was talking about Himself and His disciples. What an honour this is. Here is Christ associating you and me with His mission. What He came to do, He has entrusted to us to do in the world. This passage talks about Jesus being the light of the world, but in Matthew 5:14, he calls us the light of the world. Just as Jesus was sent into the world, He says, 'As the Father sent me, even so I send you' (cf Jn. 20:21). We carry through the mission of Jesus. In 1 Corinthians 3:9 and 1 Thessalonians 3:2, Paul says that we are God's fellow workers: that is something that should bring joy to our hearts.

When I was converted I was an extremely shy person. I never opened my mouth in public. My family was a Christian family so I was always put on the Christian committee in our school, but I never talked. Then the Lord met me and converted me, and the first thought that came to me at the age of fourteen was that God was going to make me a preacher. I dared not tell anyone, I thought they'd laugh. The first person I told was a Buddhist friend: I thought he wouldn't laugh. How could God use a person like me, who never opens his mouth, to be a preacher? But that's the thing about God, He uses *us* to do the work that *He* has come into this world to do.

Motivated by necessity

Now there's a sense of necessity in this passage. It says, 'As long as it is day, we must do the work of him who sent me.' That word 'must' really means, 'it is necessary'. There is a sense of compelling necessity, as one commentator puts it. He's telling us this is what we must be doing – as long as it is day. It's not an option for us. 'It's a good idea to do some work for God, to round up your life, to have a little religious aspect also to your life,' some people say. But that's not the way Christianity looks at mission and involvement in the service of God.

Actually, all we do is for God, but this passage really shows that what he's talking about more is work and weakness and service. In verse 6 He shows what this work is and He heals this blind man. In the book of John the Word 'works'; 'we must do the works of him' refers both to the words and to the works that Jesus did. So here Jesus is specifically talking about Christian service – as long as it is day we have to do the works of God. God's love has to go to others. That is the answer to the problem of suffering in the world, and He's going to use us to do that – we complete His mission. Every Christian therefore must take involvement in the mission of the church as a compelling necessity. Look at those words – as long as it is day we must do the work of Him, of God.

Motivated by urgency

In the second part of verse 4, He says, 'Night is coming, when no-one can work.' There's a time limit: the door of opportunity is open only for this life. Soon the night will come; after that we have no more chance to impact the world. All of us therefore are motivated by a sense of urgency.

When I was a child, a Scripture Union missionary who was serving in India came to stay in our home in Sri Lanka. He was a man called Cecil Johnston, a wonderful man of God, who became like a hero to me. I'll never forget what he wrote in my autograph book – 'Only one life, it will soon be past. Only what's done for Jesus will last.'

When I left university and went abroad to the theological seminary, I had this tremendous sense of remorse, that there were so many friends with whom I hadn't adequately shared the gospel. So I wrote to several of them, urging them to read the gospel of John. One of them wrote back and said, 'You asked me to read this gospel. I started reading the gospel – in the beginning was the Word and the Word was with God – I couldn't understand it so I just closed it.' And I realised that I had lost an opportunity. We have to use these opportunities while we have them.

The father of one of my colleagues in Youth For Christ was very sick and was dying and he said, 'You must come and talk to my father about Jesus.' I was a little apprehensive. This man was an intellectual, one of the communist pioneers of Sri Lanka. I was a little afraid, but I came because I had been requested to come. I started talking to him about all sorts of things, apart from the gospel: his health, his work ... My young colleague was getting a little impatient so he butted into our conversation, 'You wanted to talk to him about the gospel, didn't you?' 'Yes,' I said, and given that encouragement, I started talking to him about Christ. I explained the gospel and how Jesus had come into the world to save us and all that He had done. Then I asked him, 'Would you like to commit your life to Christ?' And he said, 'Yes.' I was shocked! Then I asked him, 'Would you like to pray with me right now?' And he said, 'Yes.' I prayed with him, and what a transformation in that person. He lived for seven more days, and whenever a Christian would come, he would say, 'Pray with me.' If a group of Christians visited him, he would say, 'Let's sing some songs,' and he would have worship services in his hospital room. He lived for seven more days and he died a happy man. What if I had missed that opportunity? 'When our earthly life is done, our earthly work is done,' someone has said. Don't put off the opportunity of service until it's too late.

One of the sad things for me has been to see people I've grown up with, in the church, in Youth For Christ, who had been called by God to do something special for Him, getting involved in various things and postponing responding to this call. 'Maybe a little later,' they said, 'I'll do something else for the moment.' And little by little they lost touch with the ministry. They may go up in society, but they have gone down in life, because God has not used them according to the potential with which they could have been used.

Paul says in Ephesians 5:15-16, 'Be very careful, then, how you live – not as unwise but as wise, making the most of every opportunity, because the days are evil.' With the old translation in mind John Wesley wrote, 'Redeem the time, catch the golden moments as they fly.'

People say that we are living in the post-modern era in which many people are reacting to the bondage of time, productivity and efficiency. They say that because of this bondage our person-hood was violated and we were depersonalised. And so in reaction they are talking more about freedom, about doing what we want to do, about the importance of our emotions, about obeying our thirst as the Sprite advertisement says. Just do what you want to do, they say. The result is an easy-going life where we obey our feelings rather than external factors like the needs of others. These people won't pay the price of commitment, except commitment to their own pleasure and progress. They are not willing to die for others and for a cause. In every generation however, whether it's pre-modern, modern or post-modern, Christians are people who live for others. We are not bound to time and productivity, we are bound to God, and God is love and therefore our life is compelled, as 2 Corinthians 5:14 puts it, by the love of Christ.

Motivated by love

I wonder whether these selfish people are really happy. Love is the happiest word in the human vocabulary. If love is flowing out of our lives and if we are in touch with God so that we have this inexhaustible reservoir of God's love to tap into as we serve Him, then our lives are going to glow with the joy of the Lord, because love is a joyous word.

As part of my responsibilities in Youth For Christ I used go to Pakistan quite regularly. On one visit I was in a little town in the interior of Pakistan, staying on a mission hospital compound in the home of an old missionary of about eighty. She had retired and her daughter lived with her. This old lady had come as a young wife with her husband, to the mission field. Their first child got sick, they were unable to give proper treatment and that child died. They had two other children. One of them became a minister. The daughter was a brilliant student who became a surgeon with a bright future. She gave it all up to serve in this little town, as a surgeon. Instead of driving a car, she rode a bicycle.

I was very impressed with these two people and the thing that impressed me most about this paralysed old lady was when she talked, there was one thing she kept saying over and over again – 'I am so happy.' And she would give a reason why she's happy. Then we'd go on talking for a little longer and again she'd say, 'I'm so happy.' Here's a lady who's paralysed and she says, 'I am so happy.' Her first child was killed on the field because of a lack of proper treatment, and she's so happy. Her husband has died and she's so happy. She's separated by thousands of miles from one of her children, and she's so happy. And the other child who is a brilliant student is going to work on a push-bicycle, and she's so happy. You see, when the love of God leads our lives – true we are under bondage to God, but the result of such bondage is a joy that the world knows nothing about, the joy that comes as a result of love coming in and flowing out of our lives.

I am the light of the world

Jesus goes on to give another of His reasons as to why He's the answer to the problem of suffering in the world. He says, 'While I am in the world, I am the light of the world.' Now this verse 5 constricts the concept of being the light of the world to the period of His life while He is in the world. However, it follows a passage in chapter 8 verse 12, where He has already applied the concept of being the light of the world in a broader, more all-encompassing sense, and this is just one aspect of the fact that He is the light of the world.

Let us look at this verse: 'I am the light of the world. Whoever follows me will never walk in darkness, but will have the light of life.' He is explaining what He means by saying that He is the light of the world, 'Whoever follows me will never walk in darkness.' The light is a guide to us so we don't walk in darkness.

In Psalm 119:105, we are told, 'Your word is a lamp to my feet and a light to my path.' In John 1 this word is personified and described as Jesus – now Jesus has become our light. Of course He achieves this function most consistently through the Bible. But it's more than that, by His work for us, He has become the way of salvation. And then he enlightens our eyes to accept this gospel. When we come to Him He comes to us, and He abides with us, so that Matthew 28:20, says, ' I will be with you always to the very end of the age.' He does this of course through the ministry of the Holy Spirit. So the song that we sing, 'I know where I am going and I know who's going with me,' is true.

There is so much uncertainty in the world, so much failure – politicians, ideologies, friends that we have trusted, all took us into dark swamps of uncertainty and disappointment, but with Jesus we are on sure ground. Oh there's much that we can't see. We may experience what the old spiritual writers used to call 'the dark night of the soul', which is a prolonged time of difficulty and uncertainty, when the light doesn't seem to shine through. Maybe there are some here who are going through this: you may not feel that He's there, but He is one who keeps His promises and He has said that He is going to be with us. And if He is with us we are not dismayed because He is greater than the problem.

A traveller in Africa was going through the jungle with a guide when he complained, 'There is no road, no path in this jungle, we have lost our way.' The guide replied, 'There is no way, I am the way.' He knew this jungle through and through. God knows what life is all about. He is bigger than all the problems we face. He is with us, He is committed to us. We can go through the darkness with confidence because He will see us through.

When a Muslim in Africa became a Christian he was asked, 'Why have you changed your religion and become a Christian?' And he said, 'Well, say you are walking along a street and then you come to a fork and you don't know which of the two roads to take. And at the fork there are two people, one dead and one alive. Which one do you think I would ask for directions as to where to go?' Jesus is with us and so we have the way to go.

Jesus goes on to say, 'Whoever follows me will have the light of life.' You see, the function of light is not only to show the right way, it is to give us the light of life, it is to open up for us the bright way. It is not only a right way, it is a bright way – He is the light of life. Sometimes right is not bright: that is why we have this word 'goody-goody', it's a derogatory term, good person but boring! The Christian life has the light of life in it. John Wesley said, 'The one who follows Christ shall have the divine light continually shining upon him, diffusing over his soul knowledge, holiness and joy.'

Hundreds of thousands of Sri Lankans have left our country because of its problems. Many have come to Europe and a lot of them have met Christ as their saviour. Some of them come back, some for good, others to tell their relatives about Jesus and what He has done for them. One such person went home to the north of Sri Lanka. The person who told me this story said that this person was a dull, naughty person before he left for Europe. When he met Christ, he was completely transformed. The people were surprised in his village, so somebody asked him, 'What is the secret of you being so different?' He said, 'You can imagine what will happen to you if you swallow the sun. Well, somebody brighter than the sun is inside me and that's the difference in my life.'

Through the 'I am' statements in John's gospel, Jesus expresses this truth in different ways. Also in John 10:10, He says, 'I have come that you may have life and have it to the full.' What is it that brings this brightness to our lives? It is the fact that God gives us the deepest pleasure in life, the deepest fulfilment. And what is this deepest fulfilment? Psalm 16 talks about it. 'You show me the path to life. In your presence there is fullness of joy and in your right hand are pleasures for evermore' (cf Ps. 16:11).

You see, when we get close to Jesus, as Jesus explained in John 17:3, we come to know Him, we enter into an intimate relationship with God and the spark comes into our lives. We are made for love. The deepest joys in life are from relationships of love. But human relationships of love will never fully satisfy. Only God can satisfy. So the loving tie with God is the spark that ignites the light of Christ in our hearts.

We may have temporary problems that will cloud this light. Then we linger with God till the light returns. Though we cannot see the solution to the problem, we see Jesus and we realise that Jesus is bigger than the problem and God's love is greater than all the lack of love that we have seen in life. And so in Psalm 27:1, David says, 'The Lord is my light and my salvation.' How could he say this even though he was in the midst of this deep crisis? In verse 4 he tells us,

> One thing I ask of the LORD,
> this is what I seek:
> that I may dwell in the
> house of the LORD
> all the days of my life,
> to gaze upon the beauty of the LORD
> and to seek him in his temple.

As we gaze upon the beauty of the Lord we realise God is with us, we don't have to be afraid, and the joy of the Lord returns. Don't try to serve God without that joy, without the beauty of having Him close to you, or you will be an angry, bitter, disappointed person. George Muller once said, 'The first and primary business to which I ought to attend every day is to have my soul happy in the Lord.'

Motivated by the gospel

The fact that we have this great gospel is one of the great motivations for Christian ministry; Jesus is the light to this dark world – that's the message we have. We will all have problems, people will oppose us, it's going to be inconvenient to be in God's service, it might look like we are wasting our talents and our potential because we have gone to serve amongst some unreached people who are taking so long to respond, but are we going to give up? No. We have a great message, we have the message which is the only message that matters from the perspective of eternity, that God is the light of this dark world. We can't give up.

In Jeremiah chapter 20, the prophet talks about all his terrible problems. The chief steward of God's temple has assaulted him and put him in stocks by the temple overnight and on his release he complains to God. He wants to give up his ministry. 'But,' he says, 'if I say, "I will not mention him, or speak any more in his name," his word is in my heart like a burning fire, shut up in my bones. I am weary of holding it in' (verse 9). You see, the message was burning in his heart, and that enabled him to go on and on and on serving Him.

I have a great fear for the evangelical church today. We seem to be placing so much emphasis on techniques and methods, on research into trends in this country, in the world (which is important), on helping Christians to have a great time when they come to church, on active programmes to keep our youth busy. These are all good things, but in the process we may be neglecting the great things. Christian ministry is a lofty calling, and it's a lofty calling because there is a lofty message. It is a message that gives us the urgency of the gospel. People are lost and heading for a Christless eternity and here is the answer, and here is what helps us to go on and on and on serving Him, even though there are so many problems.

The great preacher Gypsy Smith was born in a gypsy tent. With hardly any education he started preaching at the age of seventeen. He preached until he was eighty-seven years old, when he died on the way to America on a mission and was buried at sea. Somebody asked him what was the secret of his freshness and vigour? And he said, 'I have never lost the wonder.' The wonder of the gospel helps us to go on, however difficult things might be.

Different responses to the healing of the blind man

After Jesus has healed, the ordinary people ask all sorts of questions. The Pharisees get in on the act. They ask questions especially about the Sabbath and then start weighing the options. They ask the parents, who evade the issue, and then they talk to the man in verse 24, basically saying, 'Admit it, this man is a sinner.' And he gives the famous reply, 'Whether he is a sinner of not, I don't know. One thing I do know. I was blind but now I see!'

Scholars of John, like Don Carson in his wonderful commentary on John, say that John may be saying that decisive faith is characterised by personal witness. Some of us may not be great preachers, but we can always tell what God has done in our lives. It's not the whole gospel, but it opens the way for presenting the essential gospel. People may not be interested in the gospel, but they may be interested in what we have experienced.

The Pharisees asked some more questions and then end up insulting him. Look at verse 28. I think it's quite typical when big-shots are humiliated by small-fries, they end up being insulting. This has often happened when young people with a lot of enthusiasm and not much wisdom go into the church: they are a threat to the established people who insult them.

When the Pharisees insult the blind man, this former beggar becomes God's lawyer. Look at verses 30 to 33 where you hear him eloquently defending the truth of the gospel.

How often God is so eloquently proclaimed from the most unexpected sources. I work for Youth For Christ and most of our work is with poor, uneducated young people, many of them from Buddhist and Hindu backgrounds. One of the most thrilling things for me has been to see the way God uses their spontaneous, non-traditional witness for Jesus – these people you would least expect. In the last twenty-three years that I've worked for Youth For Christ I have seen many people come to Christ, and because of our humanness we are a little more excited when some people come than when others come. We think, 'Oh this is a great catch, God is really going to use this person.' And after twenty-three years I can tell you how wrong we have been. Sometimes the people we least expect are the ones that God uses so powerfully, because God delights to use weak vessels, so that all the glory, says the Bible, will go to Him. If we are open to the love of God to come into our hearts and we stay in touch with Him, and we allow God's gifts of the Spirit that He gives us to be used in our life, and are available to Him, God can use us.

Jesus will never forsake us

In verse 34 they replied to this man, '"You were steeped in sin at birth; how dare you lecture us!" And they threw him out.' He was giving his testimony, 'God did this to me.' They were talking about his past, not looking at the present work of God. How far from the mind of Christ. This also happened to Paul. When he came to the church they looked at his past sin, but Paul had a Barnabas. This man had Jesus and when 'Jesus heard that they had thrown him out ... he found him, [and] said, "Do you believe in the Son of Man?"' And then of course it goes on to record how he believed in Christ. Verse 35 is a beautiful verse. Jesus took the initiative, He heard and went in search of him. Psalm 27: 10 says, 'Though my father and mother forsake me, the LORD will receive me.' God goes after us when we have been rejected by humans. He is the light and He assures us.

I think I heard that G. Campbell Morgan, who was one of the preachers at this Keswick Convention years ago, wanted to be a Methodist preacher and in the Methodist system – I am a Methodist so I can talk about this system – we have a trial sermon if you want to be a preacher. So he preached his trial sermon. A few days later he went to the notice board to see the results and he found that he had failed. And so he sent a telegram to his father with just one word, 'Rejected.' And the father quickly sent back a telegram to the son. 'Rejected on earth, accepted in heaven. Dad.'

Jesus has a way of accepting us. He shows us, He ministers to us all through different means, maybe through reading a book, through the passage we are reading for that day and someday he comes and shows us that we matter. This applies to ministry too, where we are going to face insult and rejection from people, as the blind man did. Perhaps you are afraid because of that, perhaps you have some close person, a parent who is in the ministry. And you saw the way they were treated by the church and you say, 'I won't go into the ministry after they treated my father in that way.' So you prefer to be on the sidelines like those parents of that blind man. They didn't do anything wrong, but they are remembered right through history as the people who refused to face up to the responsibility of what they knew, who avoided the issue.

If you obey, if you pay the price, you will be hurt, you will be hurt deeply. You will weep because of what people do to you. But that's not the end of the story. Jesus will meet you if you let Him, and He will meet you in your need. He will minister to you and He will use the very rejection you got from people as the stepping stone to make you strong and more effective in God's service; so that when you look back, the overwhelming conviction you have will be that God has touched me – not how much I have suffered, not how bad they were to me, not even how much I have done for God, rather, Jesus loves me, Jesus is committed to me, Jesus goes with me as I do His work.

The great preacher Charles Spurgeon was once asked by somebody, 'Of what persuasion are you?' I suppose they wanted to hear his convictions about some of the controversies of the time. Spurgeon responded, 'I am persuaded that neither death nor life, neither angels nor demons, neither the present nor the future, nor any powers, neither height nor depth, nor anything else in all creation, will be able to separate us from the love of God that is in Christ Jesus our Lord.'

My dear friends, that's the most wonderful thing about ministry. Jesus is with us. When we look back we want to sing, 'I am so glad that Jesus loves me, Jesus loves me, Jesus loves me, I am so glad that Jesus loves me, Jesus loves even me.'

The Good Shepherd Lays Down His life
by Ian Coffey

John 10

I wonder what you've learned at Keswick this week. Life is meant to be one long process of learning, you do realise that, don't you? The word 'disciple' means 'learner'. Some of you may have known that joyous moment, when you passed your driver's test and could rip up your L-plates – that's it! Well, the good news is, that as a Christian disciple you cannot do that until you get to heaven. You and I wear the L-plates continuously because discipleship is about learning.

A few weeks ago I came across a remarkable group of sayings by people of different ages, not Christians, who talked about what they were learning at different ages in their lives. Let me give you a selection.

A little boy aged 7 said, 'I've learned that you can't hide a piece of broccoli in a glass of milk.'

A little girl of 9 said, 'I've learned that when you wave to people who live in the country they stop what they are doing and they wave back.'

A girl of 13, growing up, said, 'I've learned that when I get my room just the way I want it my mum makes me clean it up again.'

How about this, a profound thought from a 13-year-old boy. 'I've learned, if you want to cheer yourself up, you should try cheering someone else up.'

Or a 15-year-old, 'I've learned, though it's hard to admit it, I'm secretly glad that my parents are strict with me.'

Or a woman of 29, 'I've learned that brushing my child's hair is one of life's great pleasures.'

Those drivers among us will sympathise with this 29-year-old man: 'I've learned that, wherever I go, the world's worst drivers have followed me there!'

Or a 46-year-old lady who said, 'I've learned that the greater a person's sense of guilt, the greater their need to cast blame on others.'

This profound comment from a 52-year-old woman: 'I've learned you can tell a lot about a man by the way he handles three things – a rainy day, lost luggage and tangled Christmas tree lights!'

A 58-year-old man, 'I've learned that making a living is not the same as making a life.'

A 61-year-old man, 'I've learned that if you want to do something positive for your children, improve your marriage.'

A 72-year-old, 'I've learned that everyone can use a prayer.'

An 82-year-old man, 'I've learned that even when I have pains I don't have to be one.'

An 85-year-old lady, 'I've learned that every day you should reach out and touch someone.' People love that human touch, holding hands, a warm hug, or just a friendly pat on the back.

And how about this? A 92-year-old man said, 'I've learned that I still have got a lot to learn.'

As the people of God, we should be like that, we still have a lot to learn. We've been reminded as we began our communion service tonight, we all stand on level ground. None of us is an expert; all of us are in God's learning school. What have you learned at Keswick this week? Keswick, founded on the principle of biblical holiness: what it means to be God's people living in God's world, God's way. We are in that learning school. Those who plan and pray and work hard for Keswick, don't want us simply to become a spiritual version of *Mastermind*, that we can wow everybody with our Bible knowledge. They want that you and I might be different, that on the street we live in, the place we work, the people that we worship with, people might know that we have been with God, because of something that's happening in our lives. What are we learning?

As we look at John chapter 10, you'll notice the third 'I am' of Jesus, 'I am the gate.' But the 'I am' that we are looking at this evening is in verse 11: 'I am the good shepherd,' says Jesus. And we are going to look at those verses surrounding that little statement.

Jesus used many pictures from everyday life to illustrate truths about the kingdom of God. His parable teaching ministry took an earthly story and gave it a heavenly meaning. And it was natural with a crowd of people who lived in an economy that was dominated by agriculture, with sheep on the hillsides and probably some shepherds in the crowd, that Jesus would use such an analogy. If you've grown up in a town or a city it's a little bit difficult, because our minds don't quite fall into gear in that way. Yesterday as I drove past a lovely hillside on the outskirts of Keswick and watched the sheep grazing, I remembered I told one of my boys when we were here years ago, that sheep in Keswick had got two legs shorter than the other two. And he only told me a few months ago that he had believed that for three years!

The picture Jesus used was a picture that identified, not just with those who were there, but it echoed with the Old Testament scriptures. Most notably, think of King David when he wrote his famous 23rd Psalm, from his own background, his own boyhood experience – he likened the Lord to *his* shepherd. So Jesus takes not just a simple illustration from everyday life, but much richer and more profound than that, He says, 'I am the shepherd of which David said, "The Lord is my shepherd."'

Two very important theological truths come out of that analogy and also in other places in the teaching of Jesus.

1) Human beings are like helpless, lost sheep.

2) God the Father, God the Son and God the Spirit are in the rescue business of seeking and finding lost sheep.

This gives us some understanding of Matthew 9:36,

'When he saw the crowds, he had compassion on them, because they were harassed and helpless, like sheep without a shepherd.'

The heart of God is moved by people. I love poetry, I love the beauty of gardens, but there's one line in a poem that I always find very difficult: 'You are nearer God's heart in a garden than anywhere else on earth.' Now the natural world testifies to the glory of God, but people, that is wrong. If you want to get near to the heart of God, stand in the checkout queue at Tesco, at the bus stop, on the football terraces, walk through the crowded streets of Keswick, that is where God's heart is – with men and women, all colours, all shapes and sizes; Jesus was moved with compassion when He saw sheep without a shepherd. He feels the same today when He looks at us, when He looks at our world.

I want to bring out four things illustrated from the words and life of Jesus, to help us to understand what it means when we say He is the 'good shepherd'.

I am the good shepherd

His Sacrifice

Verse 11 talks about His sacrifice when it says, 'The good shepherd lays down his life for the sheep.' We are going to be thinking about the death of our Lord Jesus on the cross on that first Good Friday, remembering Him in breaking bread and drinking wine together, because He told us to. We are not just simply going through a ritual, a ceremony, but we are remembering that the one who has called us to follow Him has nail-pierced hands. The Bible tells us that Jesus laid down His life in order that you and I might find life. And Jesus speaks here in verse 11 of the good shepherd – you see his goodness in the fact that he is willing to sacrifice his life for the sheep.

Look at verses 17 and 18. It's very interesting how Jesus says, 'I have the authority to lay my life down and the authority to take it up again. This command I received from my Father.' Anticipating the cross, Jesus speaks prophetically to His disciples, to the crowd that listened, and down through the years to you and me as we sit with open Bibles. He looked towards the cross and said, 'That will be no accident. I am not a helpless victim. I choose to lay down my life in order that countless thousands might find forgiveness and a new beginning with God.'

Many of you have read, or least heard of the book, *Peace Child* by Don Richardson which tells of the ministry he and his wife were involved in among the Sawi people in New Guinea, a tribal group of head-hunting cannibals. He is very honest about the difficulty of absorbing and understanding the culture of these people. They had learnt the language, they were trying to build bridges of friendship, but found it very difficult to explain why they were there and the message of the gospel that they carried. He talks about the way in which these groups from different villages were often very jealous and feuds would blow up over the slightest thing. But one particular day a very serious incident occurred. Some cattle had wandered away and there was an argument; two men from rival villages had started fighting and one of the men had been killed. The men from the Richardsons' village came flooding back and there was going to be an all-out fight. They knew from what they had heard, that often it wasn't until many of the fit men in the village were dead that a truce would be made. As the men were getting their instruments of war together, one young man, who obviously had some influence within the tribe, suddenly rushed into his home and took their six-month-old baby boy from his wife's arms. She was distraught and hysterical, but he rushed away. He went to the other village and offered his child to the men there with the words, 'Will you plead the words of my village among your people?' And the men replied, 'Yes.' 'Then I give you my son,' he said, handing the baby over and adding, 'and with him I give you my name.' And he walked home without the child. They weren't going to kill the child, they were going to take the child within their community. Later that evening, a man came with a child from their village, and an exchange took place. Suddenly the Richardsons saw a motif of the gospel: Jesus, God's peace child. And those tribal people who said, 'Whenever there's a dispute that no one can settle, only with a peace child can a peace be bought,' suddenly saw a picture of what Jesus did by His atoning death on the cross.

Let's remember as we come to communion, maybe it's unfamiliar – we are in a tent, the words may be different, Eucharist, Holy Communion, the Lord's Table, the Lord's Supper, all those things point to the verse above my head – 'All one in Christ Jesus.' Don't let the terms we use get in the way. Let us focus on Him, the good shepherd who by His sacrifice has opened the door of heaven to us.

His commitment

If you look in verses 12 and 13, Jesus contrasts Himself with the hired hand. 'The commitment,' says Jesus, 'on My part is I lay down my life.' When trouble comes the hired hand looks after number one, that's all. But Jesus says, 'My commitment to the welfare of My people is total.' When John writes his first letter in the New Testament, he gets caught up in one of those doxology moments when he just released in praise and he says, 'How great is the love the Father has lavished on us, that we should be called children of God!' (1 Jn. 3:1). Jesus is committed to us.

I have sensed, talking to many of you this week, that there are some who understand intellectually that Jesus is the good shepherd, but the level at which we struggle is at the level of our experience of God. We say, 'I know it's true, but I find it hard because as a parent my heart is filled with pain for my children who are a long way from God.' Or some of us perhaps look at a marriage, which is not going anywhere and we've invested everything in it. Or we've known the experience of a failed or a broken relationship. You are in a church and even today you've thought about being back in that fellowship on Sunday and your heart was not filled with joy, but pain. You've been let down badly, been betrayed by people who profess to be Christians, that's what makes it so hard.

Some ask the question, 'Lord are you really the good shepherd?' I want to remind you what that goodness means, what the commitment of Jesus means. The Bible tells us that He is utterly committed to our welfare. The Bible tells us that He who began a good work in us will carry it on to completion, until the day of Jesus Christ. The Bible tells us that nothing, principalities, powers, nothing can separate us from the love of God that is in Christ Jesus. The Bible tells that worries and concerns are known to Him, the very hairs of our head are numbered. Again and again the Bible says, 'Trust and do not be anxious. Cast all your care upon Him. Put your trust and your faith in Him.' Easy to know that in theory, isn't it? You teach in Sunday School, you preach, but how do I get it from here to there?

Remember the children's story about the owl and the centipede? The centipede got fed up with walking around on the ground with all those legs so he went to see the owl, the wisest creature in the forest. The owl thought about his problem for a few days and when the centipede came back the owl said, 'I've worked out the answer. What you need to do is learn to fly.' The centipede said, 'Thank you very much, Mr. Owl, that's a great bit of advice, but how?' To which the owl is said to have replied, 'Listen, I give you the theory, you work out the practice yourself.'

But you know God doesn't say, 'You work it out yourself. Here's a book full of texts, of verses, here's a collection of theological principles, so go away and let your mind drift around them.' The wonderful truth is that God by His Spirit comes to live within us, so that when you go back to that difficult church, or back to that home, or into the office, or into the factory and say, 'Well, I knew the sense of God's presence with all the Christians and all the teaching and all the fellowship...' The wonderful truth is that He is the 'with us' God – 'Emmanuel' means 'God with us'. When He comes to take up residence in your life by His Spirit, and our lives open more and more to the influence of His Spirit, to His fruit, to His gifts, to His direction, we discover that He is the 'paraclete'. We can't get our minds around that in our English language: it's a wonderfully rich word, in fact so rich we use different words – we talk about 'the comforter', 'the advocate', 'the strengthener'.

There was a Bible Society team of translators, working with Wycliffe amongst the Karre people, trying to translate the New Testament into the Karre language in Equatorial Africa and they were struggling with that word 'paraclete'. How could they describe the Holy Spirit? One day the translators discovered in the culture of this people, a group of porters going off into the bush carrying, African-style, a whole bundle of things on their heads. They noticed that in the line of porters there was always one who didn't carry anything, and they assumed that he was the boss, there to make sure the others did their stint. However they discovered that he wasn't the boss, he was a porter with a special job; he was there if anyone fell over with exhaustion or tiredness – he would come and pick up the man's load and carry it for him. And he was known in the Karre language as 'the one who falls down beside us'. They had their word for 'paraclete'.

I would say to you people in pain, you don't have to walk alone. You can know Jesus the good shepherd, walking with you, whatever you face at the moment in your life; whatever need there might be, in your family, in your marriage; whatever pain you feel in your heart, the good shepherd is utterly committed to your welfare. That doesn't mean your problem is going to disappear with the wave of a magic wand, it doesn't work like that. But God's going to give you the grace, and you're going to find His solution in that situation, whatever that might be and however long that takes – He is with you. We are not alone.

I remember a couple of Easters ago, God really ministering to me and helping me at a time in my life when I felt deeply disappointed with Jesus. It probably shocks you to think I could be deeply disappointed with Jesus. If you've never been disappointed with Jesus, come and sign my Bible later. There are times with the Lord Jesus, we seek Him, we pray, we go out on a limb, we do something and it doesn't quite work out, the way that we had hoped that it would. And suddenly, reading in my Bible one day, I realised part of what the disciples were going through even after Good Friday, even after the resurrection, was a sense of disappointment with Jesus. And what does He do? He comes to them in the upper room and He says, 'Peace be with you.' He breathes on them and says, 'Receive the Holy Spirit.' He meets them in their disappointment. He met me in a time of disappointment. He can meet you in whatever it is that you have carried around in your heart this week and face as you go back to work. He is utterly committed.

His knowledge

Did you notice that in verses 14 and 15. 'I am the good shepherd; I know my sheep and my sheep know me…' How about this though? '… Just as the Father knows me and I know the Father – and I lay down my life for the sheep.'

It's intriguing that Jesus puts His knowledge of you and me on the same level as the relationship between Himself and the Father. Why? Because He's talking about a deep intimate knowledge. You can know people at different levels, can't you? You say, 'I know someone,' when you've met them twice. You know someone but you are not sure that they would recognise you if you met them again. But Jesus says here, at the deepest intimate level of relationship, 'I know my people in the way that the Father knows Me and I know the Father.'

And look, He says, 'My sheep know me.' That's the depth of relationship that He opens to you and to me. I believe this has come to us in different ways this week, through the Bible readings, through the evening meetings, this journey of relationship, of discipleship, of going deeper with God. He is with us, He knows us, He knows what we go back to. Does that make you feel comfortable or uncomfortable? Your response tells you where you are in your relationship with Him.

I wonder if I am speaking to someone who looks at the next few weeks and months, with a real hesitance in your heart because you are not sure quite what you face. There are unanswered questions gnawing away inside at the moment. You believe God's got something in store but you don't know what it is, you don't know where you'll be in three or four months' time. Take hold of these verses and be encouraged. The good shepherd knows you. He says, 'My sheep hear my voice and they follow me.'

I remember as a young Christian I was terribly worried

that the will of God was a tightrope – one false move, I'd fall off and that was my Christian life wrecked. An older Christian took me on one side and said, 'The will of God is more like a broad field, not a tightrope. When you start climbing over the hedge at the side He'll tell you. Now get on with it.' I needed those liberating words to be able to walk hand in hand in faith with the good shepherd.

His mission

His mission is the fourth thing I want you to notice. Look at verse16. Last night Ajith reminded us so powerfully about Jesus being the Light of the world and His heart for men and women*. Verse 16 says, 'I have other sheep that are not of this sheep pen. I must bring them also. They too will listen to my voice, and there shall be one flock and one shepherd.' I hope you realise that's the majority of us in this tent tonight. Some of you may be messianic believers, it's great to have you here, but Jesus speaking to a Jewish audience is saying, there are other sheep from another fold. There's the Gentile world with people of different colours and different languages. The picture in Revelation that John saw when he said, 'I saw a great multitude that no one could count, from every nation, tribe, people and language, standing before the throne and in front of the Lamb' (cf Rev. 7:9). That is God's mission, that heaven should be a multicoloured, multicultural praise party for the Lamb of God. And you and I need to be engaged in this mission. If it matters that much to Jesus it should matter that much to us.

Last night we were reminded of the challenge to mission, not just for those who are called in some full-time way, but all of us called to the challenge of mission in our street, mission on our doorstep, mission in the cities, the towns, the villages where we live. Jesus' heart was moved with compassion for broken people and He wants us to feel that way too.

Some of us struggle. We look back in our lives and say, 'I don't know whether the Lord can use me because…' There's been some sense of failure, moral failure, sin in your life.

*Ajith Fernando's talk 'I am the light of the world' can be found on p.181.

I hope God has met you this week and you've dealt with that, brought it to the cross and found forgiveness. But even still there's something there and it says, 'I don't know whether God can actually use me.' Have you ever noticed that little line in one of Graham Kendrick's songs, 'He turns our weaknesses into His opportunities'?* The very things we think disqualify us, actually qualify us. You see, if we felt we'd got it all sorted out with everything taped and neatly parcelled, we would become arrogant, triumphalistic people who quite frankly a lot of folk would just run away from. But because you have known pain and in that pain have found grace in our Lord Jesus Christ, because you have known doubt – and you do realise that what makes faith, faith, is doubt – because you've known doubt but exercised your will and trusted even when you couldn't fully understand, that gives you something to offer a hurting world.

I honestly believe that most lies are told in church on Sunday at ten past twelve. Why? Because people come up and say, 'How are you?' 'I'm fine,' you answer. But I'm dying on the inside. We can afford to be real. He is the good shepherd. As we put ourselves in His hands and receive His grace we need not hide our weaknesses – in fact the apostle Paul boasts about his weaknesses, because he had learnt the secret, 'When I'm weak, then I'm strong.' When I'm actually vulnerable enough to say, 'There is need in my life,' then I find the power of God flows through me in greater measure.

As we come to the Lord's Table, we come to the *good* shepherd. Now here's a question. Can you say, 'The Lord is *my* shepherd'?

I sat about two weeks ago with a member of my church who was dying. Peter wasn't a very old man; he had struggled with an illness for quite some time. Over the early part of the summer as I visited him, he obviously was finding studying the Bible, even conversation very difficult. But somebody had given him a lovely booklet of meditations on the 23rd Psalm which he could just about cope with and which gave him a lot of comfort and help.

* Graham Kendrick, 'Rejoice, Rejoice'

One afternoon he showed me what he had read that day and as we talked about it, I remembered a true story about an evangelist in the Yorkshire Dales who visited a little group of churches on a fairly regular basis. It was at the time when evangelists didn't just do meetings in church, but visited people in their homes and all sorts of informal gatherings took place. And there was one lad in that village community who had severe educational difficulties. This evangelist took quite a shine to this lad, partly because the lad looked after sheep, and he sort of connected with him over the 23rd Psalm. A number of people felt it was very strange that this evangelist would spend any time talking to this lad, who had no education and who couldn't understand most of what was going on. But patiently, over several visits, this evangelist taught this young lad the 23rd Psalm off by heart. He showed him that phrase, 'The Lord is my shepherd' – five words, count them out on your fingers. Then he showed him the important word on his fourth finger, 'the Lord is *my* shepherd,' and he talked about personal faith – not just about the Lord Jesus, but about knowing Him in a personal way in his life.

One winter the lad was lost in the hills in a blizzard; it was one those incredible snowdrifts that took several days before it cleared. When they found him, he had obviously perished and the doctor couldn't understand why he was clutching his fourth finger on his left hand, until the evangelist came to speak at the thanksgiving service and was able to explain it. I reminded my friend, on the day that he passed into God's presence, that word *my* is what makes all the difference.

I wonder if I'm speaking to someone tonight and you've sat in many communion services and may have even taken communion, but you've never really known, 'The Lord is *my* shepherd.' Well I ask you tonight, before the elements are passed around, quietly sitting where you are, to turn to Jesus Christ, put your faith in Him, believe that when He died on the cross it was to pay the penalty for sin that you deserved to pay. Trust Him, give your life to Him, turn around from the things that you know are wrong and invite Him to be the Lord of your life. And take bread and take wine as a seal of what you have asked Him to do in your life.

I wonder if I'm speaking to a Christian tonight and you've struggled with the goodness of God. And the Lord Jesus says to you tonight, 'I am the Good Shepherd.' And as you go back to face that situation you don't go back alone, the 'with us' God goes with you, the one who falls down beside us, He is there. Praise His name.

I am the Resurrection and the Life
by Liam Goligher

John 11

While you are turning to John 11, let me read you some advice that I received by e-mail from my son-in-law. I thought you might be interested in these statistics. 'For Safety's Sake' is the caption.

> Do not ride in cars because they cause twenty per cent of all fatal accidents.
>
> Do not stay at home, because seventeen per cent of all fatal accidents occur in the home.
>
> Do not walk on the streets or on the pavement, fourteen per cent of all accidents happen to pedestrians.
>
> Do not travel by air, rail, or water, for sixteen per cent of all accidents happen on these.

But did you know this, that only point zero, zero, one per cent – I'll repeat that again, just in case you didn't get it – point zero, zero, one per cent of all deaths occur in worship services.

You may just be in the safest place you could possibly be this evening!

Facing death

I suppose one of the things that we notice about ourselves is our preoccupation with our health. Health is the subject of lots of jokes. But there may be some people here for whom health is no joke. One of the reasons we are preoccupied with our health is because we have none of us really come to terms with our deaths. If the Christian faith has nothing to say about death, it has nothing to say.

When we are young of course we don't think or talk very much about death unless it intrudes into our world, and even when we are older we actually avoid the subject as much as we can. I know a man well into his eighties who admitted, after the death of his wife, that he had never really thought of either one of them dying, or of its consequences. In death we lose a parent, a child, a friend, a lover – we lose. However much we try to disguise it, to keep it away, to confine it within the sterile walls of the hospice or the hospital, death only speaks loss to us. It is, as Shakespeare called it, 'The undiscovered country from whose bourn no traveller returns' (Hamlet III:i). Sometimes we joke about death. You know Woody Allen's quip, 'It's not that I'm afraid of death, it's just that I don't want to be there when it happens.' We all identify a little bit with that.

But did you know that death is most acute as a problem to Christian believers? It raises all kinds of questions in our minds about God, about His goodness, about His power.

Does God really care?

Is God good? Then why does He allow death? Is God powerful? Then why, oh why doesn't He put an end to it all? In many ways those two questions are the sub-plot to the story that we have read this evening. For the story raises the question, does Jesus really care? Does He really care for me? Does He really care about my predicament, about my health, about my loved ones, about my family, the concerns that I have, does He really care?

Here is the story of someone who was a well-loved friend, a well-loved brother – someone around whom there revolved a whole universe of experiences, who had a whole network of relationships. Suddenly those relationships ended when his life ended. And it raises problems.

Jesus' ways

This passage of Scripture is for those of us who have problems with Jesus' ways, for the whole story in many ways opens up to us something about the ways of God, the ways of Jesus with His people. Here are these sisters experiencing anguish – it's the natural anguish of people who have seen someone they love grow sick and die. But we don't understand this story unless we understand that their anguish is actually compounded by their relationship with Jesus. There is evidence in the gospels that they enjoyed a very close personal friendship with the Lord Jesus. There can be no question of their love for Him or their trust in Him, or His love for them. So it was the most natural thing in the world for them to send for Jesus when their brother got sick. And you can see how they felt in verses 21 and 32 when both Martha and Mary express their confidence, 'Lord, if You'd been here our brother wouldn't have died.' There is no indication here that they thought for one minute that Jesus' friends should be exempt from sickness just because they believed. They knew where to find Jesus, even when the authorities were looking for Him and couldn't find Him. They come to Him, appealing to His love and their relationship to Him and they say, 'Lord, the one you love is sick.'

Now I wonder whether you can identify with these sisters. Many, if not most of us, in this tent tonight can identify with them because we have a relationship with Jesus. All God's children, all those born of the Spirit, adopted into the family of God, have Jesus as their elder brother. Once we have been redeemed by Him we belong to Him, we have a relationship with Him, we can go to Him and we can say, 'Lord, the one You love is sick.' There was an old man who was once asked what he did when he was in trouble. He said, 'I go to the Lord and I say, "Lord, Your property is in danger."' We have been redeemed by Him, you are not your own, you have been bought with a price. You are the Lord's, if you are a child of God, you can say to Him, 'Lord, the one You love is sick.'

So you can imagine the added distress that came into their lives when Jesus apparently did not act. They knew Jesus could heal, they had seen Him do it. They knew Jesus could heal from a distance, they had seen Him do that. I don't know what they expected Him to do, but they certainly expected that He had the power to make their brother better and He didn't do it. Not only did He not make him better, He didn't even come; He apparently showed indifference. You can imagine the kind of heart searching they went through. By the time Jesus arrives, Lazarus has been dead for four days and to them that made the prospect of a miracle impossible and the state of the dead man irreversible. The thing that strikes me is this – Jesus may be completely informed about your troubles, and yet apparently act as if He were indifferent to your troubles.

We learn that prayer for the sick, which is encouraged in the Bible, may not be answered. We learn that what happens in our lives and circumstances may appear to contradict the direct words of Jesus. Just look at verse 4 and you wonder what they must have thought when they heard the report of those words, This sickness will not end in death.'

Jesus' ways are shaped by His love

Have you got a problem with Jesus' ways with you? The story tells us that Jesus' ways are shaped by His love. There's a lot said in this chapter about Jesus' love for these people, and it's obvious they love Him. I think John has a theological purpose here. Lazarus, the one whom Jesus loves, is being held up as the representative of all those Jesus loves, namely all Christians. And it strikes us, doesn't it, that those whom Jesus loves especially, get sick and eventually die. You may be struggling with this question, 'Does God love me? Does Jesus love me?' And yet verses 5 and 6 in this chapter link Jesus' love with His delay – Jesus loved Martha and Mary and Lazarus, yet when He heard that Lazarus was sick He stayed. Do you see the grammatical link there? He loved them, yet He stayed where He was two more days.

What kind of love is this that does not jump when we call? What kind of love is this that doesn't give us what we ask for every time we ask it? What kind of love is this that doesn't spoil the object of the affection? The fact is that the Bible says He loves us and the fact that He loves us and that we love Him is no guarantee that we will be sheltered from the problems and pains of life.

We see this principle of love and suffering operating in the life of our Lord Jesus Himself. There in the garden as He approaches the cross, as He bears on His shoulders the burden of your sin and mine, as He sees the accumulated wrath of God against the sin of the world hanging there, ready at any moment to be poured out on His own Spirit to crush Him – there you see the tension between the love of God and suffering. God loved His Son. Three times in the Bible He says, 'You are My beloved Son.' And yet the fact that He loved His Son, the Lord Jesus, didn't stop Him inflicting on His Son the awfulness of that wrath of Calvary in order that you and I might be delivered from our sin. Jesus' ways are shaped by His love, we are being told.

Jesus' ways are shaped by His purpose

Verse 4, 'It is to my Father's glory' so that God's Son may be glorified through it. Verse 15, 'I am glad ... so that you may believe.' Verse 42, it is 'for the benefit of the people ... that they may believe'. What He is teaching us here is that He has a long-term strategy that drives both His action and His inaction in the world. His goal is doing the Father's will and achieving the Father's purpose.

When He talks here about the Father's glory and His own glory, He is thinking of course supremely of the cross. John 12:23, 'The hour has come for the Son of Man to be glorified.' If you look at the context there you will see that He is thinking of His death, because He goes on to speak of the corn of wheat that falls into the ground and dies. And in many ways it was the raising of Lazarus that was to lead directly to the death of Jesus – Lazarus taking sick, Lazarus dying and being buried, Lazarus then being raised by Jesus, was a link in the chain that ended at the cross. For John 11:53 tells us, 'From that day on they plotted to take his life.' It was the final spark needed to ignite the accumulated hostility of the leaders against Him. The sickness and death of Lazarus exposed the pretensions of the Pharisees and Sadducees and from that day on they decided they could no longer have Him around. They thought they were good until Jesus came, but against His awesome holiness they saw the contrast.

Now of course the reality is that Martha and Mary, and the friends of the family who were there grieving, didn't know the end of the story, neither did the disciples. You see, we don't get a printout at the beginning of our lives, as to the way our lives are going to take. There's no point in our experience when God gives us a printout of His end purpose and how it is that my little part in the procedure of my life is going to fit into His ultimate purpose. The Bible just doesn't tell us that, but what it does tell us is that God does have a purpose.

Jesus' concern in these events is that He finally would be glorified. That's why He says those shocking words, and they are shocking, in verse 14, 'Lazarus is dead, and for your sake I am glad.' Glad? Would you like to rephrase that Jesus? Did You really mean to use that word right there in that context Lord? Glad that Lazarus is dead? And He says to His children, 'Don't you realise that I know the end from the beginning. I am not taken by surprise, nothing just turns up for Me. Don't you realise that I am working with a much bigger picture here? There are cosmic powers and forces and your life is part of that, and eventually I am going to make you part of that bigger picture. But I have a purpose and your life is being formed and wedged and woven into that purpose as I work with you and as I work with your circumstances. Things are not just happening by chance; it's not just the roll of the dice. You are in My hands and one day you'll understand.'

Dr Sangster, the great Methodist preacher, had a brother who was severely handicapped and only lived to the age of six. Sangster says in one of his books, 'I struggled with it as a boy and I struggle with it as a man, but I know that when I get to heaven and ask Jesus about it, I'll be satisfied with His explanation.' His ways are shaped by His purpose.

Jesus' ways are shaped by His wisdom

Frankly, He knows more than you or I do. Verse 4, 'This sickness will not end in death.' As unlikely as it appears to the disciples and the sisters, there will be a resurrection from the dead and that to God's glory. In fact, in verse 11 He already begins to redefine death – 'Lazarus has fallen asleep.' You see the implication, sleep is something you wake up from, it isn't the end.

His message to us is: He knows what He's going to do. He knows not only the end, but also the means to the end, He knows when to act. The Bible asks the question, why does God delay? Because His grace makes room for people to repent. That is why we are heading towards the year 2000 and Jesus isn't back yet. God is being patient with you, He doesn't want anyone to be lost or to perish, but everyone to come to repentance.

Why does He often delay in our prayers for healing, or the meeting of a need or deliverance from a habit, or a destructive relationship, for the salvation of a loved one? I can't give you a definitive answer, all neatly packaged, but be sure of this – delays are inevitable; we are finite, we don't see the big picture. Our desires and our prayers are shot through with our own selfishness and sin, but God's delays are not final. He will act in His own time and way. We need to trust Him.

Jesus actually, you notice in this story, puts Himself in an impossible position so that He might do the impossible. And that's the Lord's way with you. If He wants you to trust Him He puts you in a place of difficulty. If He wants you to trust Him greatly He'll put you in a place of impossibility. Let's be honest as we look over our lives, what is the thing that has driven us back to Jesus over and over again? What has brought us to our knees when we have become a bit comfortable in our spiritual lives? What is the thing that has really opened us up once again to the Word of God and the Spirit of God and the things of God? Very often it has been when tragedy has struck, when there's been failure on our own part or on the part of someone close to us. Are you struggling with Jesus' ways? Then please learn from this passage of Scripture that He is saying to you, 'My ways are shaped by My love, I don't want to harm you. My ways are shaped by My purpose and My ways are shaped by My wisdom.'

Jesus' words

Let's change gear a bit. It may very well be that you are struggling, not with Jesus' ways but with Jesus' words. Maybe, quite frankly, you don't believe Him. Martha appears in this story as a very sane saint, a practical down-to-earth individual who is also a woman of great faith. Notice, will you, that she had no doubt that if Jesus had been there He could have healed her brother. Now that Lazarus was dead she had no doubt that Jesus being there would bring comfort. She can also do what many of us do in church regularly on Sunday – she can trot out the orthodox Jewish belief about resurrection on the last day. 'I know,' she said, 'he will rise again in the resurrection at the last day' (verse 24). She believed what every devout Jew believed and was ready to confess it. But you know Jesus is not happy with a cerebral faith, with a mere intellectualising or theorising of religion.

You see how personal He gets in verse 25 – 'I am the resurrection and the life,' He says. 'He who believes in me will live, even though he dies; and whoever lives and believes in me will never die. Do you believe this?' Do *you* believe this? It's in that context He makes this astounding claim. He is concerned to divert Martha's focus from an abstract belief about something that will take place on a last day yet to be defined. He wants to turn her away from that kind of abstract faith into a personalised faith. He is saying to her, 'I am resurrection, I am life. Do you believe Me, Martha?' He won't let us sit, you see, in our pews, keeping faith at a distance, talking objectively about 'the' faith, or 'the' doctrine, or 'the' truth. Jesus insists on making His truth personal to us. Wherever we are listening to this message, He is saying to us, 'Do you believe this?'

You see, when you are sick you want a doctor, not a medical textbook. When you are being sued you need a lawyer, not a book on jurisprudence; and when you are a sinner you need a saviour. Words themselves can lack power and authority unless the one who speaks them can demonstrate his ability to do what he says. That's why Jesus regularly turns the attention onto Himself. He claims to be your sufficient saviour, He claims to die for your sin, and He backs it by rising from the dead.

So just look for a moment at what Jesus says. He turns Martha's thoughts to Himself, who He is, what He can do. In the human race, in the end we all face death and there is nothing we can do about it. Somebody has said the statistics on death are quite impressive – one out of one people die. We can stave it off for a time, but when it comes it is final. What Jesus is saying here is this – there is one in the human race for whom death is not final. For Martha and Mary and most of the people of their day, as for many of the Old Testament saints, the teaching about life after death was obscure and shadowy at best. But here is Jesus, and He comes to turn the spotlight onto the whole issue of death. 'I am resurrection,' He says. By His words, by His miracles, by His resurrection, He brings life and immortality to light through the gospel. '*I am resurrection.*' It isn't just that He raises people, He has risen power in Himself. This means that He has to die for us, so that He can demonstrate that risen power of God in His own life. You and I need never to be afraid again of death, He is saying, 'because I have beaten death'. In Revelation 1 we see Jesus with the keys of death and Hades in His hands. Jesus beat death.

I stood for a moment after we had conducted the funeral service for my father, and in the silence in my mind came those words I had used in the service – 'I am the resurrection and the life.' And then in the silence the words came back to me – 'Jesus has beaten death! Do you believe this?'

'I am resurrection. I am life,' Jesus says. That means the quality of life He gives now is real. It isn't just pie in the sky when you die, it's steak on the plate while you wait! To know Him right now means spiritual life, it means no longer to be dead in trespasses and sins, to be cut off from the life of God. To be a Christian right now is to know resurrection life – it's the power of His resurrection. There are many times in my experience when I've looked at my life and I've looked at the power of the resurrection and thought, there is a big divergence here between the way I am living and the power of the resurrection life of Jesus. And yet I have to come to the Bible and say, seriously, that if I know Jesus, I know this resurrection power is available to me. And I have to say too in my experience, that there have been those moments where the resurrection power of Jesus has meshed with my life and at those points I have experienced, sometimes briefly, sometimes gloriously, the reality that Jesus is life, not just resurrection, He is life right now, eternal life, spiritual life, that is not interrupted by death, but ends in glory itself. That is a staggering claim for us. Jesus' people are the living among the dead. Those are the words of Jesus. Do you have a problem with His words? Do you believe them?

This passage is speaking of people who have a problem with Jesus' ways and with Jesus' words, but it may very well be speaking to those who have a problem with Jesus' works.

Jesus' works

It's very interesting, as we read this story, I think these women might have been asking the question, 'Is there anything Jesus can do now?' Even knowing Him as they did, even having seen Him perform miracles, as far as we know they had never seen Him raise anyone from the dead; they weren't expecting Him to do that. They were standing with their weeping friends at their brother's graveside thinking, what can Jesus do anyhow? As the story develops I want you to notice, it starts where they are and it ends where He is. It starts with His anger.

Anger

When you first heard the bad news about a diagnosis or a prognosis, you may very well have begun to feel angry. When you first heard the news of the death of a friend or a family member you may have felt anger.

This story begins with anger. We are told that He was deeply moved in spirit. The German translation says, 'He was outraged in spirit and troubled.' It wasn't that He stopped loving the sisters or people in general, but He was angry. What was He angry at? Was He angry at sin that leads to death, death is the wage of sin? Was He angry at sickness and death and the havoc they cause in people's lives? Was He angry at the unbelief of those who were standing around grieving and wailing as if they had no hope? We are just told He was angry.

Profound anger in the face of bereavement or bad news is something that Jesus has experienced. When a child dies of AIDS Jesus is angry. He stands beside you at the graveside of that young person as you are feeling anger at the end of a wasted life which was full of great potential. He is angry: let me tell you. He is angry at the rape of women in Bosnia, He is angry at ethnic cleansing in Kosovo, He is angry at the abuse of a child. He is angry about these things. And you need to know that your Jesus has felt anger as you have done, at the injustices and the evils that rock our world. Have you felt anger?

Grief

Have you felt grief? Jesus grieved; when He was shown the tomb, we are told Jesus wept – literally in the Greek it says, He burst into tears. I guess most of us know what that's like. Isaiah had predicted the Messiah would be a Man of Sorrows and acquainted with grief (cf Is. 53:3). Isn't it strange the way we so theologise things that we forget we are talking about a real flesh and blood person here, the Lord Jesus – He became a true human being of average size, same shape as us, looked like one of us. He burst into tears, confronted by the death of a friend.

There's reality there. My dear friend, if you are struggling with reality about this Christian business, you need to read the story again – here is reality, here is the gospel of John, which of all the gospels talks most about the deity of Jesus, the God-hood of Jesus, the awesomeness – the transcendence of Jesus starts with all eternity; 'In the beginning was the Word and the Word was with God and the Word was God and everything was made by him' (cf Jn. 1:1). He burst into tears.

The onlookers saw in His tears an expression of His love for Lazarus – 'See how He loved him' (verse 36). Have you spent a sleepless night in tears over some personal tragedy? Jesus has wept with you, you need to believe that. I need to ask someone who is not a Christian, is there something in this story that will touch your heart? You see we want you to love our Lord Jesus. Is there something in this story that will reach into the innermost recesses of your life and touch a chord there? Do you need to know that this great God who made the universe actually cares so much for real human beings that He weeps when they weep? Does that touch a chord in your life, that He cares for you, that He weeps with you, that He has wept over your hardness of heart and He has wept with you in your griefs and your trials, and He loves you and is calling you to Himself, and He is saying, 'Do you believe Me?' I want you to love my Lord Jesus with those tears, I want you to stand with me, apart from that graveside and see Him with His friends there and see Him burst into tears and I want you to love Him the way I love Him right now, for that – would you do that?

But there is something in this story that leaves your experience and mine. Anger, we share that with Him. Grief, we share that with Him. But there's a third element here that we don't share.

Power

We can understand the interplay with these emotions – anger and grief are often mixed up in us. But our anger and grief are often mixed, are they not, with a sense of frustration and impotence, we can do nothing. We feel powerless to change our circumstances or the circumstances of others. But not Jesus, for alongside anger and grief there is that element that is only His – power. And as we read the story we find the Lord Jesus bears down on that tomb, the way my dad used to bear down on us when as small boys we had done something wrong – there was that look of determination on his face and we knew we were for it. I tell you, death knew it was for it that day. Jesus bore down – that's what the Greek says – He just focused and terrifyingly, threateningly, He made His way towards that tomb. He was going to deal with death that day. And if death could shake in its shoes, death was shaking in its shoes right there, that day Jesus came in power.

Nothing can divert Him from the task. He comes to remove our tears and to deal with death. Isaiah had said, 'He will swallow up death in victory, the Lord God will wipe away tears from all faces' (cf Is. 25:8). And His power is in stark contrast to the hopelessness of the situation. Remember that these events happened to a prominent family before crowds of witnesses – this was nothing done in a corner. It happened in a town just two miles away from the capital city of Jerusalem. It happened at a time in Jesus' life when absolutely everything He said or did was being noticed, recorded and observed by His opponents because they were looking for something to get Him on. It happened, we are told, four days after the death of Lazarus. By this time dissolution and putrefaction would be well established. The NIV sanitises (as many of our English versions do) Martha's very practical observation in verse 39. She said literally, 'There will be a stink.' And from a human point of view the situation is irretrievable. Lazarus represents not just the recently dead, but the long dead – those who have dissolved and disappeared, the decomposed.

And what does Jesus do? Well, He takes command, He engages in prayer out loud, for our benefit, so that we might know where His power comes from – He will do nothing outside of the will of His Father. This miracle will be performed in the power of God, to the glory of God. And then He speaks to Lazarus. This tomb, by the way, was undoubtedly in a cemetery. Why did He say, 'Lazarus, come out'? One old commentator probably gives the right explanation. He said 'Lazarus, come out,' because if He hadn't said *Lazarus* there would have been a mass resurrection! Earlier in John 5: 28-9, He had said, 'The dead will hear the voice of the Son of Man and those who are in their graves will come out.' 'Lazarus, come out!'

The only loser in this story is death, and him who has the power of death, that is the devil. And the message of the story is this – He speaks, and listening to His voice, new life the dead receive. It happens right now, as people come to spiritual life, awakening to a whole new life of experience of God.

It happens now as men and women respond believingly to the claims of the Lord Jesus. And it will happen at the end of history, when the dead will hear the voice of the Son of God and those who hear will come out to be raised, to be transformed and to be with Him for evermore.

In the film *Shadowlands* the powerful story is told of C. S. Lewis and his relationship with Joy Gresham: they meet, they engage in a marriage of convenience and only later fall in love, but their time together is short: Joy dies of cancer. The film is good because in it we see two themes: pleasure and pain. It ends with Lewis's faith intact but shaky. In real life however, there was no doubt a period of shaky faith, but he emerged with a triumphant hope. He memorialised the one he loved, Joy, in a poem:

> Here the whole world (stars, water, air,
> And field, and forest, as they were
> Reflected in a single mind)
> Like cast-off clothes was left behind
> In ashes yet with hope that she,
> Re-born from holy poverty,
> In lenten lands, hereafter may
> Resume them on her Easter Day.*

If Christianity has nothing to say about death, it has nothing to say.

We used to read to our kids some of C.S. Lewis's Narnia books. In *The Last Battle* the great lion Aslan speaks to the children and tells them that their parents and each one of them is 'as you used to call it in the Shadowlands – dead'. And as He speaks, they realise that, as C.S. Lewis puts it, all their life before has been only the cover and the title page; that now at last they are beginning Chapter One of the great story, 'in which every chapter is better than the one before'. Do you have a place in that great story?

The raising of Lazarus and the rising of Jesus one week

---

* This epitaph was cut into a marble plaque which is near where her ashes were scattered at the Oxford Crematorium.

later point to the trustworthiness of His claims. You can trust His ways with you for He loves you. You can trust His words to you because He has backed them up in actions. You can trust His works. What He did for Lazarus, He will do for you. One day you will hear that voice, one day you too will rise, one day our eyes will see the King in His beauty.

The Grain of Wheat
by Ron Dunn

John 12

It's a joy to be here. Actually it's a joy to be anywhere. Next time I come over to England I'm going to drive! I'm sorry that I missed being here yesterday, I'd much rather have been here than sitting in an airport in Indianapolis for two and a half hours, and then missing two flights because of the weather over here. We are certainly happy to return after all these years to Keswick. I was here first in 1978, and then the last time in '87 and a great deal has changed, except you've still got the same old clock for the speaker up there. Sometimes I want to shoot it, and I would be justified because it struck first!

Now I have here a glass of water from which I'm going to drink. Since I was here last time I have developed a condition. I keep asking the doctor what it is and he keeps telling me and I keep forgetting. I think it starts with an 'H' and it keeps me dehydrated all the time, so I have to drink water – nothing worse than a dry preacher! As far as I know that's the only side effect, other than I have no sense of time, and so I just drink until the water's gone. As long as there's water in the glass I keep on preaching! I hope you won't be like one church in the States, I told them that. And the next service they had a little communion glass for me, but I know that you won't do that. Now would you open your Bibles to the gospel of John chapter 12 reading from verse 20 to verse 26.

Sigmund Freud, the father of modern psychiatry, who was not a Christian, had a favourite story of a sailor who was shipwrecked on an island. The natives of this island took him and declared him to be king, absolute ruler for one year. And they said, 'In this one year we will supply your every need, give you anything that you ask for, over and far abundantly more than you need. For one year you will reign and be king and have anything and everything you want. But at the end of that year you will be banished to a deserted island with no resources on it at all.'

So the sailor had two choices. He could take everything that was given to him in that one year. He could consume it, gratify his every wish and then be banished to a deserted island and starve to death. Or he could conserve all the abundance that they were giving him and take it to the deserted island with him and live there for many years in abundance. Just two choices: you either consume your life for the present, or you conserve it for the future.

There is a sense in which every person here tonight is a king, and you sit on the throne of your own life. You can do only one of two things with your life. You can consume it right now for the present. Live for the present, build for the present, and then face the future, without hope, without God. Or you can conserve this life, or reserve this life for the future so that it will be an abundant future.

When Jesus received this word from the Greeks, it's amazing we have no record of His answering the Greeks, but He says, 'The hour has come for the Son of Man to be glorified' (verse 23). Now you can actually take the gospel of John and divide it into that portion which is before His hour had come, and that portion which says, 'now His hour is come,' and it is at this point in chapter 12 that the whole thing separates. Up until now Jesus would say, 'The hour has not yet come.' They would try to take Him but the hour had not yet come. But now, in chapter 12, when the Greeks came, I believe symbolising the world seeking Jesus, and He recognised, 'Now the world is ready for My sacrifice,' now He says,

'My hour is come.' And everything He does, even washing
the feet of the disciples, is based on the fact that He knows
His hour has come.

And He says, 'Father, what could I say, deliver Me from
this hour? I could pray that, but no, that wouldn't be right.
For this is the hour for which I have come into the world,
therefore, glorify Your name.'

Now for most of us, to be glorified means to be honoured,
to have a glorious experience, but we need to understand that
when Jesus talks about being glorified He is saying, 'I am
ready to be crucified.' When He prays for the Father to glorify His name He is actually asking the Father to crucify
Him, because for Jesus, the hour coming was the hour for
which He was born and came into this world, that He might
die for the sins of mankind. And so He says in verse 24, 'I tell
you the truth,' explaining Himself. 'Why must You die, Lord
Jesus?' If you read the gospels carefully you will find that
every time Jesus talked about the cross the disciples tried to
change the subject, they didn't want to talk about the cross –
no, that's not the kind of Jesus they followed. They signed on
to follow the one who would overthrow the Roman yoke of
bondage and make them a great nation again, and so when
Jesus talked about the cross and dying they tried to change
the subject, they didn't want to hear about that.

Now Lord, why must You die? And He answers, 'I tell you
the truth, unless a kernel of wheat falls to the ground and
dies, it remains only a single grain. But if it dies it produces
many seeds.' Then He makes the application to us. 'The man
who loves his life will lose it, while the man who hates his life
in this world will keep it for eternal life.'

The dividends of dying

I want to talk to you tonight about the dividends of dying,
the rewards that Jesus is speaking about here.

Fruitfulness

Now of course the first obvious dividend of dying is fruitfulness. He says, 'If a grain of wheat remains alone, I mean does-
n't fall in the ground and die, it abides alone.' Here is a farmer

who has a grain of wheat or some seeds and he can do one of two things with them: he can consume them right then and there and satisfy his instant pleasure, or he can let them die, put them into the ground and they will bring forth a harvest. But before there can be harvest there must be death. Before that farmer can reap a harvest he has to let that seed go, cover it up where it's out of sight and let it die, and then it will bring forth much fruit.

And Jesus, if He comes and just teaches and does miracles, He still remains alone. When He goes back to heaven He'll take nobody back with Him but Himself. It is only as He dies that He will bear much fruit. And so you have enunciated here a principle that runs throughout the Scripture, that it is out of death that life comes. If I want life then there must be death, it's just that simple.

For instance, let me read Paul's words in 2 Corinthians chapter 4 beginning with verse 7. He says that we have this treasure in clay jars so that it may be made clear that this extraordinary power belongs to God and does not come from us. We are afflicted in every way but not crushed, perplexed but not driven to despair, persecuted but not forsaken, struck down but not destroyed. Always carrying in the body the death of Jesus, now, watch it, 'so that the life of Jesus may also be revealed in our body. For we who are alive are always being given over to death for Jesus' sake, so that his life may be revealed in our mortal body.'

How many times do we say, 'Oh I want people to see Jesus in me'? Isn't that right? I want to be Christ-like. Okay, it's easy, just die. I don't know that I want it that badly, I... Now here is the eternal principle in verse 12, 'So then, death is at work in us, but life is at work in you.'

We heard about, a moment ago from Jacob, the necessity for evangelism and winning those people in Indonesia to Christ, but I want to tell you something, nobody is going to be won to the Lord Jesus Christ until first of all somebody dies. There will not be any fruits until first of all there is death. And so Paul, seemingly, gladly accepted it, so death works in us, death works with us – everywhere we go we bear about in our body the dying of the Lord Jesus. Why? So that

Jesus may be made manifest in out mortal flesh – isn't that what we want? Don't we want Jesus to be made manifest in our mortal flesh? If that's to happen then you must die. There'll be no fruit, there'll be no evangelism, unless people are willing to die and that's the trouble in this age of self-gratification.

I don't know how it is in your country, but we are just stuffed and overflowing with it in the United States: get it, grab it and eat it now. This is the age of 'We won't wait for anything, we want instant gratification.' You live for yourself and you watch out for number one; you don't care about the future, you don't make a commitment to anything, except the here and the now. And to talk to that generation about dying to self!

Well, he goes on and explains that those who love their life will lose it. Later on he's going to talk about eternal life but he uses two different words there. When he talks about losing your life and hating your life, he's using the word 'psyche', which is the ego, this is the intelligent life, this is the life that chooses and plans and fulfils desires. Interestingly, Jesus says that those who want to keep this life – I'm number one, I'm not going to have anybody tell me what to do, I am the master of my fate, the captain of my soul; I'll do what I want to do, I make my own choices, I make my own plans – anybody who does that – and it's a present tense verb there – is already losing their own life; Phillips translates it 'destroying' it.

The Inuit Indians, Eskimos of Canada and Greenland, have an interesting way of hunting bear. They will take a bone, preferably a wolf bone, and they will sharpen it at both ends. Then they will coil it through a process, freeze it in blubber and lay it across one of the paths the bears travel. As the bear comes along he smells that blubber and in one gulp he takes it and swallows it, not knowing that it's just blubber on the outside, but on the inside there's this twisted, sharpened bone. And the minute he swallows that he's dead. He doesn't drop down just yet, but every move he makes, every step he takes, causes that bone to twist and to slash and to tear and the internal bleeding starts and the Indians just follow the tracks of that bear until it dies.

It's the same way as a person who says, 'I'm going to save my life, I'm going to keep my life for myself, I'm not going to give my life in sacrifice to Jesus Christ, I'm not going to die in that way, I'm going to do what I want to do.' The minute you do that you are already in the process of dying and destroying your life. Friends, there are only two things you can do with the seed, you can either consume it for the present or you can conserve it for the future. There are only two things you can do with your life, consume it right now in the present, saying, 'I want to live the way I want to live and do things the way I want to do,' and then die. Or you can say, 'I'll die now, I'll die to having my way.'

Luke puts it this way – 'If any man will follow me let him take up his cross, let him deny himself and follow me' (cf Lk. 9:23). I love Charles B. Williams' translation, 'If any man will follow me let him say no to self.' I like that, let him say no to self. Does your self ever talk to you? Yes. My self said quite a bit to me sitting on the runway! Here we were cramped in these little seats, and you know how it is, the guy in front of you lays his seat way back, and self says, 'Get it away from me.' Does your self ever tell you anything ? 'Blow your horn at that driver, don't let them do that.' Our selfs are always telling us things. Do you know what it means to die? Say no to self – not my will but Thine be done. And I choose to die to my life in this world. That's the only way to fruitfulness.

I said a moment ago, there'll be no life unless there is death. Abraham and Sarah's story is a perfect picture of that – life coming out of death, that's the way God works. It worked that way with Christ, with Paul. That's the principle. My dear friends, you and I must understand this, that if my life is to be fruitful, I must die, that's all there is to it.

I remember several years ago, right after I had left the pastorate and I had entered this itinerant ministry, a faith ministry – they call it that because you don't trust anybody to give you enough to live on so you live by faith! Anyway I struggled on, you know it does get kind of thin at times. But I went to one meeting, and this pastor shouldn't have said this to me, but he said, 'You know we are a really giving church.' And he told me how much they were going to give me, it was about five times as much as I had ever gotten in my life. Whoa, boy! I'm going to enjoy this meeting, yes Sir!' And all week long, all I could think about was, man, we can catch up on our bills and do this and do that, man. I can call my wife and tell her what we are going to get.

I remember on the Tuesday night, I was there in the motel and I was praying about the service and I was saying, the meeting was going fair, but nothing interesting was happening, there was no life there, nobody was being convicted, no one was coming to Christ. I was wrestling with the Lord and I said, 'Oh God, anything Lord, what's it going to take to see revival, what's it going to take to see life break into this meeting?' And you know what the Lord did, He brought up that love offering, just as clearly as I am talking to you, and I don't mean that I hear God with an audible voice, I don't, some people may, but I don't. But God said, 'Well, if you want to see life and fruit, then you must die to that offering.' And He said, 'I want you to give it away and here's who I want you to give it to.' I wish I could report to you that I instantly said, 'Well, of course, Lord.' No, my first thought was, 'This is the devil speaking.' You know, we never become so concerned about whether it's God or the devil until it comes to money, have you noticed that? But I knew it was God. I wrestled all afternoon until I came to a point, I fell on my knees and I said, 'Lord, that's Yours.' And I died to that.

That night, it was interesting, I finished my message which I thought I had not done very well, and in the States at these kinds of meetings we give an altar call. So everybody stood and the choir was going to sing. And I tell you folks, it was as if a heavy hand got on my chest and just pushed me back out of the way and the Holy Spirit was saying, 'Now let Me show you what I can do.' On the first verse we had twenty-eight people come to trust Christ for the first time in their life. And it went on like that all the rest of the week. I can only assume that God finally gave me the grace, broke me down where I was willing to die to something that meant a lot to me.

Now there are other things I've had to die to. I'm in this meeting and I've got a loved one, a relative who's lost. God says, 'How badly do you want to see them saved?' Would you be willing to fast and pray for seven days, eight days? Would you be willing to say, 'I'm not going to eat another bite of food until this one comes to Christ'? Are you willing to die to your convenience? Are you willing to die to sleep? Are you willing to die to your hunger? Are you committed to see fruit in your life and to see life come out of this death? It's you who must die, you're the one that must die, just as surely as Jesus died in the flesh you must die in your ego and in your convenience and your own self will.

I hope I'm not being too bold to say that I believe that when the church, or when an individual Christian takes upon himself to die in whatever way God is dealing with him, I believe He then has every right to expect fruit to come out of this life. If you want to know why there is not more fruit-bearing in our lives than there is, and why we are not winning more of our friends and families to Christ, why the church is not prospering more in evangelism, I believe the answer is, that we are not willing to die for it. There is fruitfulness when we do this.

Fullness

There is also a fullness. Remember the interesting statement Jesus makes in verse 25, 'The man who loves his life will lose it, while the man who hates his life in this world will keep it for eternal life.' Of course we already have eternal life. But in John 10, He says, 'I am come that they might have life and have it more abundantly.' Now you can have life and not have it abundantly. Go to hospital and see someone there who is alive, but you can't say it's abundant.

I tried to figure out once what abundant life was, physically, and I decided that's when everything works. [Takes off glasses] Right now I don't have abundant life. [Puts on glasses] Now I do! I've got my glasses on, I've got abundant life, my eyes are working. You understand what I'm saying? I think, in the Christian life the abundant life is when everything works – when your prayer life works, your faith life works, your witnessing life works. Oh I know a lot of Christians who have life but there's nothing abundant about it, they are just alive, but there's no abundance.

But He says we will keep it for eternal life. I think of it this way: it is a fuller life here and a forever life there. The paradoxes of Jesus are hard for us to understand, but if I want to enrich my soul, I must divest myself of everything. If I want to live I must die. If I want to save I must lose. That's why it's so hard for this world always, and especially for this generation, to understand the bare essentials of the Gospel, and that's why I think that in many of our pulpits we need to stop preaching therapeutic stuff as though on a psychologist's couch and we need to get back to the word of God. I hear more psychology than I hear theology nowadays when I go to church and I listen to the preacher. That's not going to convert anybody. Do you hear many people today calling upon us to die to our self-interest, to die to our petty allegiances, to die to our convenience, to hate our life in this world, so that somehow like our blessed Lord we may fall into the ground and die?

Faithfulness

Of course there's another dividend, I've mentioned two, fruitfulness and fullness, but there is another one that I must mention and that is faithfulness. I love verse 26. He says, 'Whoever serves me must follow me; and where I am, my servant also will be.' That's interesting – whoever serves me must follow me. I tell you what, if I'm going to serve Jesus, I need to be where Jesus is, right? Sometimes I think I'm following Jesus, but oh no, He's gone this way. Well I know, but this road's so much smoother, this path offers more prestige and actually it's easier on the body. Yes, but Jesus is over here.

Have you ever thought if Jesus came back to this earth today, if He was still alive today on this earth, where would He be tonight? Oh I think He might be right here with us. But where else do you think He would be? You might look for Him in the slums, among the homeless, among those who stink, among those who are the outcasts of society, it wouldn't surprise me at all if that's where you'd find Him. You'd probably find Him sitting down, not having lunch with the head Pharisee, but with the publicans and the sinners. Now I tell you something folks, if you are going to follow Him you're going to have to be where He is. Where is Jesus in this world? Well, He told us in Luke 15 that He leaves the ninety-nine safe in the fold and goes out and searches for the lost.

But there's a twist to that. Not only will we be where Jesus is, but if we are following Him right, He'll be where we are. I talked to a fellow the other day who ministers in India. Oh boy, he talked about the rough times and how hard it was. And I said to myself, I could never do that. But the fact of the matter is, if Jesus sent me there, He'd be there with me. What more can I ask for? If I am following Him aright, not only will I be where He is, but He'll also be where I am – you're not there by yourself, you're not there without resources, you're not there without company, you're not there without sympathy, you're not there without intercession, you're not there without the strength of God. For wherever you are He is too, if you are following Him.

Favour

Let me close with just a word about this. There is another dividend to dying and that is favour. I love that last phrase, 'My Father will honour the one who serves me.' Oh, but if I were to heed the call of God, and if I were to make of myself a nobody, I mean after all if you don't look after number one nobody else will. There are plenty of opportunities out there, both in the world and in the church, to promote yourself, gain a high position. All you have to do is just go along and make sure everybody likes you, and you never say or do anything that would offend anybody's delicate senses. And you know what, you'll be honoured. Oh yes, you'll be honoured. At the next denominational convention they'll recognise you, 'We welcome Dr So-and-so here, who led his church to...' (everybody has a doctor's degree if they've done anything). 'We are happy to have Dr Joe Blow here this morning, he has led his church to grow from this to that and he's on this committee and serves on this board and, oh his name is great in the land.' Ah, but there's no telling how many compromises he had to make to get there, and I know of some. You can be honoured in this life. How much better would it be to honoured by the Father?

Have you heard that old story? I would never tell this in the States because everybody knows it... I am going to tell it over here because I hope that maybe you've not heard it. An old missionary and his wife served in Africa for years and years. Finally they retired and it was time for them to come home. When their ship docked in New York, Teddy Roosevelt the President was also on board, returning from a hunting safari in Africa. Everybody was there to interview, to meet, to photograph Teddy Roosevelt. Nobody was there to meet the old missionaries. They got to feeling sorry for themselves. 'We've served all our lives on the mission field and now we've come home and nobody's here to welcome us.' And God said, 'Old missionary, you're not home yet.' Isn't that good? 'My Father will honour the one who serves me.'

Where Wrath and Mercy Meet
by Don Carson

Keswick Lecture

Turn to Romans 3: we shall come to that chapter in due course.

For the last twenty-five years or so, I have been engaged in university missions, and in that time they have changed a great deal. Nowadays when one preaches the gospel in most university situations in the Western world, there is one particular area that is very hard to get across. It's not the doctrine of the Trinity, it's the doctrine of sin. And this is partly because of a rising post-modern epistemology.

The fruit in this area is to drive many people (especially on the arts sides of our universities) to the conclusion that all notions of right and wrong are culturally dependent – they are either dependent finally on the individual, or the social unit – but that there is no absolute right or wrong. The only absolutely wrong thing is to say that there is such a thing as an absolutely wrong thing! This eventually has a bearing on gospel preaching, because if we cannot agree as to what the problem is, we cannot possibly agree as to what the solution is.

As a result in many evangelical circles in the Western world today, there is a kind of diluted and domesticated gospel; precisely because there is no longer any universal understanding of the nature of sin, there is an increasing temptation to trim the gospel so that the gospel is primarily given to meet your felt need. If your felt need is alienation, then Jesus is the gospel who gives you integration. If your felt need is loneliness, Jesus loves you and you will no longer feel lonely. If your marriage is on the rocks, Jesus' gospel puts your marriage together.

There is a modicum of truth in all of those things. The trouble is, it's only a modicum. And, biblically speaking, all of those things are tied to the far more central issue, how shall men and women, who by nature and choice are people rebellious against their Maker and who are therefore alienated first of all from God, and therefore have a whole host of social problems, how shall they be reconciled to God? Only when you have that kind of background, I would insist, can you make sense of the cross. If you do not have that analysis of the fundamental human problem, you cannot possibly arrive at a biblically faithful understanding of the cross. In other words, if you begin with contemporary analyses of contemporary problems, you will always domesticate the gospel. You may begin with a contemporary analysis of a human problem and then trace it back to a biblical analysis of a human problem, and then once that is established, come to the gospel without losing the gospel. But if you don't somewhere or other get across the biblical analysis of what is wrong with human beings, you cannot possibly remain faithful to the biblical gospel.

1) What is wrong with human beings?

The Bible Story (in brief)

In the beginning God made everything. He made human beings in His own image and likeness. He made everything good. The nature of evil is not that it is something that is the flip-side of good. It does not have the same ontological status as good, so there's a good principle and bad principle and they sort of duke it out in the universe, like in the *Star Wars* films where it's fifty-fifty, and you tilt the balance yourself by the kinds of things you choose. That's not the way it is at all.

In the Bible, sin is bound up with the kind of self-centredness that dethrones God, it wants to make self God.

The first question is, did God really say? And the first doctrine to be denied is judgement. You will not surely, die? With the Fall came the entire perversion of the created order, everything changed. So that in the next chapter we come across the first murder, fratricide. Sin becomes so appalling in the multiplying human race that God sends the flood. In His mercy He saves Noah and his family. Noah promptly gets drunk. God then promises never to send such a drastic judgement again, but it is not long before the race is full of violence and evil – and we have that horrendous chapter, so-and-so lived so many years and then he died, so-and-so lived so many years then he died, and he died and he died and he died – Oh, God said that death was the entailment of sin all right.

Some, of course, are still trying to build towers to heaven to escape floods and make themselves gods, in Genesis 11. But God humbles human arrogance and intervenes, to find one man, Abraham, and then a whole nation to come from him. Abraham, Isaac, Jacob, the twelve patriarchs.

Abraham is a great man though he can be a liar. Isaac is a bit of a wimp. Jacob is the deceiver. The twelve, well – one is sleeping with his daughter-in-law, another is sleeping with his father's concubine. Ten of them are trying to figure out whether it is better to murder one of them or sell him into slavery; talk about a dysfunctional family!

Eventually they go back down into Egypt, they are enslaved, and when God raises up Moses to bring them out, they have to be talked into it! God does bring them out with magnificent displays of power and control over evil, over the created order, yet at the same time it only takes a matter of months before the propensity of their hearts displays itself again in the horrible incident of the golden calf. The very time when God is graciously giving His words to Moses on the mountain, the people are in an orgy of paganism down below.

Eventually they enter the Promised Land after the first generation has died off. God gives them more miraculous signs, He preserves them through the forty years of desert wandering. He takes them across the Jordan river; Jericho falls. Whereupon the people are already so stuffed with pride that they make all kinds of mistakes with respect to the Gibeonites and Ai, to the period of the judges, endless cycles of rebellion and sin are followed by judgement.

Eventually there is so much judgement they cry to God for mercy. God raises up a judge. Some man or woman who leads the people in repentance yet again – delivers the people from all of their suffering. But it's only a generation or two before there's another spiral down the cycle of horrendous paganism; the kind of paganism where children become burnt offerings to the god Molech. In fact the cycles are so appalling that by the end of the book of Judges it is hard to read chapters 19, 20 and 21 in public, they are disgusting. And again the refrain, 'In those days there was no king in Israel, everyone did that which was right in his own eyes.' Oh God, how we need a king. But when the people asked for a king, it was not so that they could be God-like and well-governed, it was so that they could be like the surrounding pagans. Saul was the result, with horrendous implications.

Then God raises up a king after His own heart, David. He commits adultery and murder and it only takes two generations of kings before the nation splits. Now we have Israel in the north and Judah in the south. In the north no dynasty lasts more than three or four generations before it's bumped off by some new dynasty – with endless cycles of corruption and perversion until the people are carted off into exile. In the south the remnant thinks that it is safe and secure, but eventually Jerusalem falls, and in his powerful visions Ezekiel sees the glory of God leaving the temple and the courtyard, leaving the city, and parking, as it were, in a movable chariot in the mountain on the east of the city, a symbol of the judgement to come. God had abandoned His people and they would be dispersed. Do I need to go on?

As you read through the prophets you hear these thundering judgements from a God who is always saying, 'I am slow to anger, plenteous in mercy.' He is forbearing, yet the threats are horrendous, precisely because the sin is so appalling.

Now this is the Bible's story line. It's how we are to understand sin. It's not because the Jews are worse than others, but because they are typical of all of us. And until we see this pattern of human rebellion against God, this vaunted self-autonomy, recycling again and again; until we see that apart from God's intervening grace, there is no enduring fidelity anywhere, we really aren't ready to see just what it is that God accomplished in Christ Jesus.

The sin of mankind

Before we get to Romans 3:21, this wonderful atonement passage, we have chapter 1:18 to 3:20. The whole burden of these chapters is that God's wrath is against the entire human race, Jew and Gentile alike, because of our sin. And to get that across believably in our generation is extremely difficult. I read recently the testimony of Budziszewski, in an article called 'Escape from Nihilism'. He was a moral relativist who did his Ph.D to prove that all moral systems are entirely relative to their own culture and therefore there is no absolute right or wrong anywhere. Eventually he was converted. He writes:

> I have already noted in passing that everything goes wrong without God. This is true even of the good things He has given us, such as our minds. One of the good things I've been given is a stronger than average mind. I don't make the observation to boast: human beings are given diverse gifts to serve them in diverse ways. The problem is that a strong mind that refuses the call to serve God has its own way of doing wrong. When some people flee from God they rob and kill, others do a lot of drugs and have a lot of sex. When I fled from God I didn't do any of those things, my way of fleeing from God was to get stupid. Though it always comes as a surprise to intellectuals, there are some forms of stupidity that one must be highly intelligent and educated to achieve. God keeps them in His arsenal to pull down mulish pride and I discovered them all. That is how I

ended up doing a doctoral dissertation to prove that we make up the difference between good and evil and we aren't responsible for what we do. I remember now that I taught those things to students. In fact he taught them for seventeen years. 'Now that's sin,' he writes. 'It was also agony. I believed things that filled me with dread. I thought I was smarter and braver than the people who didn't believe them; I thought I saw an emptiness at the heart of the universe that was hidden from their foolish eyes. But I was the fool. How then did God bring me back?' And he begins to explain then the nature of his conversion.

We must understand the nature of sin. Last autumn I was in Poland and I went to spend the day in Auschwitz and Birkenau. There is something peculiarly powerful about seeing the camps for the first time. As you walk into Auschwitz 1, you see written above the gate, *Arbeit Macht Frei* (Work Makes You Free). The place was full of vicious ironies. In one little courtyard between the buildings where tens of thousands of people were lined up against a wall and shot, you could see the place for torturing prisoners. In one stone cell you could see where a figure of Christ on the cross has been etched into the stone by fingernails. You can still see the piles of human hair waiting to be shipped back from the East into Germany, to be made into fibre; and children's clothes and glasses and shoes all ready to be recycled. You can see it all.

In Auschwitz 2 – Birkenau, which is of course much bigger, most of the shacks had been burnt down, the ovens and gas chambers had been blown up in the face of the advancing Red Army. But in Auschwitz 1, there wasn't time, so you can still see the gas chamber where they could get rid of about twenty-one-hundred people in twenty minutes, using Zyklon B, a cyanide derivative. You can still see those original gas chambers. And do you know what? I think that we in the West have often misunderstood the significance of Auschwitz. In some ways the horror was unique, in part because it was so efficient, it combined this kind of horror with immaculate record keeping. The Germans couldn't destroy them all before the Red Army got there, you can still see them.

By contrast, when Pol Pot murdered he kept no records. It was out in the jungle, it wasn't quite as efficient. Moreover, most us haven't read stories of Cambodian survivors. In this bloody twentieth century we have not only killed six million Jews in the ovens, we have killed seven million others, that is Gypsies and other people perceived to be enemies of the state. At least twenty million Ukrainians, an estimated fifty million Chinese; then the Armenian holocaust; approximately a third of the population of Cambodia; plus of course the regional instances of genocide – some estimate as high as a million and a quarter Hutus and Tutsis. Plus the smaller things like the Balkans. And on and on and on. This has been the bloodiest of human centuries so far as we can estimate. No fewer than a hundred million people butchered and murdered apart from the wars. And in our wisdom in the West, we have concluded that there is no such thing as evil. Now that's evil.

I am persuaded that we are simply not ready to listen, to understand, to grasp the significance, the depth and magnificence of the grace of God and the gospel, until we see how deeply odious our sin is.

One of the significances of the holocaust was that it was done by Germans. Not because Germans are worse, but because before the holocaust just about everybody in the Western world thought of them as the best; they had the best universities, the best technology, were producing some of the best scholarship in the world, and were leading the flock in all kinds of ways. Which is another way of saying, that the nation at the philosophical peak of Western enlightenment values, led us into genocide. We are no better. It is because of the Lord's mercies we are not consumed.

If you were to read without background explanation, without recreating the Bible's whole story-line, these verses from chapter 3, I suspect there are some here who might think that it's a bit strong – 'There is no one righteous, not even one; there is no one who understands, no one who seeks God. All have turned away, they have together become worthless; there is no one who does good; not even one.' Wait a minute, what about Albert Schweitzer, he does good. 'Their throats are open graves; their tongues practise deceit.' 'The poison of vipers is on their lips.'. 'Their mouths are full of cursing and bitterness.' 'Their feet are swift to shed blood; ruin and misery mark their ways, and the way of peace they do not know.' 'There is no fear of God before their eyes' (cf Rom. 3:10-18).

I'm not persuaded. I'm not for a moment denying that common grace in our hearts enables even faulty, bruised, broken, rebellious sinners like you and me to do some good, but we are a rebel breed, a damned rebel breed. Unless we come to terms with that sort of thing and re-cloak it in contemporary form so that we can get it across to people, we simply can't make the gospel clear.

I am persuaded that one of the reasons why this so-called new perspective on Paul that redefines justification in very substantial ways has come along, is because the whole notion of sin grounded in the Fall has been shifted to one side, and now the paradigms have much more to do with the place of Israel, its identity and themes of exile and the like, without seeing that all of those themes in the Bible story-line are nestled into the bigger theme of creation and fall, which has to do with sin. We cannot agree on the solution unless we agree on the problem. It cannot be done.

2) God's wrath

It takes only a few hours of fast reading of the Old Testament to recognise that all of this horrible sin in the Bible elicits, as its appropriate response, God's wrath. It is always presented as God's, as it were, last resort. He is forbearing. Yet there are pages and pages in Isaiah and Jeremiah and Amos and Ezekiel, where there is threatened judgement and it is threatened as a function of God's wrath. In other words, the judgement that follows is not pictured in the Bible as a kind of independent result of some bad choices – you do some naughty things and there are social entailments. It's pictured rather as the consequence of God's wrath. But God's wrath is not portrayed as a vile temper, as an arbitrary burst of anger outside of God's control. It's pictured rather as a function of His holiness. If God was able to say in effect, to a Hitler or to a Don Carson, 'I don't give a rip what you do, you do what you like, I don't care,' will that make you morally better? His sheer holiness demands that those who have been made in His image and are but creatures, and who defy Him to His face, meet the judgement that He Himself has already told them that they would meet, it is personal.

3) God's righteousness

Now we come to the argument in verses 21 to 26 that we Christians are justified because of the cross of Christ. The controlling expression in this paragraph is 'the righteousness of God'. which occurs four times in these verses. And the verb 'to justify', cognate with it, twice. I think that we shall get at the heart of the issue if we reflect on four elements.

1) Paul establishes the revelation of God's righteousness and its relationship to the Old Testament (verse 21).

The 'But now' is not a logical 'now' – but now the next step in my argument. It's rather a 'now' that's eschatological, it is a 'now' at this point in redemptive history. In the past there has been this, but 'now' God is doing a certain thing. That is made clear once we understand that the expression 'apart from the law', is not connected with the righteousness of God, but with 'is made known'. In other words, we are not to read, 'But now our righteousness from God apart from law has been made known.' We are to read, 'But now, a righteousness from God has been made known apart from law.' That is, apart from the law covenant; which prescribed its own sacrificial system by which men and women could know the righteousness of God and be justified before Him. But 'now', at this point in the sweep of redemptive history, but 'now' with the coming of Jesus Christ, but 'now' with the coming of the new covenant, a righteousness of God has been made known apart from the law covenant.

But it is not so independent of the law covenant that it has nothing to do with it. No. It has been made known now apart from law, yet it is that to which the law and the prophets testify (verse 21). That is to say, the law and the prophets prefigured it; they announced it; they modelled it, but they did not provide it. That has happened 'now', at the end of the age. And this righteousness is bound up, as we see in the following verses in ways that still need to be unpacked, with the death of Jesus Christ with His atonement on the cross. That has been made known 'now', at the end of the ages. That's the argument.

In my view, one of the best commentaries on the epistle to the Romans is by my colleague Douglas Moo. However, at this point I have to depart from his understanding of the 'But now'. He thinks that it runs a bit like this. 'But now, over against the time of wrath and judgement in the Old Testament, "now" there is a time of mercy in the coming of Jesus.' So he sees the significance of 'now', as 'now' at this point in redemptive history. But that's not quite it here. This is a common mistake, to think that then there was judgement and now there's grace. The truth of the matter is, in the Old Testament God is the God of judgement and of grace, and in the New Testament He's still the God of judgement and of grace. In fact if you push me I would argue that you ratchet up on both fronts.

As you move from the old covenant to the new, you see the grace of God progressively disclose all its clarity and beauty, until you see it climaxing in the cross. And if you look at the theme of judgement, yes, this horrible judgement in the Old Testament, it climaxes in the New, with the teaching of Jesus, the apostles, and Paul, on Hell. The only reason why we don't see that judgement likewise reaches its climax, is precisely because we have relegated Hell from our thinking. And so we do not read Revelation 14 in all its horrific imagery, and say that all of the pictures of divine judgement in the Old Testament are quite frankly, as horrible as they are, tame compared to that. And do you know who introduces most of the innovative metaphors regarding Hell in the New Testament? Jesus.

Oh no, as you move from the old covenant to the new, it is not that you move from wrath to grace. You move, in fact, from a ratcheting up of the pictures of wrath, to wrath, and from the ratcheting up of the pictures of grace, to grace. The significance rather is, that 'now' a righteousness from God, has been made known apart from the law of covenant. It's come in a new covenant. It's come in a covenant that is sealed with Jesus' blood. That's the connection. And yet the old covenant did predict and prefigure this. It had its lambs and its sacrificial system and its priestly system, and ultimately they would find their fulfilment in the ultimate temple and the ultimate priest and the ultimate sacrifice. They bore testimony to the great sacrifice that was to come.

2) Paul establishes the availability, now, of God's righteousness to all human beings, without racial distinction, but on condition of faith (verses 22 and 23).

What Paul has been doing in the previous two and a half chapters is establishing universal guilt, that is of both Jew and Gentiles – *all* are under condemnation. Now he says that likewise this righteousness from God that has now appeared, is for all without racial distinction – Jew or Gentile. That is, there is a logical connection between this paragraph and the preceding chapters. 'This righteousness from God,' he writes, (verse 22), 'comes through faith in Jesus Christ to *all* who believe. There is no difference, for all have sinned and fall short of the glory of God…'

I should pause here long enough to say that in recent years there has been a new interpretation of the phrase rendered in the NIV, 'faith in Jesus Christ'. It could be taken to mean, 'faithfulness of Jesus Christ': the Greek could be understood that way. The word faith can either mean 'faith', or 'faithfulness', it depends on the context. So it's possible to read, 'this righteousness from God comes through the faithfulness of Jesus Christ'. After all, that is a biblical theme, the faithfulness of Jesus Christ takes Him to the cross – that's one of the great themes of John's gospel and of the epistle to the Hebrews – He obeys even unto death; so this righteousness now from God, comes through the faithfulness of Jesus Christ to all who believe. And some who argue for this position say that it is clear more in Greek than in English, because in English we have two different words here, 'faith' and 'believe', whereas in the original it's the same root. And then it sounds really strange. If I were paraphrasing, it might sound a bit like this – this righteousness of God comes through faith in Jesus Christ to all who have faith. That seems a bit redundant, doesn't it? If we take it in the traditional sense, isn't that what you are forced to believe, this righteousness from God comes through faith in Jesus Christ to all who have faith? But if 'faith' really means 'faithfulness' then there's no problem, they say. But with all respect I think that's profoundly mistaken.

Rather, the point of the additional phrase 'to all who believe' is precisely to establish the fact that it is not for a particular racial group, as in the old covenant which was focused on the Israelites; we are to read like this – this righteousness from God comes through faith in Jesus Christ, to all who have faith. In other words, that's why you have the repetition, precisely because you are stressing the '*all*'. That fits the context superbly – this righteousness from God comes through faith in Jesus Christ, to all who have faith, for there is no difference, for all have sinned, and now it comes to all who have faith – that's the point of the argument.

So what Paul establishes then, in this next point in the paragraph, is that this righteousness from God is available to *all* men and women, without racial distinction, but on condition of faith. In other words, it is unlike the old covenant which is bound up with the Israelites and those who become Israelites. But a righteousness from God has been made known apart from law, and it is for *all* who have faith in Jesus Christ, for we are *all* lost, we are *all* sinners. He's taken two and a half chapters to prove the point, and now this righteousness from God is available to us, on condition of faith.

3) The source of God's righteousness in the gracious provision of Jesus Christ is His propitiation for our sins (verses 24 and 25a).

We '… are justified freely by his grace through the redemption that came by Christ Jesus.' Christ's death buys us back. God presented Him as our (older versions have) 'propitiation' in His blood, received through faith. God presented Him as a sacrifice of 'atonement', the NIV has. Now what is at issue in these various translations?

Expiation has as its object, sin. You expiate sin, you cancel sin: expiation cancels sin. Propitiation has as its object God. You propitiate God, you make God favourable. So the argument in the past has been, Christ's sacrifice was a propitiation in that, instead of God standing over against us in righteous wrath, His wrath was turned aside since Christ absorbed it, so that Christ is now favourable towards us; He's propitious towards us. Christ's sacrifice is an act of propitiation which makes God favourable toward us. So most Christians believed till the 1930s in the Western world.

However, in the 1930s there was a Welsh scholar by the name of C.H. Dodd, who argued that this can't be propitiation, because it's so different from what propitiation means in pagan circles where you propitiate the gods by your sacrifices in order to make the gods favourable. We, then, are the subject to propitiate the gods to make them favourable, the gods are the object. But that's not the way in Christian circles, Dodd said. After all, *God* so loved the world, that He gave His Son. If He was already so favourable toward us that He gave His Son, in what sense does He still need to be propitiated? He's already so propitious that He doesn't need to be propitiated. So therefore this can't be propitiation, it has to be expiation. This is not turning away the wrath of God, it's just the way God cancels sin.

Then the question comes, why do you have two and a half chapters about the wrath of God, starting at 1:18? And he says, well the wrath of God is not really wrath, it's just sort of an outworking of what goes wrong. You do naughty things and naughty things happen to you; it's a kind of moral principle in the universe.

No, this really won't work at all. For in fact, the way the Bible has disclosed the wrath of God throughout Scripture in both Testaments, is in exceedingly personal terms. If you can depersonalise God, why not depersonalise Him also in His love? And then you retreat to a kind of deist concept of God: He wound the whole thing up, but He's so distant and absent that He doesn't really have much bearing on the present state of play.

No, the fact of the matter is that God's wrath is a function of His holiness. God is not necessarily wrathful; He is wrathful only as a function of His holiness. When His holiness confronts sin, He responds with judgement. But God's love is a function of His very character, God is love, He cannot be anything other than loving. An example I sometimes use is this: picture Charles and Susan walking hand in hand along a beach. He turns to her and says, 'Susan, I love you, I really do.' What does he mean? Well, he could mean a lot of things. He might simply mean that he wants to go to bed with her. But if we assume for a moment that he has a modicum of Christian virtue, then the least that he means is that he finds here utterly lovely. That is to say, he is saying something like, 'Your eyes, they transfix me. You smile and you poleaxe me from about fifty yards. Your personality is wonderful, I love to be with you, it's hard for me to imagine life without you. I really do love you, I want to marry you.' He does not mean something like, 'Susan, quite frankly your manners are grotesque, your halitosis, well it would frighten a herd of unwashed garlic-eating elephants. Your knobbly knees would put a camel to shame. Your personality rivals that of a mix of Genghis Khan and Attila the Hun. But I love you.' He doesn't mean that does he? In other words, when we proclaim our love, in part we are proclaiming our estimate of the loveliness of the loved, aren't we?

Now, when God says, 'I love you,' to us, what does He mean? Is He saying, 'You people, your smile transfixes me, I can't imagine heaven without you. Eternity without you would be just boring, I can't imagine it. Your personality is so brilliant, your education is so charming. You pray, I listen and I am thrilled to the depths of my being, really I love you because you are so loveable.' Is that what He means?

The fact of the matter is that God's love towards us is self-originating. He loves us because He is that kind of God, not because we are so loveable. And that is why wrath and love can coexist in God. It's hard for us to have love and wrath coexist in us, because in us, most of the time, love and wrath are in some measure a function of how we are reacting to externals. If I get angry at one of my kids because he hasn't come in on time, I know there's some deep part of me that says, 'No matter what you do, I'll still love you.' But on the other hand, the reason why I'm upset is because they said they'd be in at such a time and they're not there. And the closest we get to seeing something of this mix of righteous indignation, wrath and love, is perhaps when we are rearing our kids. But all parents recognise that sometimes we just lose it and we shouldn't – that's wrath that is not principled, not accounted for, ungodly. And we certainly don't want to get into the position of those parents who start withholding their love, precisely because the kids aren't doing what they want – 'Well, if you don't do that, I'm just finished with you.' Isn't there a sense in which Christians will always love their kids, no matter what they do?

So we can begin to glimpse what's going on in the mind of God. God stands over against us in wrath, because His holiness demands it and we are sinners. But He stands over against us in love because He's that kind of God.

'Morally speaking,' He says to us, 'you are the people of the halitosis, the horrible personality, the knees like a camel, and I love you anyway just because I'm that kind of God.'

So in that sense you see, God loves us so much He gives His Son. But His wrath must still be satisfied or God becomes an amoral being. So God presents His Son in such a way that His Son's death removes the wrath of God. In the pagan way of things human beings offer a sacrifice and the gods are propitiated. In the Bible, God is the subject who sends the Son to bear our sin in His own body on the tree – to absorb the curse, to satisfy God's demands for justice. And the just dies for the unjust and removes the wrath of God – so that God is the object. God is both the subject and the object. It is in that sense that propitiation, unlike pagan propitiation, is a biblical doctrine.

The word that is used here is sometimes used for the top of the ark of the covenant where blood was poured out, on

Yom Kippur, the Day of Atonement, to offer up a sacrifice, both for the sins of the people and for the sins of the priest, to set aside the wrath of God before the covenant community. And here Christ shed His blood on our behalf, because God placarded Him. He presented Him as the propitiation in His blood.

4) The demonstration of the righteousness of God through the cross of Jesus Christ

Sometimes in Christian circles we hear this little illustration. A judge pronounces sentence on some criminal and then steps down off the bench, takes off his robes and offers to take the place of the criminal. Have you heard that sort of illustration? Now I'll tell you what's the matter with it. In our justice systems the judge is merely an administrator of justice, that's all. The judge is not personally offended by the crime, he is merely an independent arbitrator of a system. But in the case of God, the offence is against Him. There is no system of justice bigger than God. God is not an independent administrator of justice, it is His justice system. And sin in its essence is not merely against a system of which He is the arbitrator, it is against Him; that is precisely why He is wrathful and why He's offended. It is precisely why, unlike our judges (who couldn't conceivably have the authority to take the place of the criminal), He can step off the bench as it were, and provide a propitiating sacrifice that satisfies His own justice, while at the same time reconciling rebellious men and women to Himself.

God does this, we are told, to demonstrate His justice; because in His forbearance in times past under the old covenant, He even left the sins committed beforehand unpunished; they faced temporal punishments, but the final handling of the sins of Abraham, or Isaiah, or Jeremiah, was not by the temple sacrifices, but in the present time, in the death of Christ, so that God might be just and the one who justifies those who have faith in Jesus.

This view of the atonement is not the only model used in the New Testament. There are other complementary models of how to understand what Christ did on the cross. But I want to say in the strongest possible terms, that this understanding of the cross lies at the heart of all of the rest of them. And if you lose this one you lose the gospel. Now I know that point is widely disputed, but I would argue it very strongly.

Take, for example, the theme of reconciliation. Many people today say that the heart of the Pauline doctrine of the atonement is not propitiation, it's reconciliation, alienated people being brought back together, sinners and God being brought back together. And there's no doubt that reconciliation is an important theme in Paul. The question is, why is there a need for reconciliation? Because we are alienated. What has alienated us? Our sin. Why is God alienated from us, why doesn't He just accept us? Because His holiness demands that He condemn us. How is it then that men and women are reconciled to God? Because Christ pays for our sin, He absorbs our guilt, He takes our punishment. And you are back to wrath and substitution and propitiation, as the very grounding of reconciliation.

I think that you can demonstrate those sort of points exegetically and theologically. One could treat other models of the atonement in similar ways. You discover that if you push hard enough they all come back first and foremost to this fundamental issue: what is sin? What is God's response to it? How does He deal with it? What is the purpose of the cross? And if we cannot see how ugly, how death-dealing, how God-defying sin is, we shall not see how utterly satisfying the cross is, by which men and women alone are reconciled to God.

Long I have pondered the curse of the cross,
Sinless the Christ bears my guilt and my pain.
Thundering silence, a measureless cost,
God in His heaven lets Christ cry in vain.
Now I can glimpse sin's bleak horror and worse,
Christ dies and bears the unbearable cross.

Keswick 1999
Tapes, Videos and Books

Catalogues and price lists of audio tapes of the Keswick Convention platform ministry, including much not included in the present book, can be obtained from:

ICC (International Christian Communications)
Regency Mews
Silverdale Road
Eastbourne
East Sussex BN20 7AB

Details of videos of selected sessions can be obtained from:

Mr Dave Armstrong
STV Videos
Box 299
Bromley
Kent BR2 9XB

Some previous annual Keswick volumes (all published by STL/OM) are still in print and can be ordered from:

The Keswick Convention Centre, Skiddaw Street
Keswick, Cumbria CA12 4BY;

from your local Christian bookseller;

or direct from the publishers, OM Publishing, STL Ltd, PO Box 300, Carlisle, Cumbria CA3 0QS, England

Keswick 2000

The annual Keswick Convention takes place each July at the heart of England's beautiful Lake District. The two separate weeks of the Convention offer an unparalleled opportunity for listening to gifted Bible exposition, experiencing Christian fellowship with believers from all over the world, and enjoying something of the unspoilt grandeur of God's creation.

Each of the weeks has a series of five morning Bible Readings, followed by other addresses throughout the rest of the day. There are also regular meetings throughout the fortnight for young people and a Children's Holiday Club.

The dates for the 2000 Keswick Convention are 15-21 July and 22-28 July. The Bible Reading speakers are John Stott and Jonathan Lamb respectively. Other speakers during the fortnight include Luis Palau, Vaughan Roberts, Anne Graham Lotz, George Verwer and Vinoth Ramachandra.

For further information, write to:

The Administrator
Keswick Convention Centre
Skiddaw Street
Keswick
Cumbria CA12 4BY
Telephone 017687 72589